SHE'S A BOY

SHE'S A BOY

The Shocking True Story of Joe Holliday

Joe Holliday with Louise Chapman

THISTLE
PUBLISHING

First published in 2015 by:

Thistle Publishing
36 Great Smith Street
London
SW1P 3BU

www.thistlepublishing.co.uk

ISBN-13: 978-1-910670-40-8

FOREWORD

She's a Boy is the autobiography of Joe Holliday, detailing his life and the months preceding his arrival into the world.

The book was compiled from the best recollections of actual events as remembered by Joe and his mother Julia Farmer.

Conversations recorded in the book are, of course, not the words spoken verbatim, but are the memories Joe and Julia have of conversations they have had together and with others. While the conversations and facts recorded are true to the interpretation and memory Joe and Julia have of events, it is accepted that others may have a different memory of the way in which things were said or meant.

PROLOGUE

January 24, 1988

'So, what have I got?' Mum asked, urgently. 'A boy or a girl?'

'All in good time,' the midwife responded as she rushed to wrap me in a white sheet, seeming determined that Mum would not see me. Her colleague had already darted out of the door.

'Penny has gone to ask one of the doctors to come along to have a little look at you both. You've got a bit of a tear that is going to need some attention.'

The moment I was delivered, Mum had felt the sudden change in atmosphere in the room. As I was lifted into the air, she'd seen a huge red lump drop down between my legs and she'd seen the look of horror that crossed the midwife's face. She was trying to pretend she hadn't noticed any of it.

My dad, with a better view of me and of what was going on, was standing silently at Mum's side, apparently having gone into some sort of shock.

Mum's mind began racing through the books she had read in preparation for labour and she remembered one of them saying boys' testicles can sometimes be very enlarged when they are first born. Maybe that was the lump she'd seen?

The room started to fill with doctors as the midwife lifted me towards the scales.

'See if you can see what we've got,' Mum urged my dad as she tried to sit herself up enough to see, but though my dad took a step forward, he didn't say anything. Mum says it was as if he had shut down. She hadn't heard me cry yet and could feel fear rising.

'5lb 5oz,' Mum overheard as I was placed into a see-through fishbowl-like hospital cot and someone started to wheel it towards the top of the room. I was all wrapped up, with only the top of my head and part of my face visible. As I passed by her, Mum could see that my eyes were open and I looked incredibly alert. I was making a sort of humming noise. It was a strange noise, like she'd never heard a baby make before, but she found it reassuring.

Half of the doctors began peeling off and gathering around me, making it impossible for Mum to see me. The other half crowded around her. There was a general urgency about the way everyone was moving around. One of the doctors introduced himself and started explaining that Mum had lost a lot of blood and the placenta had not come down as it should.

'But what about the baby? Is everything okay with the baby?'

'My colleagues are looking after the baby, Miss Baker. I can assure you the baby is in very good hands. We really need to get you down to theatre and get you sorted out and then we can tell you all about Baby.'

'But can you just tell me what I've got? Is it a boy or a girl?'

'Not yet,' the doctor replied.

'Not yet?' Mum was indignant. 'What do you mean, not yet? Can't you tell the difference?'

'I know this is a difficult time for you but just try to remain calm for us. You need to get down to theatre and we'll look after Baby.'

Mum could not have realised that my abdomen, pelvis and entire mid-section was so malformed, so incomplete, that no-one knew the answer to her question. She also did not know that the umbilical cord had snapped inside her and she was haemorrhaging so badly her life was at risk.

As she was wheeled away to theatre, Mum pleaded with a nurse to tell her if I was okay.

'It looks like Baby may have a hernia or something,' the nurse said kindly. 'The doctors will have a look and talk you through it when you get back from theatre.'

As her bed was rushed out of the delivery room, through some double doors and towards theatre, Mum tried to tell herself that if it was just a hernia it could be easily resolved. Her niece had been born with one and it hadn't been a big problem. At the same time, Mum's mind kept snapping back to the nightmare she'd had the night before, which she'd somehow known was more a premonition than a dream. She'd always had a deeply spiritual side, a sixth-sense about things, and she was rarely wrong. In her nightmare, she'd just given birth and as the baby was lifted into the air all of its limbs had started falling off.

In theatre, someone placed a mask over Mum's face and told her she was about to go to sleep. She felt her eyes roll back and she drifted into unconsciousness. Both she and my dad were only 19 years old and neither of them had expected to have to deal with any of this. They hadn't even expected, or wanted, to have to deal with a straightforward pregnancy, labour or baby, let alone face what they were about to.

CHAPTER ONE

Like me, my mum, Julia Baker, was an unexpected and unplanned baby, but she too was very, very loved. My nan and grandad only had a fairly short-lived relationship with each other and split up when Mum was tiny. Nan had been 39 when Mum arrived and Grandad was 44. They'd each been married to other people previously and had both thought their families were complete well before they met, but even after they separated Nan and Grandad shared the upbringing of Mum 50/50 and remained close friends.

My grandad, Ernie Baker, lived in Spalding, the south Lincolnshire market town once famous for tulip growing. Similarly to a lot of the population of the area, he spent a lot of his working life on the land, mostly on the sugar beet campaigns. He was always a hard worker, but never had a lot to show for it, being one to live for the moment rather than plan for the future. One of the bar stools at Grandad's local pub practically had his name on it. He had his own glass behind the bar and was never happier than when he was in there with a pint of Mackeson Stout in one hand, a cigarette in the other and the day's racing tips laid out in front of him. Mum grew up surrounded by the old boys in that pub, who spoiled her with bags of crisps and glasses of lemonade whenever she went in. Many years later, Mum would sometimes take me in there and they all used to greet me in exactly the same way.

Grandad's two sons and daughter were much older than Mum and lived away with their mother. Grandad still saw them quite often but Mum was very much the baby and got lots of attention. In theory, Mum's home was with Nan, but she spent almost as much time at Grandad's and even on the days she didn't go to Spalding, Grandad would generally drop in to see her and have a cuppa with Nan.

Nan's house, in the village of Pinchbeck, was about ten minutes away from Grandad's by car or around 20 by bike, which was how all of them got around because no-one in my family drove back then. Nan, Jean Ives, also had three elder children – all sons. Kevin was 15 years older than Mum, Terry 12 years older and Gary nine years older. By the time Mum has any recollection, Kevin and Terry were very much grown up and living their own lives, though Gary was around more. He and his girlfriend April lived with her and Nan for quite a few years and Mum was quite close to Gary.

Nan was one of those people who was always busy and always doing something and she seemed to be good at everything. She was a fantastic cook, an amazing gardener and she could turn anything into something special on the sewing machine. She worked in bars and pubs her whole life, as a cleaner and barmaid and it was while Nan was working in The Bull, in Pinchbeck, that Mum first met my dad, Gary Holliday.

My dad was born and grew up in Kent where his father was quite a success story and owned a motor business as well as a load of other property, but his parents separated and his mother came to live in Pinchbeck. My dad's uncle owned The Bull and he and Mum were children when they met in there for the first time. Mum had gone along with Nan and was 'helping' her clean and playing with the chickens that roamed free in the beer garden at the back and my dad was there with his mum visiting his uncle. It's fair to say it wasn't love at first sight. In fact, Mum says they took an instant dislike to each other and whenever no-one was looking, my dad would pull her pigtails and she'd call him names.

Throughout their school years, Mum and my dad were aware of each other, but didn't have a lot to do with one another. They both went to the village primary school, but, aged 11, my dad, always the academic, passed the 11-plus and went off to grammar school in Spalding. Mum, always the popular joker, did not pass and was bussed each day to a secondary school in Crowland, a village beyond Spalding and halfway to Peterborough.

My dad got his head down, completed his O-Levels and went on to the grammar school's sixth form. Mum, on the other hand, only just made it to the end of school without getting kicked out. What she got up to was more mischievous than malicious – smoking behind the bike sheds and sneaking out to the chippy at dinner times – but it left her with a pretty booked-up detention diary. Nan would try to tell her off, but often couldn't help but laugh at what she got up to. She knew Mum had the brains to do whatever she wanted but couldn't be pushed to use them how or when someone else dictated. Mum ultimately left school with a couple of CSEs and a vague idea of taking up an apprenticeship as a hairdresser. She was happy, so Nan and Grandad were happy too.

The hairdressing didn't last more than a couple of weeks before Mum couldn't bear the bitching and sniping in the shop. She got a job behind the till at the Spalding branch of the old DIY chain Texas Homecare and started doing some shifts with Nan at the village Snooker and Social Club.

The old snooker club had burned down when Mum's brothers were teenagers and it had left them with nothing to do in the village. Nan was a part of the team that raised money to get a new social club set up above the village hall at the back of The Bull. When the villagers managed to get the money together to kit it all out, Nan worked behind the bar and cleaned free of charge until it became established. She ultimately became club secretary and did everything from running and managing the bar to taking all the bookings they got for private functions and, by the time Mum left school, Nan had full-time paid work at the club.

The phrase everyone-knows-everyone was invented for Pinchbeck and because Nan had been in the village forever and worked in the pubs it was pretty much literal in her case. She had grown up with, gone to school with, worked with or spent years serving drinks to every Tom, Dick and Harry or their sister and she got on with them all. When people drank in Nan's bar they always seemed to know they had to stay in line, but she never had to upset anyone. She loved the social club and all of its characters and everyone loved her.

Once Mum turned 18, she started serving behind the bar with Nan and they giggled and chatted their way through their shifts like best friends. On Saturday nights, they'd stack up all the drinks that customers bought for them throughout the night and have them back-to-back while clearing up at the end of the night before staggering home together. On Sunday lunchtimes, they'd often end up waltzing round in front of the bar with the old gents who went along for a 'quick half' week in week out while their wives prepared lunch.

'Come on Jean, let's have some music on,' one or other of the customers would call out from the tables around the dance floor where they all sat playing cards.

Nan would crank up a bit of Max Bygraves or Charlie Pride and the playing cards would soon be abandoned for a minute or two. It was the mid-80s and Mum was a child of her time, with very big hair and purple eye shadow up to the brow, but she was just as comfortable with the music of Nan's youth. Nan had a lovely singing voice and I can just see her dancing, head thrown back, singing along.

The younger crowd at the club tended to spend their time at the other end of the room, beyond the huge floor-to-ceiling red velvet curtains that were only ever closed when there was an evening do on, around the big old dark wood snooker tables. Mum had been busy serving when my dad went into the club one Sunday and headed down to the tables. She only noticed him as he made his way back down the room towards her with two empty pint glasses. Mum always says that my dad – skinny and a bit geeky looking – appeared so unsure of himself walking towards her. He was a total contrast to Mum, who is so like the comedienne Dawn French that she once won a lookalike contest. Mum shares not only the star's looks, but her apparent bubbly confidence. Mum really felt for my dad and plastered on one of her big welcoming smiles.

'Hiya Gary, how you doing? I haven't seen you in ages. What can I get you?'

'Oh, hi,' he replied awkwardly. 'Just a couple of pints of Coke please. I'm good thanks. You?'

'I'm great ta,' Mum said as my dad handed her the glasses he was carrying and she began filling them one by one with draught cola from the pumps. 'So what you doing with yourself these days?'

'I'm still at the grammar school. Just finishing my A-levels. Hoping to go to uni in September,' my dad replied looking down at the bar as if a bit embarrassed by it all.

'Wow, uni? That's brilliant,' Mum said, genuinely impressed. 'What are you hoping to study?'

Dad looked up, seeming pleased that she was so interested and wasn't going to make fun of his ambitions. 'I want to go to Warwick to do maths. It's a really great place but it's quite tough to get in so I'll just have to see how it goes.'

'Good for you. God, I was useless at maths. Didn't have a clue what the teachers were going on about most of the time. Actually I could probably say the same for most subjects!'

Mum laughed loudly – she has an uproarious cackle – and my dad chuckled along before taking his drinks and turning to walk back up the room to his game of snooker. Mum watched him go and has said she felt drawn to him from that moment.

Until she met up with my dad again, Mum hadn't been particularly interested in finding a boyfriend. On Friday nights she usually went over to Spalding with one of her many friends and spent the evening with Grandad and his mates in The Northern. Grandad wouldn't hear of Mum or her friends buying any of the drinks all night. Then, at the end of the evening, he'd jump up onto his bike and insist on giving Mum and whichever friend was staying over a lift back. He'd balance one of them on the seat and the other on the handlebars and Mum can't believe they never had a horrible crash. The hedge around his council semi in Spalding's Edward Road did have a big dent in it, though, from him using it as a braking system. Mum laughed so much on those nights out that she couldn't imagine having a better time with anyone else.

Something about my dad made Mum feel differently about the prospect of having a relationship and when he started coming into the social club regularly they began chatting more and more. Mum felt my dad had a slightly damaged quality and she had a subconscious urge to make him feel better about himself, but it wasn't just that. They found it easy to talk to each other and generally just got on well. Mum always used to ask my dad how his studies were going and he seemed to enjoy the encouragement she gave him. They also discovered they both shared a love for the rock group Queen and, with his long curly hair, Mum even told herself my dad had the slightest air of the band's guitarist Brian May.

On a beautiful Sunday afternoon in July, my dad was standing at the bar when Nan was talking to Mum. 'Shall we have Trivial Pursuit out in the garden when we get home? Get everyone round?'

'Trivial Pursuit?' Dad asked. 'I love a bit of Trivial Pursuit.'

'Well get yourself along then,' Nan told him.

It was typical of Nan to invite anyone and everyone around to her house, which was always full of waifs and strays either just visiting or staying for a while. She couldn't ever see anyone in trouble for somewhere to stay and it meant there were always plenty of people around. Her brother – my Uncle John, who has mild learning difficulties – was just one example. She took him in when Mum was about 14 and he lived with her continuously after that. A huge roast on a Sunday for whoever happened to be around and a game of Trivial Pursuit was a bit of a tradition.

That Sunday in the garden, playing Trivial Pursuit, was the day Mum and my dad got together. They both knew it wasn't the best time to begin a relationship, with my dad due to start university a few months later, but became inseparable. My dad's mum Barbara was so against the relationship, fearing Mum would try to hold my dad back, that they let her believe it wasn't happening.

That September when my dad left for Warwick in his little yellow Vauxhall Viva, he and Mum both cried their eyes out, but promised to write every day. As it turned out there was a communal phone in my dad's halls of residence, so they were able to speak daily instead. Mum would go out to the phone box in front of Nan's house at a prearranged time and call him from there so as not to run up Nan's phone bill. My dad told Mum all about the fantastic time he was having and all the people he had met and Mum did her best not to show her concern that a lot of them were girls.

Not long after my dad left, it was his birthday and he convinced Mum to go down and spend it with him. He wasn't supposed to allow anyone to stay with him in the halls of residence but was sure they'd get away with it. He was so keen for Mum to meet all of his new friends.

Mum got the National Express coach down to Coventry and my dad met her in his car the other end. They ran into each other's arms and took up exactly where they'd left off.

Within a couple of hours of Mum getting off the coach, she was in Mandela's, one of the Student Union bars and had fitted in with my dad's friends as if she were another student. There was Richard, who was exceptionally clever and would later become a commercial airline pilot, Rebecca, who seemed a bit cool at first but bonded with Mum after telling her she was a bit spiritual and did tarot cards, and Jason. Jason was studying art and media and, as English has always been Mum's secret passion, she found his explanation of his media studies fascinating and they really hit it off. Mum made everyone laugh with stories of the social club and the things she'd got up to with Nan and Grandad and my dad was happy to sit back and let her be the star.

The following day, my dad, Jason, Rebecca and Richard wanted to show Mum some of the beautiful surrounding area so they all dived into my dad's car and headed to Stoneleigh Abbey, in Kenilworth. Mum loved the imposing country house, which was set in beautiful grounds where peacocks roamed and, wrapped up against the autumn chill, they had a lovely relaxed afternoon there. That day's giggles were provided when they all decided to invest some spare change in jumping aboard a little kiddies' train that motored around in a circuit close to the house.

Mum left on the Monday, a little sad to be going back to reality, but already looking forward to her next visit. In fact, 'reality' did not last very long because within a couple of weeks of being back Mum lost her job at the DIY store. On the instructions of the deputy manager she'd left the till to help unload a delivery. When she returned her manager was waiting for her and began screaming and shouting at her for leaving it unattended.

Mum made an initial attempt to explain herself, but was infuriated by the manager's attitude. 'I tell you what,' she told him. 'Don't worry about it. You can stick your job.'

Mum threw her Texas apron at him and stormed out. Once she'd got back home and cooled off, she starting to regret what she'd done and, a bit worried about it all, she rang my dad.

'I've just had a row with my boss and walked out of my job.'

'Great,' he said. 'Now you can come down here at the weekend!'

They had another amazing weekend and when Sunday night came round neither of them wanted it to end.

'Why don't you stay?' Dad said. 'Why do you have to go back to Pinchbeck?'

Mum realised she didn't really need to rush back and agreed to stay on for a few days, which turned into a couple of weeks. They had some wild nights out, drinking cheap vodka and, on one memorable occasion, pushed Richard home in a trolley. At the weekend, my dad drove the gang to The Virgins and Castle, in Kenilworth, a beautiful country pub, and they spent a much more sober afternoon there.

Mum went home to do a few shifts in the social club the following weekend, but got another National Express ticket and returned to Warwick a week or so later. Over the next few months, she shuttled backwards and forwards, spending as much time as she could with my dad in Warwick where they survived on his student grant and the little bit of money she was earning at the club. When Mum came home, Grandad would often bung her a packet of cigarettes and, more often than not, she'd find he'd folded a fiver inside for her. He and Nan were quite happy to see her enjoying herself.

Occasionally when she was home, Mum would bump into Barbara, who would delight in telling her how well my dad was doing at university. Mum had to keep a straight face and pretend she hadn't seen him.

At Easter my dad drove back with Mum for the holidays and seemed a bit quiet in the car. Mum thought maybe he was concerned that they wouldn't be able to see a lot of each other in Pinchbeck with his mother about, but he was preoccupied by something else.

'I've been thinking. You know what we should do? We should get married.'

'Married?'

'Yes, why not? We know we want to be together so why wait? I'll be moving into a house-share with the guys next year and you could come with us. You can find a job in Warwick or you could even go to college and get your CSEs.

You're brilliant at English. Some of the poems and stuff you write are really good, you could do really well and I could help you get through your maths exam then you could do whatever you wanted in life.'

Mum couldn't imagine being any happier than she was then and didn't have to think about it for long. 'Let's do it!'

They weren't sure how they were going to break the news to Barbara, but broaching the subject didn't turn out to be as difficult as my dad thought. Barbara found one of Mum's E-cup bras mixed up in my dad's washing from uni and it didn't take much to work out who it belonged to. She wasn't very happy about it all but seemed to realise she couldn't do anything about it. My dad introduced Mum to the rest of his family back in Kent, who were much more accepting of her and she quickly became very close to his Aunt Di and Grandad.

Nan and Grandad were completely relaxed about Mum's plans and when she decided to have an engagement party back at uni, Nan even said she'd travel down for it. Mum put a notice up in the dining room of halls: 'Party here, 8pm Saturday, all welcome, bring booze.'

Loads of people turned up and they had an hilarious night. Gary's girlfriend April drove Nan down for it and Nan danced harder, drank more and sang louder than any student there.

In the following weeks, Dad began coaching Mum on maths out of old CSE textbooks and she signed up to start college the following September. She managed to move into his halls' room without anyone official finding out. The halls' cleaner twigged it, but she and Mum had become really friendly and she even helped them keep it quiet. Mum would often make the cleaner a cup of tea or even help her get the vacuuming done and one day, when there was an unplanned inspection of halls to make sure everything was in order, the cleaner tipped Mum off quickly so she could hide in a wardrobe!

Mum spent the days hanging out with whoever didn't have lectures, often going into town with Jason to watch films, supposedly as research for his media course. When everyone was tied up with uni, she'd surprise them by taking all their washing down to the launderette or cooking them a proper meal. A lot of evenings were spent just huddled up with my dad in his room, sometimes listening to music, other times quizzing each other out of text books. Each morning, she rang Nan for a natter about the latest social club gossip and Grandad was inevitably sitting at her kitchen table having his daily cup of tea. Nan would pass the phone across and he'd worry over whether Mum had enough money, enough food and was looking after herself properly.

With the most time on her hands, it was left to Mum to get in touch with estate agents to try to find somewhere to live in September. Richard had made his own arrangements, which left Rebecca and Jason, who had become a couple, and Mum and my dad looking for a place to share. Mum set up a load of viewings and they all loved one little cottage they found out in the sticks a bit. It was circular and really quirky, but when a train roared past they realised it was right on top of the tracks. A couple of places they looked at were filthy dirty and one stank of dogs. Then they went to a semi in the village of Lillington. The house fronted on to a well-to-do street and had a beautiful bay window at the front. Inside, it was a little dated but homely and each bedroom had its own pink porcelain basin. At £380 a month it was on the pricey side, but they all loved it and agreed to take it.

Everything would have been perfect if it wasn't for the fact Mum had started to feel really ill.

CHAPTER TWO

Mum had always had a fuller figure but the weight had started to drop off her and she felt sick all the time. Of course, pregnancy crossed her mind, but she and my dad had always been doubly careful about contraception. To rule it out, they did a home pregnancy test and were both relieved when it came out negative.

A few weeks later though, Mum's symptoms were no better and she'd started to feel so dizzy in the mornings that she couldn't get out of bed until she'd had something to eat. She was pale and her eyes were sunken in her face.

Knowing Mum was far away from her family, the cleaner was really concerned for her. 'Are you sure you're not pregnant love? I really think you ought to see a doctor.'

'I haven't got a doctor here and we're going home for summer in a couple of weeks. I'm sure it's nothing serious. I'll go and see my doctor then.'

Jason wasn't happy about Mum putting off seeing a doctor either. He went and sat on the side of her bed one morning and handed her one of the Rich Tea biscuits he'd discovered could help settle her stomach. 'You need to go to the chemist, you know. You've got to have a proper pregnancy test there to be sure.'

Mainly because she didn't have the energy to argue, Mum agreed to get the bus into town with Jason and go to a chemist. My dad was sitting one of his end-of-year exams as she and Jason sought out something for her to use to take a urine sample with them – in the end settling on a rinsed out Daddies Sauce bottle.

They took it to the chemist where the snotty assistant looked down her nose as she took the sample from them. Mum thought it was all a bit of a laugh until she and Jason returned for the results an hour-and-a-half later as instructed. As they walked in, Mum suddenly had a terrible dread and wrapped her arm around Jason's.

When they went to the counter, the assistant gave Mum a sneering smile. 'Well, congratulations,' she said. 'I'm sure you'll be pleased to know, you are pregnant.'

If Mum hadn't have already been holding onto Jason's arm she fears she would have fallen down in shock. Neither of them said anything as he guided her out of the chemist.

They went to the nearest pub where Jason led Mum to one of the tables and pulled out a chair for her. She sat down, put her elbows on the table and rested her head in her hands. 'What am I going to do?'

Jason was very calm. 'You're going to have a drink then get the next bus back to uni, wait for Gary's exam to finish then talk it through with him. It's going to be okay.'

So that's what they did. Jason walked Mum back to the room she and my dad shared and she sat on the swivel chair next to my dad's desk wringing her hands and dreading what she had to tell him. The clean and simple room contained just about everything the pair of them owned and despite being tiny, didn't even look cramped as a result. They had nothing, how would they manage a baby?

Mum heard my dad's footsteps coming up the stairs and hardly even breathed until he walked into the room. He looked across at her and before he'd even shut the door behind him, Mum told him.

'But how?' he said, all the colour draining from his face as he stepped in and sat down abruptly on the bed opposite her.

'I don't know either,' Mum replied, hating seeing the pain and worry on his face. 'But I am. I've been to the chemist and had a test. It's why I've been so ill. I don't know what we are going to do.'

Dad stared silently at a spot on the floor for a moment, then took Mum's hand. 'Don't worry. We can sort this out. We'll get you an abortion. No-one even need ever know it happened.'

Even the word abortion sent shivers through Mum and her eyes filled with tears, but she looked at the fear on my dad's face and didn't say anything. She told herself there was no other choice.

When Nan called to speak to Mum as normal the next day, Mum ended the conversation as quickly as she could. She knew Nan would pick up that something was wrong but she couldn't speak to her while she was keeping such a big secret and she knew if she stayed on the line too long she'd break down. It was the same the next day and the next. In the meantime, my dad found a private clinic in Coventry that charged a few hundred pounds to carry out abortions. He rang his father and told him he needed some money for books and before Mum knew it, she and my dad were arriving at the clinic, the money in their hand.

The clinic had a real back-street feel to it and the chairs they sat on in the waiting room were old and dirty. Mum felt physically sick as they were shown into a consultation room and took their seats across the desk from a female doctor. Looking back, Mum cannot remember a single word that was said to her during that meeting. She knows the procedure was explained and a date agreed but she had slipped into her own world. All she could think was that she couldn't go through with it.

Back at the residences, Mum went off for a bath, wishing she could just sink her head under the water and make everything go away. The thought of telling my dad she didn't want the abortion was as bad as the thought of facing Nan, Grandad and Barbara with the news that she was pregnant. She felt she'd let everyone down. She just lay there and sobbed and sobbed until the water went cold.

The next thing Mum was aware of was Jason standing over her with a towel. She didn't know exactly how he'd got into the room, she may have forgotten to lock it, at the time it didn't matter. She didn't even know how long she'd been in the bath crying. As Jason wrapped the towel around her she felt like a small, lost child.

Jason took Mum back to his room and once she was dressed, pressed her to tell him what was going through her mind. 'You don't have to get rid of the baby, you know. Just because Gary says so.'

'I don't want to trap him,' Mum said, crying again. 'Really I don't. It's his first year of uni but I just don't think I can do this. I'm willing to leave him. I don't want to, but I could and then he wouldn't have to have anything to do with me or the baby. I wouldn't have to ruin everything for him, but how can I tell him? How can I do that to him?'

'But, Julia, you have to. You can't just keep quiet and go along with it. Has he ever asked what you want? This is insane. Let me talk to him. You stay here. I'm going to go across and make him understand that you mustn't just be pushed into this.'

Jason headed straight for the door and Mum wasn't up to trying to stop him. To begin with she just sat there crying and worrying over my dad getting the brunt of Jason's anger. It didn't seem fair. Unable to stop the tears, she made her own way down the corridor.

Outside my dad's room, she could hear Jason's voice, calm and level. 'You can't just bulldozer her into getting rid of the baby. It's not on mate. She's in a right state.'

Mum stepped into the room where my dad was sitting in the chair, listening to what was being said, looking down at the floor. She couldn't bear to see his misery and couldn't handle having this conversation. Jason and my dad both turned towards her, but without a word to either of them, Mum just climbed onto the bed, curled into a ball and closed her eyes. As the boys continued to talk, Mum fell to sleep.

The next morning, the first thing she saw was my dad sitting in the office chair beside her, clutching a handful of leaflets. She glanced at them and wondered what was going on.

'I've been to the student welfare office,' my dad said. 'About benefits and stuff that are available. And we could manage, you know? So I've been thinking. Sod what everyone else says, let's have the baby.'

Mum couldn't help the grin spreading across her face as she sat up. 'What? Have the baby? But what about uni?'

'That's what I'm saying, it wouldn't have to affect uni. We could scrape by for a couple of years. It'll be tough but we can do it and then I'll have a degree and I can get a decent job. We were going to have a family at some point anyway, we're just speeding it up a bit.'

'Oh my God. This is incredible. You really mean it? We're going to be parents?' As they hugged, Mum says it felt like a cloud had lifted. She was so over the moon that she didn't really consider that perhaps my dad was just doing it to make her happy.

They decided to continue to keep things quiet until they could tell their parents face-to-face. It wasn't easy for Mum to keep up the deceit when she spoke to Nan and Grandad on the phone, but equally she was dreading telling them the truth. At uni only Jason and Rebecca and a handful of others knew about the baby and they all promised their support. Jason and Rebecca even agreed they could all still move into the Lillington house.

With the plans all set, Mum and my dad headed back to Pinchbeck for the summer. The last time they'd made the journey they'd excitedly agreed to get engaged. This time the 100-mile trip felt much longer as they sat in silence thinking about the scenes that lay ahead at the other end and the reality of their situation began to sink in.

They'd decided to go to Nan's house first, but when my dad pulled the car to a stop outside, Mum was paralysed with fear. 'I can't do it,' she said. 'You're going to have to tell her.'

He could see there was no point arguing. 'Okay, wait here.'

To my dad's credit, he got out of the car alone and sought Nan out in the back garden where she was hanging washing. 'What's wrong,' she said. 'Where's Julia?'

'It's okay Jean. She's in the car. She's asked me to come and tell you something before you see her.'

'Oh my God. I knew she wasn't well. What is it? Come on, tell me.'

'It's okay, it's okay. It's not that bad.'

'Oh thank God. I thought you were going to say she was pregnant.'

The next thing Mum saw was Nan flying down the side of the house in floods of tears, pushing her bike at her side. She glanced at Mum in the car, but didn't acknowledge her or stop. Mum was mortified and leapt out of the car. 'Mum! Where are you going?'

'The bloody wool shop,' Nan replied as she cycled off, tears still running down her cheeks.

Nan never bothered to lecture Mum over her pregnancy or be angry with her or my dad about it. She came back from the shops, piled down with pastel coloured wool and gave Mum a huge hug. 'So, I guess you better tell me what you want me to bloody well knit.'

The next morning, Grandad came round for one of his visits and Nan handed him his mug and got straight to the point. 'Julia's having a baby.'

He spat half his tea across the table. 'What, a real 'un?'

Mum was the apple of Grandad's eye so it didn't take him long to get used to the idea.

My dad went alone to tell Barbara and Mum never found out exactly what was said, though it isn't difficult to figure it out.

That summer, Mum and my dad stayed with Nan while they tried to build up some savings before returning to Warwick. Spalding and Pinchbeck are full of large food factories where temporary work is usually available on the production lines, piling ingredients onto packed salads and sandwiches and my dad got a job in one of them. Mum still felt very unwell and had even had a bleed, which seemed like it might lead to miscarriage at one point so she stayed at home resting while my dad went out to work. Mum thinks my dad's resentment of her and the situation had started to build up even then.

In the evenings, my dad would often come back in a foul mood and would snap and growl at whatever Mum said. She tried not to react and would keep out of his way until he seemed a bit happier again. Mum hated the thought of Nan seeing my dad behaving that way and made excuses for him. Mum realised he must have been tired and she appreciated that he had a lot to think about with finances so stretched, the baby on the way and his degree. On occasion, he'd seem more like himself and they'd cuddle up in bed and talk about what life would be like when the baby arrived and Mum would try to convince herself it was all going to be okay.

When the holidays were over and it was time to return to the Lillington house, nothing seemed so magical any more. I was due at the beginning of February and Mum knew those four months would quickly pass and she'd be caring for a baby miles away from Grandad and Nan. As none of them could drive, the distance seemed even greater. Mum climbed into my dad's car with a great sense of dread, but did not dare to share her feelings with him or anyone else. She'd made her bed and felt she had to lie in it. She and my dad drove back in near silence and their relationship never really recovered.

All Mum's daydreams about living in a house-share collapsed pretty quickly as she discovered she found Rebecca particularly difficult to live with. Mum had learned from Nan how to make a house a home even on virtually no budget and with a bit of paint and a couple of trinkets she got it looking nice, but it didn't help the atmosphere. Mum likes to keep things spotlessly clean and was happy to do a lot of the cleaning, but whatever she did seemed to irritate Rebecca and she found herself getting angry in return. Though Mum was still close to Jason, his loyalty was ultimately to his girlfriend and as neither Rebecca nor his parents were particularly impressed at the prospect of them living in a house with a baby there was an added awkwardness. The rows grew gradually more intense until, just before Christmas, the other couple gathered all their things and moved out.

Mum felt the tension between her and my dad thicken as his concerns about their finances stretched even further. She didn't even mention that she didn't have a winter coat and made do without. Her health remained awful – she'd developed a hiatus hernia, which gave her horrendous chest pain and heartburn that she'd vomit with. On top of that, she had a constant feeling that something more serious was wrong. Mum told the midwives at her appointments that she was convinced there was something wrong with the baby but the scans did not show anything and they told her it was just first-time-mum nerves. The only unusual issue they found was that Mum had a slightly twisted pelvis and as a result they recommended and booked her in for a caesarean.

Nan and Grandad phoned regularly and though Mum knew they could tell she wasn't happy, they remained upbeat and supportive just as she wanted them to. Nan even went and stayed with her for a week and sought out a second-hand cot that she worked her magic on, making beautiful white cotton drapes and a tiny matching duvet for it. She planned to return the week I was due, to help Mum out in the early days.

Two weeks before I was scheduled to arrive, my dad drove all the way up to Lincolnshire in thick snow to collect Grandad so that he could be with Mum for a few days. Mum had been particularly unwell that week and a midwife had actually wanted to admit her to hospital because her blood pressure was so high. Mum couldn't bear the thought of missing her time with Grandad and had convinced them to let her go home so long as she rested and wasn't left alone.

On a good day the round-trip to Spalding would have taken my dad just over four hours, but in those weather conditions it must have been much longer. As soon as he left, Mum developed a raging headache – a symptom she had been warned could indicate pre-eclampsia and meant she needed to get to hospital urgently. She didn't have a phone and did not want to face the fact anything could be going wrong so she went to bed and tried to pretend it wasn't happening. It was as she tried to sleep that she had the nightmare about my arrival and during it she experienced contraction pains that were so real she wonders now if she were actually in labour even then.

It was late when my dad and Grandad finally got back and Grandad bustled in with shopping bags full of food to fill the cupboards he knew would be nearly bare. Mum threw her arms around him and felt immediately better knowing he was there. She convinced herself her headache had eased and tried to forget about the dream and concentrate on enjoying her time with Grandad.

Late the following night, when Mum's waters broke she couldn't ignore what was happening any longer. As Grandad and my dad battled to dig the car out of the snow, she realised she'd probably already been in labour for hours. Grandad waited at the house while my dad and Mum zoomed off to Warneford Hospital, a tiny place in Leamington Spa that was little more than a cottage hospital.

Mum wasn't surprised when an examination showed her labour was quite well progressed and a decision was made to allow her to try to have me naturally. She and my dad were taken straight through to a delivery room and though Mum had never been there before she recognised it instantly – from her dream. At the foot of the bed there was even the same ticking clock that had seemed to make her headache worse in the dream. She told herself not to be so stupid and did not mention the dream to anyone. She tried not to even think about it and she managed not to until that moment when I was being whisked off to special care and she was on her way to theatre.

CHAPTER THREE

Mum's two memories from the moments she began to regain consciousness have blurred into each other over time and she is no longer sure which came first. She suspects her first memory was of hearing, for the first time in her life, Grandad shouting in anger. As well as shouting, Grandad was grabbing at Mum and pulling her into a sitting position. She found out later that he had walked into the recovery room and found her lying on her back and beginning to vomit. He was shouting at the nurses.

Mum thinks she fell back into unconsciousness for a time after that and her next memory is of opening her eyes and seeing Grandad's usually happy-go-lucky, reassuring face, strained and pale, his eyes red from crying. Next to Grandad was a vicar, regally dressed in white robes. Mum had the worst imaginable pain banging through her head and various drips feeding into her arms. She wondered what the vicar wanted and, to begin with, she didn't even remember that she'd just had a baby.

She looked at Grandad. 'What's happening?'

He took Mum's hand and struggled to speak through his emotion. 'Listen to what the chaplain has to say, me duck.'

Memories of what had gone on in the delivery room started flooding back for Mum as she looked to the chaplain. He laid his hand over hers. My dad was sitting across the room, still silent and bewildered.

'Hello Julia, I'm Reverend Read – the hospital chaplain. I've been asked to come along because Baby has been taken to special care and the doctors felt it might be wise to have a christening.'

Mum filled with dread. She knew babies were only baptised in hospital because they were going to die. She turned to Grandad for some sort of explanation or reassurance, but he couldn't speak. He just nodded for her to agree.

'Okay,' she said, through sobs. Grandad put his arms around her.

'I'll be back shortly,' the vicar said, squeezing Grandad's shoulder as he left the room.

'Have you seen the baby?' Mum managed to ask Grandad. The physical pain in her head almost as unbearable as the emotional pain of realising her baby was going to die.

'Yes, the baby is beautiful.'

'Does Mum know what's happening?'

'She knows. She's on her way.'

Some nurses and a porter arrived to wheel Mum's bed across to the maternity ward where she was put into a side room. There was one other bed in the room but it was empty and Mum realised they were making a conscious effort to keep her away from all the other new mothers who had their babies with them.

Given the circumstances and feeling as unwell as she did, it must have been impossible for Mum to take in what was going on. She had an horrendous labour, had ended up having 46 stitches during her operation and had needed a blood transfusion. She vaguely remembers someone coming to the room to give her some kind of explanation of what my situation was. All she really took on board was that I had a hole in my stomach.

My dad and Grandad sat either side of her bed until the vicar came back with a nurse at his side. He was holding a short form, which he needed to complete before the service.

'Have you agreed upon a name for Baby?' the vicar asked.

'No-one has told me if the baby is a boy or a girl,' Mum said, suddenly feeling panicked. 'How can we choose a name?'

'What names have you discussed?' the vicar asked gently.

'Well, Joel for a boy, but we haven't got a girl's name yet,' Mum replied, glancing towards my dad, who had said so little it was as if he were unable to speak.

'Joel for a boy is perfect,' the vicar said.

'So I've got a boy?' Mum asked, confused. She glanced up at the nurse.

'Joel is a lovely name,' the nurse said. 'If it's not right, it can be changed later.'

Mum assumes Grandad and my dad had been given an explanation about my gender being uncertain. Perhaps she had too, but she had been unable to absorb it. Nothing seemed to make any sense. In hindsight, it's clear that no-one expected me to survive and they were all just trying to ensure I had an identity to die with.

The door opened and there stood a midwife, cradling me in her arms. My body had been carefully wrapped in sheets so that only my shoulders and feet were poking out. I was dressed in a mishmash of different coloured knitting – little yellow booties, a blue jacket, mint mittens. My eyes were just as wide and alert as they'd been in the delivery room.

'We didn't have too much to fit this little one, but we've done our best. Got to make the little 'un look good for a christening,' the midwife said, placing me down on Mum's chest.

'But there's nothing wrong,' Mum said as she looked down at me.

'Perfect little face,' the midwife replied softly. 'Just leave the little poppet dressed, my love. Don't you go delving around and upset yourself.'

Mum watched as, even at a few hours old, I appeared to be trying to lift my head off her chest as if in defiance at being told that I wasn't strong enough to live. Mum and Grandad were so close that they often seemed to share the same thought and, with his arm around her, he noticed what I was doing too.

'Does that look to you like the face of a baby that is about to die?' he whispered in Mum's ear. 'I'm telling you, he's going nowhere.'

Mum felt certain Grandad was right.

As the brief christening was conducted, Mum was so weak that she was terrified she was going to drop me and had to ask Grandad to take me. It was all she could do just to keep her eyes open. As soon as it was over, I was taken back to special care and Grandad told Mum to rest. She couldn't argue and gave in to sleep.

When Mum opened her eyes again, two suited and important-looking men were coming into the room and my dad and Grandad had gone. One of the men was in his late 50s or so and the other was closer to 30. They introduced themselves as doctors from Birmingham Children's Hospital and told her they had been called in to assess me and decide what should be done.

Mum's family were all hard workers, but none of them were academic and the well-spoken and obviously highly-educated doctors made her feel very small. She wished some-one were with her.

The doctors said they needed to explain what was wrong with me, but from the start, the terminology they used went straight over Mum's head.

'We can't feed the baby at the moment' she recalls one of them saying. 'There's nowhere for the waste to go,' 'the baby has no anus,' 'a colostomy is a priority,' 'there's a hole in his stomach.'

Mum couldn't keep up. She had no idea what they were telling her.

'Stop!' she eventually shouted, angry at being made to feel stupid and inadequate. 'I don't understand what you are saying.'

The doctors were quiet for a moment.

It was Mum who broke the silence and she was still rag-ing. 'What do you mean you haven't been able to feed him? Is it even 'him'? Is that right? Is he a boy? No-one seems to know!'

'We think so, but we can't be sure.'

'Well does he have a penis?' Mum spat back, thinking it must be the most simple thing in the world to be sure about.

'Joel's genitalia is incomplete. We think he is a boy, but at the moment we must concentrate on some of the more critical issues. The biggest priority has to be whether we can find a way for him to feed and process waste. I'm afraid he is a very, very poorly child. If Joel is going to survive, he will certainly require surgery and we need to decide whether operating on him is in everyone's best interests. Joel may not be able to withstand surgery and even if we do operate successfully, his long-term needs could be very, very substantial. It would be an awful lot for you to cope with. As difficult as we understand it is to face, in these cases, it can sometimes be better for everyone if we do not intervene.'

Mum may not have understood a lot of the what the doctors had said but she understood that part and she was enraged.

'What do you mean 'better if we don't intervene?' she screamed. 'What are you, God? If you have the skills to help of course you must! Don't stand there and ask me if it's in my best interests that my baby survives! It's my baby, of course it's in my best interests for it to survive! And how can it not be in a baby's best interests to survive? Surviving is what people are born to do. My baby was not born to die. Babies are born to live!'

The doctors remained totally calm. 'Miss Baker, we realise how difficult this must be for you. We have a duty to explain to you just how poorly this child is and to make it clear that even if we operate and if he survives, just how ill he will continue to be.'

'I don't care,' Mum said through sobs. 'I don't care how ill he will be. I will look after him. Please, please just give him that chance.'

The doctors exchanged a glance. When the elder of the two of them spoke, Mum felt as if he was pleased she was so adamant. She felt a bit like he'd been testing her.

'Miss Baker, we'll do everything we can. We'll arrange to get Joel to Birmingham today. Until we get him into theatre we can't be sure exactly what we are dealing with. A lot of Joel's stomach is on the outside and we will try to put that in. We will certainly have to make him a colostomy.'

'Can I come with him?' Mum asked, still not knowing what a colostomy was.

'Unfortunately Birmingham is a children's hospital only. You'll need to stay here to recover yourself, but I promise you, we will do our very best for him.'

Mum managed to hold herself together quite well as the doctors shook her hand and left, but once they were gone she collapsed back on her bed and broke down. She couldn't believe any of what was going on was real and it was just beginning to hit her how poorly I was. A nurse went to check on her and explained that, once they'd organised an ambulance for me, they'd bring me in to see her before I was taken to Birmingham.

The next person who walked through the door was Nan and as soon as they saw each other, she and Mum were both in tears. Gary and April had driven Nan down and, walking into the room behind her, they quietly pulled up a couple of chairs and sat in the background.

'Have you seen him, Mum? Have you seen Joel?'

'Not yet darling, but I've just seen your dad and Gary. They've told me what's happening. Gary has just nipped off to drop Dad back to your house for a bit. He was up all night waiting for news so he's going to get some rest and come back tomorrow. Gary will be back soon.'

In the meantime the nurses cleared the dayroom where there would be more space for everyone to go to say good-bye to me. Mum was loaded into a wheelchair and wheeled across by a porter and within a few minutes of getting there, the nurses brought in trays full of cups of tea and plates of toast for everyone. No-one could really stomach it but they all appreciated the gesture.

A few minutes later the door swung open and I arrived in my little see-through cot, looking just as alert and healthy as I had when Mum had seen me before. Nan, who'd expected some monstrous-looking baby, rushed straight over to the nurse.

'I'm so sorry, but you've brought the wrong baby.'

'No, no, this is Joel. This is your grandson.'

Nan burst into tears. She couldn't understand what was going on either, it didn't look like there was anything wrong with me. Nan and Mum both had a hold of me and a nurse took a Polaroid photograph of me in Mum's arms. We still have the picture and Mum looks so sad in it – a drip still in her hand and her face all red and swollen.

My dad returned just before the ambulance crew arrived with the biggest incubator Mum had ever seen and took me from her so they could link me up to all kinds of monitors and things. As they wheeled me away, Mum lost it completely, finding it impossible to let me go, knowing that she might never see me again.

Mum, Nan, Gary, April and my dad remained in the day-room for a while. The others tried to make conversation but Mum did not want to talk. She felt totally lost and empty. It was getting towards evening again and Mum's brother, April and Nan, who'd dropped everything to get there, had to get back. Nan had to make sure someone was available to keep an eye on Uncle John and to cover her shifts at the social club, but promised to get back as soon as she could.

Mum and my dad were left alone, just waiting for news. My dad hadn't had any sleep for almost two days by then and decided to go back to Mum's room where he had been given permission to stay in the other bed. For Mum, sleep wasn't an option. She couldn't bear to move from the spot where I'd left her. She sat in her wheelchair looking blankly at the wall going over and over everything that had happened. She thought of the months she hadn't realised she was pregnant and all the nights out she'd had in that time. She worried and wondered if the drink she'd had or something else she'd done was to blame for the way I'd been born. She thought of me miles away in an operating theatre and was eaten up by the fact she wasn't there with me.

Throughout the night, the nurses popped in every half an hour or so just to sit with her for a few minutes or to deliver cups of tea. One of them even went to the shop and got Mum some cigarettes. They were lovely to her, but all Mum really wanted was a call from Birmingham.

In the early hours the call eventually came through and a Chinese nurse, who was so caring that she'd made Mum feel she was living the trauma alongside her, answered it. The nurse ran the entire length of the corridor before bursting into the day room in floods of tears.

'He's out of theatre and guess what? He's not even in intensive care. He's made it!'

The nurse took Mum back to her room where they woke my dad and told him the news, before the nurse convinced Mum to get a few hours' sleep herself.

At 7am, Mum's eyes snapped open again as the curtains on the ward were pulled back. It was the first time she had felt completely free of the anaesthetic and able to think straight and all that was on her mind was me all alone in Birmingham. She asked a nurse if there was any news.

'We've not heard anything, but I can give them a ring for you?'

'I need to be there myself.'

'They just don't have facilities for mothers to recover there. It's not possible.'

'But I need to be there. I'm serious, I can't stay here.'

'You've got an horrendous amount of stitches. You need to stay here and get well, then you'll be much more use to Baby.'

'Honestly, staying here isn't an option. I need to be in Birmingham.'

'Look, let's wait and have a word with the doctors when they come round, okay?'

'What time is that?'

'There'll be round about 11. I'll go and call Birmingham for you and get an update, then I'll pop straight back. Just give me a few minutes.'

As soon as the nurse left, Mum looked over to my dad and they both knew she wouldn't be staying. She knew there was little point waiting for the doctors – they'd only tell her she couldn't go. There was still a drip in her arm and Mum thought it would only delay things if she waited for someone to come and remove it properly. She got hold of the tube and yanked it from her skin. It bled, but she didn't care. She shuffled off the side of the bed and threw the tube into a sink in the corner. My dad got her clothes and, with Mum moving gingerly, he helped her get dressed.

The nurse walked back in moments later. 'Oh, no, what have you done? The doctors will never discharge you.'

'I'm going,' Mum said. 'Just give me whatever paperwork I need to sign.'

'I knew you were going to do this,' the nurse said. 'Okay, well if I can't talk you out of it, at least let me sort that arm out before you go.'

Once Mum's arm was bound, a couple of the midwives helped my dad gather their things and then walked right out to the car with them. They each gave Mum a huge hug.

'If it was me,' one of them said. 'I'd do exactly the same.'

Mum was told that a midwife would visit her at home in the morning to check her over.

Travelling in the car was horrifically painful for Mum and every bump and jolt caused her a lot of discomfort. They went to Lillington first, where they collected Grandad, who wasn't at all surprised to see Mum. He knew she wouldn't be able to stay away from Birmingham.

The trip on to the children's hospital took 40 minutes and Mum was in agony. Every now and again, Grandad would break the silence in the car by asking if she was all right. She'd just grit her teeth and nod. As they drew into the city all she could think was 'my baby is here somewhere all alone and I don't even remember what he looks like'.

The area around the front of the hospital was covered in graffiti and looked dirty and uncared for, which made Mum's guilt worse. It looked like a dump and Mum was mortified that she'd allowed them to take me off and operate on me without knowing anything about the place. Inside, thankfully, it looked far better.

Grandad was one side of Mum and my dad the other, both of them having to prop her up because it was so difficult for her to walk. They got in a lift and made their way to special care where they found a lady sitting at a desk out the front of the unit.

Mum stepped forward. 'My son is in here. We've come to see him.'

It was the first time Mum had said 'my son' and she always remembers how strange it felt to realise she was someone's mum.

'What's Baby's name please?'

'Joel Holliday.'

'I'll just get someone to come and take you through.'

Mum already felt dizzy and sick through the exertion of getting to Birmingham and the ward. As it dawned on her that she was about to be reunited with me, she felt even more ill, worrying what state she would find me in. She thought about the warnings the doctors had given her about how ill I would be even if I got through surgery. Were my problems all physical or mental too? Could she cope? She'd told the doctors she could, but, in reality, she did not know if that was true.

CHAPTER FOUR

I didn't look anything like the same, apparently perfect, baby they'd all seen the day before. Fast asleep in one of six incubators in the room, I was covered in tubes and drips. Mum says it looked as if both my arms and legs were broken as they had all been bandaged and splinted to keep various cannulas in place. I was wearing a white babygro, deliberately too large so that it was loose around my abdomen. The poppers at the bottom had been left open to allow tubes to feed into my feet. At the side of my incubator an electronic monitor displayed my heart rate and oxygen saturation level and beeped every few seconds.

The nurse pulled up some chairs to allow Mum, Grandad and my dad to sit at my side.

'He's doing absolutely fine,' she said. 'Got a great set of lungs on him, that's for sure. Everything went very well in theatre and he has been nice and settled since. He hasn't needed any assistance at all with breathing, which is really very good. The doctor will be best placed to tell you about everything in more detail and he should be round quite soon. Until then, I'll show you how the portholes in the incubator work so you can reach in and give his little face a stroke.'

After showing Mum how to unclip the portholes, the nurse left them to it and carried on with what she was doing. She told Mum that she only had to ask if there was anything she needed. Mum, my dad and Grandad sat quietly at my side, taking turns to reach into the incubator and allow me to grip their fingers. They didn't say much to each other. Seeing me like that brought home to Mum just how poorly I was and she worried over exactly what was wrong with me and whether I would survive.

At the other incubators in the room other sets of worried parents sat quietly, watching their own babies. Everyone spoke in the kind of voice people use in libraries. Through the constant beeps of the monitors and intermittent baby cries, both from the room I was in and those on the rest of the ward, there was a general hush. Every now and again a nurse would come in to fiddle about with the machinery and drips around me or one of the other babies or change a nappy or give a tube feed. One of the nurses asked Mum if she was planning to breastfeed and when Mum said she was, they explained she'd need to express regularly to begin with as, for the time-being, I too was being fed through a tube. They returned a bit later with a breast pump and explained how and when to use it.

When it was my turn to be changed, Mum was asked if she'd prefer to leave for a few minutes. She got the feeling the nurses suspected she wasn't quite ready to be confronted with the full detail of my condition just then and she didn't disagree. Mum found it a bit confusing that it took two nurses half-an-hour to change my nappy, but didn't question them about it.

A little later, the elder of the two doctors Mum had spoken to at Warneford Hospital appeared at my incubator. He said he'd been the one to operate on me and wanted to explain what he'd done. To Mum's recollection, he did his best to explain it all in layman's terms, but it was like an in-depth science lesson. Mum was so overwhelmed by everything and suddenly had to try to understand the technicalities of how a baby was formed in the womb and what had gone wrong with me.

Mum was told that all babies start out with the bladder and bowel fused together and as development progresses the two separate and then the abdominal tissues close round to form the abdominal wall. The doctor also explained that in those early days of pregnancy, boys and girls look the same. It is only later that either testes or ovaries form and hormones take over to develop either male or female genitalia. At some point during those processes, my development had stalled.

My abdominal wall never grew, my urinary and digestive system was incomplete and my genitals were never created. I literally had an opening in my abdomen where my bladder and some of my intestine poked through. Before that first operation, my bladder had been in four pieces and even afterwards it was still in two. It was essentially useless and urine just flowed straight out into the cavity in my stomach. There was so little flesh either side of the gaping hole that the surgeon had been unable to close it. He said that, over time, a kind of clear skin would naturally grow over to hold everything in place, but until then the infection risks were great. Once I'd had time to grow, he hoped there would be enough flesh to pull round and close the hole.

Mum asked if I really was a boy and the surgeon confirmed I was – he had found two undescended testes inside of me. Mum said he even implied that the presence of them meant I might be able to father children one day. Not naturally, of course, but the thought of it gave her a lot of comfort anyway. She asked if it would be possible to construct a penis for me and she was given the impression that she shouldn't worry about that yet. I had to survive first. The surgeon made it clear I was far from out of the woods, but at the same time Mum felt he seemed so positive. He told her he was pleased with what he had achieved in the operation, especially as he'd managed to make a colostomy.

Mum still didn't know what a colostomy was but she felt too stupid to admit it until the surgeon had left and a nurse came over to ask if she was okay with everything. It was the nurse who had to explain that a colostomy was the formation of a channel for faeces to leave the body. She said part of my intestine would have been drawn to the surface to create an exit point – a stoma. When the nurse said colostomies were sometimes reversible, Mum thought it meant mine might be temporary. She just hadn't grasped how little of my body was properly formed.

'No-one expects you to take all this information in straight away,' the nurse said. 'Just keep asking questions. We can get you a pen and paper so every time you think of something to ask you can jot it down and ask the doctors when they next come round.'

By early evening, the stress of the day and everyone's general exhaustion was taking over. The thought of leaving me behind at the hospital wasn't easy for Mum, but another part of her needed to get away. It must have been so stressful for her – she was still recovering from major surgery herself.

On the way home, they stopped off at a phone box so that Mum could ring Nan and update her. She stuck to the positives and told her how pleased the surgeon was with the operation and how well I was recovering from it. Those were the bits Mum was trying to cling to. Nan told Mum she hoped to get back to Lillington to be with her by the weekend.

That night, Mum, Grandad and my dad ate fish and chips and fell into bed. My dad had said so little that Mum became convinced he too thought my situation was all her fault. She lay in bed thinking about the baby she had dreamed of having then sobbed herself to sleep.

The next day a midwife came to see Mum and told her she'd developed an infection. Mum felt awful, but took the prescription for antibiotics and just carried on. Her only priority was getting back to Birmingham to be with me. That day turned out to be the worst of all for Mum.

Initially, when Mum got to the hospital things carried on much as they had the day before. She, my dad and Grandad all sat around me and watched the nurses come back and forth to see to me and update them on my good progress. Then, late in the afternoon, one of the nurses said it was time to change me and suggested that perhaps Mum would like to see how it was done. Mum's stitches were pulling painfully and she felt quite ill, but she was pleased they were going to show her how to begin doing something for me.

The nurse and a colleague both pulled on hairnets and scrubbed their arms to the elbows as if they were about to go

into surgery. They pulled out trays full of disposable tweezers, a pile of dressings and gauzes and saline solutions. They
opened the top of the incubator and put a heat lamp above
and Mum, my dad and Grandad all stood close by, watching.

Mum was very aware of the heat from the lamp on her
face and could feel herself sweating. The nurses undid my
babygro and underneath Mum could see for the first time
just how large the bulge of dressings on my stomach was. It
was the first time she had seen for herself that I wasn't perfect. The nurses began to lift the layers of wadding and Mum
started to see things that she hadn't been expecting – areas of
red and black on the dressings. She was starting to feel sick.
The final dressing was stuck to my skin and I howled as the
nurse pulled it away. It was the first time Mum had heard me
cry. Underneath the dressings, Mum has always said it just
looked as if a bomb had gone off. She could not believe the
mess that was there. It looked as if my legs had been snapped
back and a butcher had slit me up the middle.

Mum glanced at my dad and Grandad, wishing someone
would tell her it was all right. They were both as white as
she was and looking ahead in disbelief too. The nurses were
continuing to explain what they were doing. They began
pouring saline solution into my stomach to wash out the
urine, which made me scream even louder. Then one of them
picked up a set of tweezers with a lump of gauze on the end
and began plunging it into me and wiping it round.

Mum thought she was going to pass out. She couldn't
take any more. She knew she had to get out of there. She
turned around and ran. She ran straight out of the unit and
across to the lifts. A lift was waiting and she hurried inside,

crying hysterically. She bashed at the numbers to get down to the ground floor and when the door opened, she ran again, out of the hospital and into the underpass at the front. The pain from her stitches was tearing through her, but she told herself she deserved it. In the underpass she bent double and vomited. She was still crying and just wanted to get away. She walked through the underpass and spotted a greasy spoon café. She didn't even have any money but considered going inside. As she stepped towards the door, she realised Grandad was beside her.

Grandad sat Mum down and ordered them both a cup of tea.

Mum let her thoughts spill out. 'I can't do it, I can't even look at him. I'll never be able to look after him. I'll have to have him adopted.'

Grandad was very gentle. 'You'll find the strength from somewhere. It's just going to take time.'

'But I can't do it. I won't ever be able to do what they were doing. How can I have a baby I can't look after?'

'Don't worry about that bit yet. One step at a time. You'll get through this. You will. It's a lot to take in, that's all.'

Grandad convinced Mum to have her drink and then ordered a plate of chips. 'Just give yourself a few minutes to get your strength back,' he said.

When they were done, Grandad walked Mum back to the hospital. She clutched his arm, wincing from the pain of each step, but feeling calmer. He walked her to the ward and back to my incubator. The lights had been dimmed for the evening and I was lying awake and serene, dressed again.

Grandad left Mum to be with me on her own for a moment. She poked her hand into the incubator and, looking into my eyes, she knew she would learn to cope just like Grandad had said. She made a promise out loud to me that she'd never run out on me again.

Grandad returned a few minutes later with my dad, who said so little that Mum, again, felt he was angry with her. When one of the nurses came round again, Mum apologised for what she'd done.

'Oh, don't you worry yourself, you did very well. It's all going to take time. I tell you what you need, a little cuddle. Would you like to have a hold of Joel?'

It was a bit of a task for the nurse to lift me out of the incubator and pass me into Mum's arms, with all the tubes to contend with, but it meant so much to Mum. She held me carefully for a few moments, worried she might hurt me, before swapping places with my dad and then Grandad so everyone could have a hold before I was put back in. After a short time the nurse said I'd better be put back in the warm and lifted me into the incubator again. Mum sat and stroked my face through the portholes until I went to sleep and then she, Grandad and my dad headed back home again for the night. Mum was hurting all over and just wanted her bed.

The next day, Mum was determined to watch me being changed again and though it was awful, she did it. Every time the nurses pushed the gauze into my stomach, I screamed and Mum wanted to grab me and run away with me. She made herself keep watching and keep listening to the instructions and explanations of the nurses. She kept thinking, if it was horrendous for her, how was it for me?

At the end of the procedure the nurses applied a waxy Jelonet dressing over the wound and, from that moment on, that was the part Mum always looked forward to. She could breathe out then. Over the top of the Jelonet dressing went a huge pad of wadding and then a nappy held everything in place.

The nurses said my colostomy needed to be sorted out too, but as I was quite distressed by that point and Mum had been through enough for one day, they said they'd just get it done quickly and show her that another time. They whipped the old bag off and put a new one on.

Later that day, Mum asked if she could do something to help in the process of changing me. The nurses were amazed she was asking to do that within 24 hours of running out of the room during a change, but encouraged her. My dad seemed pleased too and Mum scrubbed up along with the nurses. On their instructions and shaking all over, Mum managed to pour the saline in, steeling herself to my cries.

The nurses said over and over again how important it was to use a new set of tweezers at each stage. One to remove the dressings, another to wipe me round and a third to replace fresh dressings. Mum wondered how I'd manage to avoid an infection with such a huge, gaping wound and how she would ever remember all the steps in the process of changing my nappy.

For the next few days, Grandad stayed at Mum's house until Nan was able to swap places with him. Then, when Nan had to go back up to Pinchbeck, Barbara said she'd stay for a bit. Mum found it difficult having Barbara staying in their house but appreciated the effort she was making and knew she and my dad needed the support. They were travelling backwards and forwards to Birmingham every day and were both exhausted.

Things carried on in a similar way for a couple of weeks and, as my condition seemed to be stable and Mum was much better, Mum and my dad agreed he needed to start thinking about getting back to university. The hospital had some flats that Mum was allowed to stay in and she suggested it would be a good idea for her to do that for a few nights a week. The flats were just outside of the hospital site, in a not particularly nice area of Birmingham and Mum had to walk back to them on her own in the dark. She used to be on edge from the minute she left the hospital until she had climbed out of the old fashioned cage lift and got into her front door. Once inside she would sit and run through the stages of changing me correctly in her mind and try to write it down in order without making any mistakes.

The doctors seemed really pleased with how I was doing, though no-one made any firm predictions about my future. They always implied that Mum should just take things one day at a time. The most they hoped for was to get me feeding normally so that Mum could take me home. They knew my biggest problem would be trying to avoid infection and trying to fight it off if I got one. If Mum could manage to keep me free of infection, they hoped to operate at some point in the future to close my abdomen. She always got the feeling it was a very big 'if'.

Gradually the various drips and monitors came off and Mum and my dad learned to change me without any help. In the middle of all that was going on, the day they went along and formally registered me as Joel David Holliday wasn't even particularly memorable. It was just another job done.

The final thing to be removed was my feeding tube, which had been my only means of taking the mix of expressed milk and formula I was being given. A nurse tried me first on a bottle of purely expressed milk, but I seemed to prefer SMA! Once formula was added to the mix, I took the feed well and the successful move to being fed by bottle was the final leap in my recovery. It meant Birmingham Hospital did not feel that I needed to be there any longer and that I was ready to be transferred to Warwick Hospital.

I'd been in Birmingham for five weeks and Mum and my dad were relieved to think I'd be moving to Warwick, which was much closer to Lillington. Nan was back staying with Mum again and they were all really excited that I was obviously getting stronger. Mum expected I'd be in Warwick for a couple more weeks then she'd finally be able to bring me home and take me out in the pram and try to enjoy some of the things she'd be looking forward to about being a mum.

The morning after the transfer, Mum and my dad went in to Warwick Hospital together to see me. Things were still strained between them, but they had odd moments where Mum felt some of the warmth they'd used to share and that morning was one of those times.

A nurse was at the side of my cot. 'Morning, he's had a lovely settled night. He's getting on very well. It looks like we'll get him home today.'

Mum couldn't quite believe what she was hearing. 'Today?' she said, panicked.

'You don't want to be here longer than you have to, do you? I should think you're dying to have your little boy home finally.' The nurse ticked a couple of things on the chart that was kept at the foot of my cot and walked away.

The prospect of bringing me home was terrifying to Mum, but she knew she had to do it some time. As usual, my dad didn't have a lot to say about it and Mum did not want to show how worried she was. She didn't want him to get annoyed with her and she didn't want the nurses to think she wasn't capable.

Another brisk nurse came across. 'Right, I hear this little one is going home today, so I'm just going to give you a quick refresher on how to change his colostomy and then we can get you on your way.'

Mum had seen my colostomy changed quite a few times, but she'd never done it herself. She watched with extra attention to detail as the nurse whipped off one bag and stuck another around the little belly button-like stoma where my intestine left my body with a flange – a large rubbery, sticky plaster. It was all done in a minute or two and Mum told herself it must be very straightforward.

'Right, that's that then,' the nurse said giving them a quick smile. 'We'll just get you loaded up with all the prescription you need and get you on your way. Congratulations.'

Mum realised she was shaking and decided to go outside for a cigarette. On her way back to the special care unit, she stopped at the phone box to call Nan.

'Hi Mum, it's me. We're bringing him home.'

'Bringing him home?' Nan exclaimed unbelievingly. 'What, now, today?'

'Yep. In a few hours. They're just getting everything we need together and then we'll be able to leave.'

Nan hadn't even been able to stay in the room yet while Mum changed me. 'Well, can you cope?' she asked, worried.

'We'll soon find out,' Mum replied. She knew it wasn't the most convincing reply but it was the best she could manage. She kept telling herself she was going to be all right, but she really didn't know if she would. It's probably a good thing that she had no idea how difficult things were about to become.

CHAPTER FIVE

As Mum walked into the house with me for the first time, her emotions were an even mix of excitement, fear and pride. Nan had a cup of tea waiting and my dad followed behind, weighed down with a pile of cardboard boxes full of my prescription stuff – saline solutions, colostomy bags, Jelonet dressings and all the rest. For half an hour or so, I slept and they chatted and tried to convince themselves everything was going to be fine. Then, as I stirred and began to cry, Mum realised she could smell that my colostomy needed changing.

My dad rushed off to get everything that was needed to transform the dining room table into a makeshift nurses' station. He laid out all the various sterile coverings and got the dressings and solutions to hand and Mum started undressing me. It was only then that she realised the side of my babygro was brown. As she began lifting my layers of dressings, with me screaming my head off, she could see excrement had leaked everywhere, including into my open stomach - the area that was so vulnerable to infection and needed to be treated with such care.

Mum was so horrified that she froze in panic. 'Oh my God, what the hell are we going to do? It's everywhere. It's all in his stomach. Look at it. Oh my God.'

'We're just going to have to get him cleaned up,' my dad said. He spoke as if he was calm and in control. 'Let's just follow the usual steps and get him clean.'

I was howling at the top of my lungs, which wasn't unusual during a change, but Mum felt even more panicked and guilty about it than usual. The nurses had always told her that a lot of my noise was just the normal protests of a small baby unhappy at having its warm clothes removed, but Mum knew the saline stung me as it went on and that day she feared more than ever that I was hurting. She couldn't believe that I'd only been out of hospital a bit over an hour and already she'd allowed this to happen. She worried again over whether she was really up to looking after me.

My dad kept Mum focused on the process of cleaning me up and reminded her to warm the saline solution before pouring it in and to use clean tweezers for each piece of clean-up gauze. They worked together as a team until the mess was clear and then started to look at what needed to be done to reapply the colostomy.

I was still only around 5lb, having dropped then regained weight in hospital, and the colostomy bags and flanges available in those days were almost as big as I was. They knew the rubbery plaster-like flanges that went between bag and body had to be cut to fit around my tiny stoma. They also remembered that the flange needed to be applied to my skin without any creases before they could place the bag on it, but every time they got to the final stage the flange kept springing off. They tried and tried, the levels of agitation and concern constantly rising, until an hour-and-a-half later the process was finally complete. They'd got the bag to stick, but what neither of them had remembered was to apply the clip that held everything in place so when, moments later, my body erupted again, they were back to square one, my vulnerable organs covered in excrement again.

Again, my dad remained calm. 'We just have to clean him up again. We obviously got something wrong. We'll have to do it again.'

The process was a little quicker second time around, but not a lot and when they got to the end they were both nervous about whether they'd got it right this time. Either way, Mum knew I was due a feed and that would have to be the next priority. Mum assumed she'd be able to feed me herself now that I was home but however hard she tried to get me to latch on, I didn't want to know. The most I managed was a minute or two then I'd come off again and start screaming. Mum persevered until she could take it no longer and asked my dad to get a bottle. They offered me that, but I didn't seem any more interested or content with it. I took a bit of milk, screamed for a bit, took a bit more, then screamed again.

'Could he have wind?' Nan suggested.

Mum stopped trying to feed me and instead attempted the difficult task of trying to help me bring up wind. She couldn't lay me flat on her shoulder and pat my back like you might with a normal baby because it put too much pressure on my open abdomen. She had to make sure that however she held me, she wasn't pressing on my organs. Her rubbing and patting, seemed to bring me a bit of comfort and eventually I dropped off to sleep. My parents climbed into bed, already exhausted, but it wasn't long before I was screaming again and my colostomy had exploded once more.

I didn't become any more content about taking feeds from Mum or a bottle and spent much of the night screaming. By morning, the house was a tip, covered in packets from dressings, half-drunk bottles and dirty baby clothes. Mum's confidence was at rock bottom and she feared the impact of a night where my colostomy had leaked into my wound over and over again. She needed encouragement and support, but instead she got what she has always described as the health visitor from hell.

Mum was sitting up in bed trying, for the millionth time, to get me to feed from her when my dad let the health visitor in. 'You really need to get this house cleaned up,' she said, without even wasting any time on introducing herself. 'And you're doing that all wrong.'

Mum looked up mortified that the woman had not only confirmed her suspicion that she was to blame for me not wanting to feed but also that she thought she didn't care about the state of the house. She didn't get a chance to say anything before the health visitor started grabbing at her breast and trying to manoeuvre things more to her liking.

'Did no-one show you how to nurse your baby?' she snapped.

The health visitor's barked instructions did lead to me taking something like a full feed, but by the end of it, Mum knew she couldn't bear to risk having to go through that again and would be giving me bottles in future.

They talked about how the night had gone and Mum admitted she and my dad had struggled, particularly with the colostomy.

'Well, it's clear you are not coping,' the health visitor said. 'I'm going to have to contact the hospital and arrange for someone to come to see you.'

As she left, Mum was convinced the health visitor didn't believe she was up to caring for me and was terrified someone would be sent to take me away.

Later that day, the stoma nurse who had delivered the colostomy 'refresher' to Mum and my dad before discharging me from hospital the previous day, arrived on the doorstep. She turned out to be lovely and, after a quick chat, realised that Mum had no previous experience of changing my colostomy.

'I'm so sorry,' she said. 'I just assumed you'd done it hundreds of times and didn't want to insult you by going through it all again. I feel so awful. No wonder you had such a terrible night. Don't worry. I will stay with you today until you know exactly what you are doing.'

The visit from the nurse left my parents much more in control of the changing side of things and they could crack that in about 40 minutes. What it didn't resolve was my feeding or sleeping, both of which I seemed to refuse. Mum tried over and over to give me a bottle but I just screamed. My dad tried and Nan tried but I wasn't interested. Mum pushed me backwards and forwards in my pram to try to settle me, she winded me as best she could, she tried to cuddle me, even though that frightened her because she'd been warned handling me too much could cause me more pain.

For two days, I cried morning and night with barely any breaks, until Mum became convinced something was wrong and called a doctor in.

The local GP came out to the house and agreed my cry sounded pained rather than discontent and sent us back to Warwick Hospital. In the car on the way there, I dropped into a deep sleep and by the time we arrived no-one would have thought anything was wrong. The doctors and nurses were kind and understanding and listened to Mum's concerns, but after a night there where I displayed little or no symptoms, it was put down to colic and we were sent home again.

Unfortunately, it did not last and Mum spent the following days going back and forth to the GP, insisting that something was wrong and that she was sure I was not taking enough milk. He gave her all sorts of advice but none of it seemed to help. The only time I did take an entire bottle Mum's relief was short-lived. I projectile vomited the entire thing up moments later in a gush of mint sauce-like fluid, which she did not recognise at the time as bile. Mum called the doctor once again and he sent the dreaded health visitor round, who convinced Mum she was most likely working herself up over nothing. Meanwhile, my dad was still trying to keep up with university, but like Mum was getting very little sleep and everything was very fraught.

I'd been home from hospital ten days when, after another night of rocking, winding, cuddling and cajoling, I eventually fell asleep in the early hours. Mum crawled into bed, exhausted and knew I'd be screaming again as soon as she closed her eyes. When she woke up at 9am, realised my dad was still asleep beside her and everything was quiet, she knew immediately that something was wrong. Mum leapt from the bed and ran to my cot. Inside she found me grey and motionless, my head tilted slightly to one side with green fluid running from my mouth.

Fearing I was dead, Mum reached in and snatched me up into her arms, almost deliberately being rough to try to get a reaction. I didn't make a sound but she could hear I was breathing at least.

'Gary!' she screamed. 'He's ill. We've got to get him to hospital.'

My dad bolted out of the bed, took one look at me and started pulling on some clothes. Mum handed me to him and, while she got dressed, he wrapped me in a blanket. They grabbed my change bag, ran downstairs and out to the car and sped back to Warwick Hospital. They headed straight for the children's ward and a nurse took one look at me and said they needed to get me back to Birmingham.

My parents and I were put in a cubicle as everyone bustled around organising an ambulance and Mum gathered herself enough to realise she needed to change me. She laid me down in the hospital cot and whipped through the process, which she was getting down to a fine art. I lay glassy eyed and unresponsive throughout, not even making a murmur when the saline was poured on.

As soon as Mum was finished, the ambulance was ready and Mum climbed in with me, while my dad followed behind in the car. When we arrived, the surgeons were already waiting. Birmingham Hospital had heard enough to suspect I'd got inflamed internal scar tissue, which can lead to a life-threatening blockage. As I disappeared into theatre someone was left behind to sit Mum and my dad down in a side room and explain what they planned to do.

The surgery was expected to take around an hour-and-a-half, but my parents ended up sitting on the cold plastic chairs in the waiting room for five long hours. During that time there was very little information and Mum just prayed I'd come out alive.

Eventually one of the surgeons appeared. 'Joel's out of surgery and he is doing amazingly well. He is one tough little man.'

Mum was told they'd found an incredible amount of adhesions and had to remove a lot of my large intestine, but the colostomy was still able to function. I was back on the special care unit and she and my dad were taken through to see me. It was the most ill Mum had ever seen me look. I still had the glassy and empty look to my eyes that I'd had when she got to my cot that morning and was covered in all the tubes of the early days. On top of all that I had a graphic wound across my middle where they'd had to slice me from one side to the other, above the area where my bladder and intestine already lay exposed. Mum took up her position at my side again and this time she didn't even leave to sleep, too terrified she would come back and find me gone.

For the first few days it was touch-and-go and Mum was worried to touch me again for fear of making things worse. She almost had to go back to the beginning to find the courage to care for me, but this time, as I got stronger, so did she. She realised that she had been the one who knew something was wrong with me even when her doctor, the health visitor and the hospital put it down to colic. She realised that not only was she capable of looking after me but her mother's instincts meant no-one would do it better.

After a fortnight I was ready to be discharged again, first to Warwick Hospital for a few days and then back home as before. Before I left Birmingham, Mum met with two of the surgeons who had been involved with me and asked, for the first time, what my future held if I did manage to bypass all the infection risks that everyone knew could finish me.

No-one really knew the answers and all predictions were always made with a great deal of caution, but, Mum walked away from that conversation believing that almost anything was possible. If I could get through the first few months, in the long run my abdomen could be sealed, a penis created and the only real problems I'd have would be a few scars.

When Mum got me home this time, it was more like the normal experience of a first-time mum bringing her baby home. It was exhausting and relentless, but Mum had a lot more confidence and started to get into a routine. Nan, Grandad and Barbara all took a step back to allow her and my dad to build their own family life.

Although things were a little easier with me, Mum felt the distance between her and my dad was wider than ever and their financial situation was not good. My dad managed to negotiate a reduction in rent with their landlord based on their circumstances, but they knew they'd probably have to find somewhere else to live after the summer holidays. He and Mum tended only to talk about me and practicalities and it was very tense.

Mum tried to put everything else to the back of her mind as she enjoyed watching me grow and progress. I hit all the milestones on time – smiling, cooing, clapping my hands and sitting myself up when required. Mum missed home, she missed Jason and even Rebecca and all the other friends she'd made at my dad's university, who she barely saw now her life was so far removed from theirs. She also missed how things had once been between her and my dad, but she loved having me and told herself none of the rest of it mattered. She concentrated on the positives and even organised a trip back to Pinchbeck and a proper christening for me where her brother Gary was named my godfather and one of her oldest friends Mel Harley, my godmother.

Birmingham Hospital sent an appointment through for a follow-up check that fell when I was around six months old. Mum was looking forward to showing the doctors how well I had progressed and hoped to find out more about when they'd be able to close my abdomen and start on the reconstructive operations she was expecting me to have. A couple of weeks before the appointment, she was lifting me into a standing position on her knee as she sang and chattered to me, when she noticed my feet were sitting incredibly awkwardly and appeared almost to be turning backwards. She tried not to let it panic her and just logged it as something else she must remember to ask the doctors about.

On the day of the appointment, Mum sat with me on her lap and my dad at her side, in front of a number of the familiar faces they'd seen after my two surgeries. The older of the two surgeons she'd originally met at Warneford Hospital in the hours after my birth seemed to be at the head of the meeting. They all smiled and nodded as Mum happily jabbered on about how well she thought I was doing and told them that I hadn't even had so much as a cold. She also told them about her fears over the angle of my feet and they nodded and made a few notes.

'I'm wondering if you can tell me a bit about the future for Joel, like when you expect to be able to do the surgery to make a penis?' Mum asked.

The tone of the meeting seemed to change in that instant. It was the older surgeon from Warneford Hospital that replied. 'Oh, my dear, I don't think that's an option.'

'Sorry? What do you mean, not an option?' Mum said in disbelief.

'Making Joel a penis just isn't a realistic surgical proposition.'

Mum turned to the young surgeon who'd told her it was possible before I'd left Birmingham. 'But you told me that's what you'd do.'

The young surgeon looked at his feet and mumbled a response. 'I'm sorry if there was a misunderstanding. I did tell you what was possible in some cases, but it wasn't meant to be specific to Joel's outcome.'

The leading surgeon interrupted his, obviously junior, colleague. He looked Mum straight in the eye. 'As difficult as it might be to face, we have to be realistic about the limitations of Joel's future and I am afraid the future is rather bleak. I have always tried to be honest with you about the very many challenges Joel will face and they are challenges that cannot be ignored.

'Joel will never have a penis. He will never be able to function as a man. That in itself will be very, very difficult for him. He will have sexual urges, but he will not be able to act upon them. I'm afraid the psychological impact of that could well be unbearable for him. The physical aspects of Joel's condition will make it highly challenging for him to reach the age of 21 and the emotional difficulties he will face could well mean that he will choose to end his own life before then.

'In addition to those issues, you are right to identify the serious misalignment of Joel's pelvis, which you have noted through the angle of his feet. In very simple terms, if Joel does manage to walk, he will do so with a very odd gait. It is quite likely he will have a duck-like waddle. However, that is not the most concerning of the issues relating to Joel's pelvis. The thing that ought to be most prevalent in our minds is that the main function of the pelvis is to protect the organs and Joel's pelvis does not do that effectively. A simple fall for Joel could be a very serious affair. One would, of course, expect numerous falls and tumbles during childhood, but for Joel any one of those falls could have fatal consequences.'

The surgeon glanced between Mum and my dad who were both staring at him, shocked and destroyed. 'I realise I am being rather frank about all of this and I do appreciate how difficult it must be to fully face Joel's situation. However, there really is no value for anyone in not doing so.'

Mum knew this man wasn't being unkind or malicious and was just trying to give her a wake-up call. Perhaps she had only heard the bits she'd wanted to when she had spoken to the doctors previously? She looked at me, her beautiful and happy little boy and wondered why I had survived everything if this was all I had to face. Why had God saved me?

She and my dad left the meeting in a daze, not quite able to deal with everything they had been told. Mum has said it was as if their worlds had just crashed and neither of them really asked the other how they were. I suppose it seemed a bit pointless really, how could they be? In the car on the way home, Mum thought about everything the doctor had said. She kept coming back to the point that even if I got through all the physical problems, he thought I'd be so psychologically scarred that I'd commit suicide. She could not bear the thought of all that pain and turmoil for me. If I'd have been brain-damaged and unable to understand how different I was to other men, I'd actually be better off. She almost wished that were the case.

CHAPTER SIX

'Have you ever thought that what the doctor told you about Joel's future was just one person's opinion?' Diane Bentley said to Mum. Diane was a health visitor that covered the area around Nan's house.

'What do you mean?' Mum asked.

'I mean you don't have to accept that there's nothing that can be done for Joel. You should get a second opinion. Why don't you try Great Ormond Street?'

It had been four weeks since Mum had been given the terrible prognosis for my future and she had felt totally defeated ever since. She had said a tearful goodbye to the Lillington house when the summer holidays began, knowing that she and my dad could not afford to return to it. They'd gone to Nan's for the holidays and my dad was back working all hours in the factory while trying to figure out where they would live in September.

Diane had been informed that Mum would be in her area for a number of weeks and had been asked to visit her at Nan's. To begin with, Mum hadn't really wanted to know her, expecting her to be like the health visitor in Lillington, but Diane had kept coming round every few days and continued to be warm and friendly. Diane had been able to see that Mum was deeply unhappy and had picked up that things were strained between her and my dad as well.

Mum had finally confided in Diane about what the doctors had said about my future and told her she was finding it impossible to deal with. Diane's suggestion about getting a second opinion felt like a lifeline to Mum. She had never even considered questioning whether the Birmingham doctors were wrong about me and had just accepted their word as gospel.

'How would I get Great Ormond Street to see him?' Mum asked, suddenly hopeful.

'Leave it with me,' Diane replied. 'I'll get you an appointment.'

Within days, Diane had got me an appointment for December and it changed everything for Mum. She'd had four weeks of feeling like there was no point to anything, but the prospect of seeing another doctor and being given other possibilities gave her back her hope and optimism.

A week or so before they needed to return to university, my dad heard about a house in Coventry that was within their tiny budget and drove down there after work one night to see it. It was dark when he arrived and the lights in the house were poor but he could see it needed a lot of cleaning up. The area, Foals Hill, wasn't the best either, but as it was the only thing they could afford, he signed a tenancy for it. That weekend, he took Mum, Nan and I to see it and, in the light of day, the house was worse than any of them had imagined.

'There's no way I'm letting you stay here,' Nan said as soon as she saw it.

The house's previous tenants had written swear words across the walls inside the front door. The kitchen window was so thick with grease that the net curtains were embedded into it.

'I knew you were going to hate it,' my dad said. 'It was the best I could do, all right?'

'It'll be fine,' Mum said with more bravery than she felt. 'We just need to clean it up a bit.'

The house was so disgusting that neither Mum nor Nan were prepared to stay there as it was so they got my dad to drive them the two hours each way backwards and forwards to Pinchbeck for the next three days while they scrubbed, bleached and painted everything. They found the only way to clean the kitchen windows was to use a hair dryer to melt the grease and a fish slice to shovel it off. The carpets were beyond hope and they took them out and burned them. It was never going to be possible to make the house nice, but they got it habitable in time for Mum, my dad and I to move in before his lectures started again.

That house became a very lonely and isolating place for Mum where she had almost no-one to turn to. She never felt accepted by the predominantly Asian community and as I became more mobile, Mum lived in constant fear of me getting an infection in the still far from perfect house. I'd started pulling at my dressings and delving around in my own stomach and she'd sometimes find me squeezing on my exposed bladder or emptying the contents of my colostomy all over myself.

Mum had always been bigger than average and her clothes were usually a size 20-22, but she was so miserable in

Coventry that she ballooned to a size 28. As the weight piled on, so did Mum's dislike for herself and, she was convinced, my dad's dislike of her. They began having terrible rows and one winter's night he told her to get out, which she did, clinging on to me and without even a coat to wear. Mum walked to the nearest phone box and waited outside for a woman to end her call. The woman kept glaring at Mum and finally came out full of rage.

'Get off my patch,' screamed the woman at Mum, who hadn't realised she was a prostitute.

Mum had me in her arms but that didn't seem to colour the woman's perception that Mum was trying to steal her trade and she smashed her fist into Mum's face. Mum ran back home and up to her room where she sobbed into her pillow as her eye turned black. The only thing that got her through the following weeks was focusing on the Great Ormond Street appointment which she had convinced herself would be the answer to everything.

The night before the appointment, Mum, my dad and I stayed at Aunt Di's in Orpington to break up the journey and we were due to stay there on the way back too. As we set off for London, Mum had butterflies in her stomach.

Mr Ransley, Great Ormond Street's head of urology, examined me while a junior colleague took notes.

'A severe, classic case of cloacal exstrophy,' he dictated to the colleague. It was the first time Mum recalls hearing a label for my condition. It's an extremely rare condition that, depending on who you ask, affects between one in 250,000 or as few as one in 400,000 births. Research seems to show that it is unavoidable and not caused by anything either parent did or did not do.

When the examination was complete, my parents sat in front of Mr Ransley's desk, me propped on Mum's knee, and waited to hear what he had to say.

Very matter-of-factly, Mr Ransley told them what he thought. 'You're raising this child as the wrong sex. This child needs to be raised as a female.'

There was a second of silence as Mum took in his words, then she exploded with anger. This was the man who she had pinned all her hopes on and that was what he had to say?

'Are you stupid?' she raged. 'I'm not listening to this shit. Come on Gary, the man's an idiot. Let's go.'

Mum stormed out of the room and my dad followed, apologising to Mr Ransley as he chased after her. A nurse, who'd overheard the conversation, ran after them. Mum was fighting to hold back tears and was shaking with rage and disbelief.

'Just step in here for a moment,' the nurse said, leading Mum and my dad into a side room and guiding them towards some chairs. 'Look, you can't go speaking to Mr Ransley like that.'

'Well, I just did,' Mum retorted and got up to walk out again, thinking the nurse just wanted to give her a telling off.

'Wait, wait, sit down for a second,' the nurse said. 'Look, Mr Ransley really knows his stuff. I'm sure what he said was a shock to you, but you should hear him out. If anyone is going to be able to help your child, it will be him.'

Mum thought for a moment and realised she didn't have any other options.

'Let me take you back through,' the nurse said.

Mum allowed herself to be led back to the room, but was openly hostile towards Mr Ransley as he tried to explain the science behind my condition. The jargon, as always, made her head spin, but then he started outlining how he could repair my pelvis to give my organs some protection, create a pathway for my urine and close my abdomen as she'd always hoped and she was forced to start taking note.

'If Joel had been born in my care, I would never have assigned him to the male sex,' Mr Ransley said. 'In my clinic, we would have treated your child as female from the start.

'I realise what I am saying must be very difficult to comprehend and I think it is something you need to go away and think about. There are other doctors in this field and you really must consult one of them if you feel you need a further opinion. I can only tell you what my own view is.'

It was another medical appointment where my parents left in a daze, not quite believing what they'd just heard.

Before they left, Mr Ransley had a parting piece of advice. 'Should you go down the route I suggest, I think it would be wise to select a date to make the switch and give yourselves a proper opportunity to let go of your son and welcome your daughter.'

Mum knew my dad was annoyed at the way she'd dealt with the news and the atmosphere between them was frosty. He was, presumably, also trying to get his head around what had been suggested and the trip back to Orpington was another near-silent one. Mum couldn't quite comprehend that the 'son' she'd spent the past 11 months bonding with, might not really exist. That, had I have been born in London, instead of Birmingham, I would have been a daughter. Her thoughts leapt between wondering why she should listen to this doctor if they were all so clearly capable of making such catastrophic errors to thinking about all the things he'd said he could do for me and feeling a glow of hope that my future did not have to be so awful.

It was Aunty Di who really helped Mr Ransley's advice to seem like an actual possibility.

'It's really only a matter of different clothes isn't it?' she said when Mum and my dad explained what they'd been told. 'Joel is still the same baby, they're just telling you that he should have been wearing pink instead of blue.'

Mum could see that Aunt Di was telling her not to allow what she had been told about who I was before that day to stand in the way of allowing me to have a future. As a boy, I faced all the problems Mum had been told about in Birmingham and there seemed to be nothing but misery ahead of me. As a girl, it seemed as if I'd be almost normal.

Aunt Di knew Mum would have a sleepless night worrying over it all and in the morning she crept in and got me out of my cot to give Mum a lay-in. She took me to the shops and bought Mum a little present, which she wrapped in a little box with a big bow. When Mum came downstairs she opened the box and inside was a pair of pretty pink socks.

'Just try them,' Aunt Di said to her. 'I've always said he's too pretty to be a boy anyhow.'

Mum recalled that Aunt Di had said that to her before and strangers had often thought I was a girl when they'd seen me in my pram. She took a deep breath and slipped the socks onto my feet. I smiled up at her, exactly as I had before and she was surprised how 'right' it felt.

'I can do this,' she thought.

She went through to my dad. 'I think we should do it,' she told him.

'So do I,' he replied.

The whole thing was a shock to everyone else in the family too but once it was all explained it seemed to make sense. Initially, Mum and my dad thought that perhaps they could keep my name unchanged but then someone suggested Joella and they decided to go with that. My middle name was to be Beatrice – the same as Nan's.

I was only a few weeks off my first birthday and, remembering Mr Ransley's advice, Mum and my dad decided to make that the date of the switch. They went to Nan's and Mum visited the village GP and asked him to write to Mr Ransley and tell him they wanted to go ahead with the treatment he'd suggested.

To begin with, Mum found it difficult to start looking at girl's clothes in the shops and initially she bought me a not-too-feminine denim dress to wear on my birthday. Later, she decided that she just needed to throw herself into the change and bought a pretty white dress that was covered in frills for the day.

On the night before my birthday, Mum bathed me as normal and deliberately put me into a neutral white babygro. Once I was asleep she put all of my boy's clothes into a bin bag and got out the pile of girl's things she'd built up.

She had expected to find it difficult to put me in the new dress the next day and was amazed by her own reaction. She took one look at me in it and felt like something had clicked into place. Mum didn't feel as if she had just dressed her son as a girl, she felt as if I should always have been a girl.

Mum carried me downstairs where Nan was pottering around in the kitchen and Grandad was already sitting at the table. Nan had worked herself up into such a state, worrying about how Mum was feeling that she took one look at her and had to walk away. Mum knew it was because she was fighting to hold back tears. For quite a while afterwards, Nan would struggle to remember to call me she, not he, and Joella, not Joel.

Grandad was able to, pretend at least, to cope with it easier. 'Now here's my beautiful princess,' he said as soon as he saw me that morning and took me out of Mum's arms. 'How's my little girl today?'

Three days later I took my first steps and although it was a real plod because my pelvis was still in its original state it meant I was even more difficult to contain. I climbed on everything, emptied cupboards, grabbed everything and Mum couldn't take her eyes off me for a second. She was constantly worried I was going to fall and badly hurt myself and was always running around behind me. It helped her to realise that there was no way she could continue to cope in Coventry, especially with the surgery I was going to need.

On the positive side, my full-on nature helped reassure Mum that my development was continuing to be unaffected by my condition. I started talking in reasonable sentences very early too and seemed to adopt my dad's love of cars.

He'd sit and show me car magazines and books with cars in and one of my first proper words was Lamborghini. It was my dad's favourite car and I could soon identify a Lamborghini and wouldn't be happy until he turned the page to one. It registered with Mum that it was very boyish of me to be so interested in cars, but she told herself not to be so stereotypical.

Mum wanted to go back to Pinchbeck to be close to Nan and Grandad and when she told my dad he didn't argue. They agreed that if my dad could get accommodation back at university, they could get a house in Pinchbeck that he could come back to at weekends. Mum got in contact with Diane Bentley to tell her what was planned and, being as perceptive as she'd been when Mum first met her, Diane suggested Mum could do with some additional support. She knew things had already been strained between Mum and my dad and rightly predicted that their relationship would become even more fraught with the added distance. She suggested that Mum should be referred to a social worker, who would be able to ensure she got all the help available to her. Mum trusted Diane and as soon as she met Dave Mann she trusted him too.

On the first day he and Mum met, Dave went to the council offices and got her fast-tracked for a house of her own. The house she was given was in Brownlow Crescent, where Barbara lived.

Brownlow Crescent was a very long cul-de-sac and Mum's house was well away from Barbara's, tucked down towards the end near a big green where all the street's kids played football and tried out all the swear words they'd learned at home. At the back was the River Glen and if you walked all the way along it, you came out not far from Nan's. Mum will never forget the date she moved in – April 15, 1989 – because it was the day 96 people were killed in the Hillsborough football disaster and the day after her 21st birthday.

Mum already had connections to a lot of the street's most established residents and very soon various neighbours would be constantly in and out for cups of tea and chats. She and Nan both knew everyone through working in the social club and going to school in the village. Mostly, being surrounded by people she'd known all her life was good for Mum, but she also had to put up with a lot of ignorance. People in Pinchbeck knew from talking to Nan and the Chinese whispers that go on in small places that Mum's baby wasn't well and there'd been a problem with my sex, but most of them didn't understand my condition.

Mum was mortified when a girl she'd been at school with stopped to talk as she wheeled me through the village in my pram one day. 'Oh so this is *the* baby,' she said. 'A girl now, isn't it? You're happy with what you've got now?'

Did people really think that she'd changed my sex because of a preference for a girl? Mum was so upset and angry.

'No, she's not okay actually,' Mum said, trying to hold back tears. 'She'll be having major surgery in a few weeks.' Mum walked away, knowing that if she tried to say any more she would end up either sobbing or screaming.

The surgery date was set for July and, although no-one out rightly said that I might not make it through the operation, the possibility hung in the air whenever the surgery was discussed. The doctors outlined the risks of anaesthetics and underlined that the operation was going to put a lot of demands on my body.

The bones of the pelvis in a cloacal exstrophy baby are basically open like a book and the aim of the surgery was to saw through my pelvis and pin it more closely together. They would then be able to reconstruct my bladder and put it and my intestine inside my abdomen before doing a repair of my abdominal wall. At the same time, they planned to remove the 'gonads' that were within me, which Mum was told were of high risk of developing some form of tumour. Further surgery was planned for the future to form the appearance of female genitalia and give me a form of continence using catheters.

By the time the operation came around, my dad was back for the summer holidays, but being back together did neither him nor Mum much good. My dad was working at the factory again and was tired and, no doubt, had his own fears about my operation and Mum couldn't think of anything else. The day before the surgery, they had their most furious row ever over nothing in particular. Though, looking back, Mum can see the stress of the situation had got to them both, at the time she felt my dad really hated her. Regardless of that, they both got up the next day focused on what lay ahead. By then, Mum was quite experienced at the long waits for me to appear from theatre, but nothing had prepared her for the 11 hours I was gone that time or for the sight of me afterwards.

CHAPTER SEVEN

I lay on my back, crying quietly, covered in tubes and drips and in so much pain Mum found it difficult to even be in the room. To allow my pelvis to set in position, both my legs were set in plaster and were splayed with a metal rod between my knees. I had stitches from my breast bone right the way down to and around my undercarriage and across my middle from one side of my spinal cord to the other, where they'd sealed my abdomen. My undercarriage had all been left uncovered to heal and Mum felt the skin looked so stretched it could all tear apart at any time.

I'd had a tube down my throat throughout the operation and was desperate for a drink.

'Bot bot,' I said in a dry and husky voice, but I wasn't allowed to have anything by mouth. It must have been impossible for Mum to explain that to a 17-month-old baby.

'Mummy knee,' I pleaded, wanting Mum to pick me up. She couldn't do that either and had to just lay her head down beside me and stroke my face.

I was swollen all over and the doctors were struggling to get my morphine correctly balanced. On occasion it caused my body to have little mini fits that jolted my pelvis and shot more pain through my body. Desperate for comfort, I started getting cross that Mum wouldn't give me a bottle or pick me up. She said she could see that I wanted to paddy, but I was so restricted that I could only cry and scream. I spent the next few days switching between angry, pained and pitiful tears. The only thing that seemed to help was listening to my favourite Spot the Dog book over and over so Mum read it again and again.

A few days after the operation, Mum's fear that my stitches would burst came true and a hole opened up in my front, from which urine started leaking. I was rushed back to theatre again to be patched up and my body was so weak there were a couple of touch-and-go moments when my blood pressure dipped massively.

Mum gained strength from the other families on the ward who all knew what it was like to have a seriously ill child. She got to know some of them well and grew to love some of the children, especially a little Cockney boy, who was about five or six. He was completely bald through cancer treatment and looked like an angel, but had the most filthy potty mouth. His parents, like most of the others on the ward, had been soft on him because they hadn't wanted to spend precious moments telling him off. Mum realised she was already being exactly the same way with me.

The little boy would sit at the side of my cot and chat away to Mum, using every expletive there was. When she left the room, he'd even actively teach me some of his vocabulary. As I recovered, there was one phrase in particular that I picked up and seemed to understand the meaning of, but couldn't quite pronounce.

Whenever the doctors were on their rounds and started approaching to examine me, which I knew would be uncomfortable, I shouted it at them. 'Pid off! Pid off!' Luckily, I was small enough for it to seem cute.

After a couple of weeks, my dad suggested that he ought to head back to Pinchbeck to get back to earning some money. Mum didn't want him to go but knew they needed him to and Nan offered to come and stay with her in his place. That day, a nurse brought a tray full of paints and a pile of paper over to my cot and managed to get me propped up into a sort of sitting position to let me slap my hands in the paint and all over the paper. I loved it and it was the first time since the operation Mum had seen me seeming really happy. The nurse didn't care how much mess I made so long as it made me laugh and a bit later she even let me cover her face in lipstick. Nan told Mum to take the chance to go and get something to eat and have a few minutes to herself and she sat with me until, worn out, I fell asleep.

'What's she got under the blanket?' Mum asked when she came back and saw a big lump under the bedclothes. She pulled back the cover, expecting to find a book laying on top of me, but it wasn't a book. The lump was my stomach, which had swelled to a massive size and seemed to be tearing open again. Mum saw me starting to flinch with pain and screamed for a nurse to come.

They called a surgeon and he took one look at me and said they needed to get me to theatre again. Mum was overwhelmed by an intuition that I couldn't survive another lot of surgery so soon and the feeling was too intense to ignore.

'You're not taking her,' she told the stunned surgeon. 'She won't be able to cope with it. We'll have to find another way.'

They thought I had adhesions of the bowel again and were insistent that whatever the risks of surgery, if I didn't go to theatre, the writing was on the wall. Mum stood firm and refused to sign the consent forms even when I started writhing in pain again. Mum called my dad, who turned around and began the two-and-a-half hour trip back again. It was 3am when he arrived and Mum had gone to sit in the playroom for a moment to collect herself.

'Why isn't she in theatre?' my dad asked her.

'She's had enough, Gary. I just know that she can't take it. If we let them take her, she won't come back.'

Mum has always been surprised that my dad didn't argue with her and seemed to accept she knew something that no-one else did. The nurses had accepted her decision with minimal argument too. She wonders now whether they all thought I was going to die either way and were prepared to let it happen Mum's way.

One of the doctors suggested using a nasal tube to try to release some of the air from within me to make me more comfortable. That eased the swelling a little, but no gas or solid had passed through my colostomy and unless it did, things would only get worse again. Mum sat next to my cot, willing my bag to work.

A number of hours passed with no movement and exhaustion started to overcome Mum. With one of my cot sides lowered, she laid her head down on my mattress. It was then that my body let out an enormous noise and wind gushed out of me, then my stoma opened and everything came shooting through into my bag. Mum was elated.

The doctors examined what I'd passed and within it was a navy blue button, exactly like the ones the nurse who had played with me all morning had on her uniform. No-one had a clue how it had come loose or when I'd put it into my mouth, but I must have done and it was that, not adhesions, that was causing the blockage. That particular crisis was over.

My condition never became quite so critical again but there were still a lot of setbacks, with infections and things. For the first six or seven weeks, it felt to Mum as if there was something new to deal with every day and it was two-and-a-half months before my plaster casts finally came off and I was ready to go home.

My legs were in a much better position but were scrawny and weak through lack of use and Mum was told it could take months for me to move independently again. It amazed everyone when after only a couple of days at home, I was pulling myself up to standing and it was no time before I was crawling and then walking again. Mum says I just had a fight about me – the fight she and Grandad had seen in my eyes from day one and it was like a vicious determination to survive.

While I was in hospital, Mum had asked a couple of times how she'd go about getting my birth certificate changed and she'd been told to write to the head of urology for advice. She'd got the impression that altering my name and sex would be a simple formality in the circumstances, but the reply she received to her inquiry letter was the first indication it might be a bit more complicated.

The senior registrar in paediatric urology's letter said that any change to my birth certificate would have to be made by the General Register Office at St Catherine's House. While he thought it would be relatively easy to have my name changed, he said it might be 'more difficult' to change my sex.

Mum mentioned the letter to Dave Mann.

'A lot of solicitors offer a free half hour consultation,' he told Mum. 'Why don't you book to see someone and get their advice before you do anything else?'

Mum called Knipe Miller, one of the firms in Spalding and explained the problem. It was such a unique query that the receptionist wasn't even sure who to book Mum in with initially, but settled on Dianne Miller, a specialist in family law.

Mum arranged for Nan to sit with me while she and my dad went along to Dianne's office in a big, detached, Georgian building close to the river in the centre of town. She expected Dianne to be snobby and stand-offish and to look down her nose at her and couldn't have been more pleased when Dianne appeared with bright purple hair and a huge, warm smile. She wasn't at all what Mum had expected a solicitor to be like and didn't even seem to notice when their meeting ran well over the free half-hour slot.

Dianne listened carefully while Mum explained what had happened when I was born and later when I was referred to Great Ormond Street. Dianne seemed genuinely moved by what Mum and I had been through and once the story was complete, Dianne looked over the letter Mum had been sent from the hospital. She then referred to her computer and a couple of large legal books she had in her office.

'From what you have said, I would think Joella's doctors would be able to confirm that it was wrong to assign her to the female sex originally,' Dianne concluded. 'You just need them to write a note to that effect to St Catherine's House on your behalf.'

My parents shook Dianne's hand and thanked her for her kindness, expecting never to see her again.

A few days later, Mum went to our family GP in Pinchbeck and explained what Dianne had said. He was more than happy to help and said he'd write to St Catherine's House and to Great Ormond Street to advise them they may be called upon to corroborate everything. Mum expected my new birth certificate would arrive in the post any time.

Christmas and my second birthday followed and distracted Mum from thinking too much about my birth certificate. It wasn't until February that a letter arrived from the Registrar General's office, which confirmed they'd had a note from my doctor and asked for some additional information. Mum wrote them a long letter explaining my entire history and referring them to Dr Dewan, the senior registrar in urology at Great Ormond Street Hospital for confirmation.

She didn't hear anything else until May when the Registrar General's office wrote to Dave Mann. The letter informed him my application for an amendment to my birth certificate had failed.

'I must explain that every certificate of a birth occurring in England and Wales must be a true copy of or extract from the relevant entry in the register of birth,' the Registrar General's letter began. 'That entry is a record of the facts about the birth and parentage of the child as at the time of birth. A birth certificate is simply a certified copy of that record. It is not a copy of current identity.

'Under the provisions of Section 29 (3) of the Births and Deaths Registration Act 1953, an entry in the register of births can be altered only on the basis that an error was made when the birth was registered i.e. that at birth the child concerned was not of the sex recorded. If it is alleged that at birth the child concerned was not of the sex recorded in the birth entry we will consider a correction of the entry if medical evidence of the error is submitted, preferably by the doctor in charge of the case.

'Where, however, a person undergoes treatment to enable them to assume the role of the opposite sex, then clearly an error cannot be said to exist in the entry and no amendment made in respect of the sex. We have consulted Dr Dewan and our own medical advisers and it is clear that Joella was born male. No error can therefore be said to exist in her birth entry in this respect. Moreover when someone changes his or her name it is not possible for the birth entry to be amended to record the assumed name. Neither is it possible for a birth entry to be re-registered where a child is to be brought up in the opposite sex. It is not possible therefore for birth certificates to be obtained showing Joella's new name and sex as female.'

The letter went on to say that my parents could consider making a statutory declaration in front of a magistrate stating that I was born male, but would be brought up as Joella, to get an official record of the link between my 'assumed' identity – Joella – and my 'true' identity – Joel. Forever more, whenever I had to produce my birth certificate, I'd have to produce the original certificate and the statutory declaration stating I'd had a sex change.

Mum was so convinced that my birth certificate would and should be changed that even when she got that response, she felt sure it could be easily resolved. She thought she must have not worded her letter to the Registrar General correctly and even though she used her free half-hour with Dianne, decided to give her a quick call in the hope she would help. Dianne asked Mum to come in to see her as soon as possible.

'It's clear to me that the law was not written with a case such as Joella's in mind,' Dianne said. 'I suggest we make an application for legal aid to get a barrister's written opinion on how to get this whole thing back on track.'

Mum happily agreed for Dianne to pursue the barrister's opinion and felt confident it would soon be sorted.

That summer, my dad finally completed university and, despite everything, he'd done okay. He and Mum talked about his plans and she wasn't surprised when he said he had concerns about moving in with us full time.

'I'm considering getting a flat in Spalding for a while to give us a chance to see what's best for everyone,' he told Mum.

It wasn't long before Mum and dad's relationship ended and my dad started seeing one of Mum's neighbours from Brownlow, Shirley, who had a daughter Donna, who was a similar age to me. Everyone tried to get along for my sake, but after my dad and Shirley moved 20 miles away to Peterborough I saw less and less of them.

More bad news was waiting for Mum as soon as the New Year began when Dianne called her into the office and told her she'd had the barrister's opinion back.

'You're not going to like this any more than I did when I read it,' Dianne warned. 'But this is not the end. I'm going to fight this with you for as long as it takes.'

Dianne handed Mum the barrister's opinion and it filled her with shock and rage.

'In reference to this case, the law is absolutely clear,' he'd written. 'Quite simply, it does not recognise a change of sex. Thus, Joel's sex as male was, in law, fixed for life on the 24th January 1988.

'A birth certificate may only be changed if a mistake was made in compiling the register. Thus, even if the law were otherwise and it was possible legally to change sex, it would still not be possible to change a birth certificate as the birth certificate would have been correct in respect of the state of affairs existing at the date of birth.

'In the case of Joel/Joella, there was no question of a mistake. The medical records disclosed the existence of male gonads, which were testicles and two small phallic structures. Although they have since been surgically removed, it makes no difference. Joella is, by her birth certificate and in law, Joel.

'Joel, if wished, could of course legally change name, but never sex.

'The future will hold many problems and difficulties not least the question of legal identity. The most obvious problems will occur should Joella wish to marry. A marriage is void if the parties are not respectively male and female.'

The opinion went on to discuss the existence of a number of transsexual pressure groups that were canvassing for changes in the legislation and advised Mum to join them.

'Is this a bloody joke?' Mum fumed. 'He actually thinks my daughter is a transsexual? She isn't even three yet. She's not some kind of cross-dresser for God's sake. And anyway, what 'small phallic structures' is he on about? She didn't have any phallic structure at all.

'There's no way I am standing for this. All these pompous dick-heads with their technical speak. Don't they realise what they're doing to a three-year-old little girl just saying 'well sorry, but she'll just have to get used to the fact that really she's a boy?' I bet he wouldn't bloody say that if it was his daughter. None of 'em would. Hasn't she got enough to deal with without all this shit?'

Dianne was absolutely supportive. 'I felt exactly the same when I read it and I totally agree. This isn't just about whether Joella will be able to marry in the future either. In theory, she could get into trouble for using a female toilet. If, God forbid, she were to get into trouble in the future and face prosecution she might be sent to a male prison. Together, we are going to get this resolved.'

Dianne still believed that a correctly worded letter from my specialist at Great Ormond Street could change everything. She'd tracked exactly what had happened after Mum's request for her GP to help with the application and had discovered that there had been quite a lot of correspondence between my GP, the General Registrar's office and Great Ormond Street and, although well-meaning, not all of it had been helpful to our case in terms of the law. However, among it all, there was one crucial note written by Mr Ransley. 'There is no doubt that an error was made in assigning the child originally and she should be re-regis-tered as female,' it said.

Mr Ransley was saying a mistake had been made in assigning me to male, which is exactly what the law required in order to make an amendment to my certificate. Dianne assumed the General Registrar's office just needed a more detailed explanation as to why it was correct to say a mistake had been made. She decided to send the barrister's opinion to Mr Ransley and to ask him to nominate a fee to write a report to address the issues it raised. Dianne secured legal aid to cover whatever Mr Ransley's fee might be, but despite a number of attempts to contact him, Dianne did not get a response.

CHAPTER EIGHT

While Mum was beginning her legal battle for my birth certificate and coping with the departure of my dad, I was busy growing up. Obviously, as I was three, I was oblivious to the birth certificate stuff, but I was very aware of my dad having gone. My very first memory is from sometime quite soon after he left.

I'd spotted him talking to a neighbour in the cul-de-sac, who he must have come to visit and, standing on a chair next to our front window, I was calling out to him.

'Dad! Dad!' I'm convinced he could hear me but he did not want to look. He finished his conversation, walked back down our neighbour's pathway, got in his car and drove off. I don't remember seeing him for a long time after that but there were plenty of other people around to make a fuss of me.

Nan and Grandad were a huge part of my life and each of them would cycle to our house every day. Grandad would sometimes still be a little drunk from the night before, but he'd always get there, usually with sweets or comics for me! Nan was often on her way to or from the shops or the club and, whenever she wasn't too busy, I'd be allowed back to her house with her, where I played with her Boxer dog and ran around the garden with a hobby horse. Nan's garden was absolutely huge and was the most fantastic place to be. The first section was a yard with a shed, then there was an area with gooseberry bushes, apple trees and raspberries. She had a huge greenhouse with tomatoes in it and a pond and huge trees at the back that were perfect for climbing.

I was an outdoorsy kid who loved nothing more than getting covered in mud, running around and using my imagination. At home, I had a Little Tikes house that Nan had bought me, but I could never just sit inside it. The house had to be a boat or a rocket and I had to climb onto the roof to steer it. The doctors had told Mum I ought to be very careful about things like that and shouldn't ride a bike either because of the surgery I'd had, but that's all I wanted to do and Mum wouldn't allow me to be a martyr to my condition. She refused to stop me enjoying myself even though it would often make her cringe with fear. She also refused to let it be an issue that I was so clearly a tomboy. In her mind that's what I was – a girl who was a tomboy.

From an early age, I was used to being surrounded by adults and, especially after my dad left, Mum always had loads of friends around at our house. Mel, my Godmother – Mummy Mel, as I called her – even moved in with us for a while and loved to get me doing cheeky things. She'd teach me to blow raspberries and stick my tongue out, while Mum fruitlessly tried to control the pair of us. Mel is one of those people who gets away with doing and saying things no-one else could. When she laughs, which she does non-stop, you can hear it three doors down and her and Mum together are like a pair of hyenas.

Whenever Mum tried to pull me into line in front of Mel, she'd step in and take my side.

'You take no notice of her,' Mel would tell me. 'She's 'orrible.'

When we went to the supermarket, Mel would take half the shopping out while Mum wasn't looking and replace it with toy fire engines and things that I'd asked for on the way round. By the time they got to the till there'd be food and nappies for me, a bottle of vodka for them, a couple of eggs, some milk and a pile of toys. Mum was finally starting to feel like her old self again after all the stress and misery of what had happened with me, life in Coventry and the breakdown of her relationship with my dad and she'd just roll her eyes at Mel and laugh.

I was still very small for my age, which was all part of my condition and it meant people tended to think I was cute, which didn't always please me. There's an infamous story about one day when the three of us went to a cafe in Spalding together, which was full of well-to-do older people, who were cooing over me because I was so cute.

'Argh, our little angel,' Mel said to me in a baby voice.

'I'm not an angel,' I said grumpily.

'Oh, you are though,' Mel replied, the mischievous glint in her eye. 'Our sweet little angel.'

'I'm not!' I said, loudly.

'Leave her Mel,' Mum warned.

'Oh, but look at her. She's so cute.' Mel said.

That was it, before Mum could stop me, I'd climbed up onto the table and grabbed the salt cellar on my way. I hurled it towards Mel.

'I'm not your f-ing angel,' I screamed. I still remembered the vocabulary I'd learned in hospital and had added to it with what I heard around our neighbourhood and seemed to know exactly when to use the words for best effect.

Mel wanted to laugh, while Mum wanted the ground to open up and swallow her. She pulled me down off the table and shoved a milkshake at me to keep me quiet. Mum's the first to admit that she was useless at being stern with me.

I still associated all men with doctors and, barring Grandad and Uncle John, was terrified of them. Once, the gas man came round and I screamed and cried and hid behind the sofa until he left and, partly because of that and partly because of all the other stuff that came with me, Mum didn't expect to ever bring another man into our lives. She wasn't even keen to have someone else to think about because she felt her time with me was precious and always feared it might be cut short, but fate had other plans.

Nan and Grandad badgered Mum to let them help with me so she could have some proper nights out and let her hair down and towards the end of the year after my dad left she started taking them up on it. She used to go to The Bull, in the village, at weekends and got to know one of the older guys in there – a flamboyant, arty guy, who was always entertaining a crowd of people. One night he introduced Mum to his son Jason Farmer, a 6ft 2ins biker with long, black hair and a full beard. He was a year younger than Mum, hinted at a bit of a chequered past, but had a kindness about him that Mum was drawn to. After an hour and a half talking to each other, he was pestering for a date to take Mum out for a drink.

Farmer – as I have always called him – came to pick Mum up a few nights later while I was playing with Grandad. Mum realised she needed to go outside and put some coins in the electricity meter before she left for the evening and expected me to stick to her leg and want to go with her rather than be left in the house with a strange man about, but to her surprise, I didn't. When she came back in, she found me sitting on Farmer's knee, stroking his beard and asking him to help me open some Smarties he'd brought round for me. She stood in the doorway gobsmacked while Farmer chatted away to me.

'Shall we go then?' Mum said after standing there for a bit.

'In a minute,' Farmer said. 'She's just telling me something.'

That night, Farmer kept saying what a lovely child I was and Mum told him bits about how I'd been ill and admitted I'd been spoiled and was a bit of a handful. None of it put him off.

Mum invited Farmer to spend Christmas with us, along with most of her friends and we all went to Nan's as normal. Mum has said there were 16 for dinner that year, which was nothing unusual and she and Nan would have cracked open the sherry by 9am and been tipsy by the time they served the food. Apparently, Mum, Farmer and I walked back to our house afterwards and they were both a bit drunk and caught up in the moment.

'I don't ever want to go home,' Farmer said.

'Well don't then,' Mum replied.

She has admitted since that, once it was out of her mouth, she could barely believe what she'd said, but Farmer never did go home. That January – the month of my fourth birthday – he brought her a ring and asked her to marry him and she accepted. Then a few weeks later, she discovered she was pregnant. When she told him, Mum expected Farmer to walk out the door and never come back, but he amazed her by being thrilled at the news – and so was I. Although it was all a bit of a whirlwind, Nan and Grandad were both totally behind their relationship too and what should really have been a disaster just worked out for the best.

Farmer had a full time job, working with his dad making model engines, and I'd spend all day asking when he was going to be home. Once he was back, I'd want him to help bath me and put me to bed.

Learning about my condition was a gradual thing for him, but he never shied away from it. I was in the bath when he saw my colostomy for the first time.

'What's all this about then?' he asked.

'It's my bubble. If I eat peas I can shoot them out into the bag!'

Everything that came with my condition was just normal to me and I didn't think anything of it. I'd show off my operation scars, or zips as I called them, to anyone who'd look. The whole neighbourhood and all the other kids in the street grew up knowing all about my colostomy and 'zips'.

The one thing that did cause me ongoing problems was the sores I got from having to still wear nappies because I had no urinary control. I was so used to pain that I didn't make much of things that would probably have been a big issue to a child who hadn't been through what I had, but it was something Mum wanted to deal with.

Not long after Farmer came into our lives, it looked like a solution was on the horizon. I went into Great Ormond Street Hospital for a day to have an exploratory procedure in advance of the operation that had always been planned to allow me to control my urinary flow – a Mitrofanoff. It would have involved inserting a catheter into my abdominal area to allow me to periodically drain urine off and at the same time they planned to begin creating some kind of vagina for me.

I do remember little bits about that trip to hospital, but I wasn't worried about it at all. I think I was so used to going to hospital by then that it was just ordinary to me. I know Great Ormond Street seemed very big and that after I'd got back from theatre I sped around the ward on a little trike. Whatever they'd done obviously didn't hurt.

There was a bit of tension on that hospital trip between Mum and the doctors partly because Dianne still hadn't had a full response from them and it was starting to infuriate Mum. The hospital administrator had written back once to say he'd spoken to my specialist and a report would follow, but we were still waiting. It made Mum question everything about the hospital and her doubts were furthered when a junior doctor mentioned that my Fallopian tubes could be used in the operation.

'Fallopian tubes?' Mum asked quickly.

A senior doctor leapt in. 'No, no, not in this case.'

'Does Joella have Fallopian tubes?' Mum demanded.

'No, we'd be using intestine.'

I am sure that Mum's dented faith in the hospital contributed to the decision she later took to not allow the Mitrofanoff to go ahead, although it wasn't the main reason. Mum had found out that the Mitrofanoff wouldn't be just one simple operation but could entail a series of surgery over a number of years. She felt I had been through enough at that stage in my life and didn't want my condition to dominate the rest of my youngest years. She also understood that once I had a catheter inserted, I'd have to be very careful not to get it bumped or knocked.

I was just starting to develop a passion for running around with a football and Mum didn't want me to have a procedure that might stop me enjoying myself. She got our GP to write to the hospital and tell them that she wanted the Mitrofanoff to wait until I was old enough to choose whether to go ahead for myself. It meant that nothing would be done to create any kind of vagina until later either.

I was too young to have an opinion about it at that stage or even to understand that the operation had been put off. I cared more about Mum's growing bump and the wedding she and Farmer were planning. The baby was due in September and the wedding was going to be two months later. We knew Mum was having a boy and I couldn't wait to help look after my little brother. I loved seeing Mum's bump move and we'd sit in the bath together some nights and I'd put bottles on her stomach for the baby to kick off. It was excellent!

Secretly Mum was quite terrified about being pregnant again in case a similar thing happened with the new baby as had happened with me. She had to have lots of extra checks but she was told everything was okay.

One day, I disappeared off into my room and came out with a gift I'd prepared for the baby, which consisted of a colostomy bag, a flange and various other of my prescription bits and pieces. I'd assumed the baby would look like me when it was born and would need all of those things too. Mum took the things from me and gave me a huge hug. I had no idea how emotional it had made her.

'Jo, you're extra, extra special and that is why you have a bubble on your tummy and your zips. I think it would be greedy of me to expect another baby that is special in the same way as you so this one probably won't have those things, but it is lovely of you to want to share.'

Mum has told me since, that, for a second, she almost wished the new baby was going to be like me so that I could continue to feel that everything about me was so 'normal'.

The way Mum always explained things and the fact she was so honest meant that none of it was a big deal to me. I think kids tend to just accept things are normal if you tell them they are. Even at that age I knew that when I was born, I'd originally been called Joel. Mum always told me that I'd been very poorly and because the doctors were so busy making me better they'd been really silly and had got mixed up and thought I was a boy to start with. She'd never hidden my baby pictures away and had always insisted that Joel was a part of me and a part of my history and neither she nor I should be ashamed of it.

I knew about Dianne Miller too because Mum spoke to her on the phone for updates on what was happening every now and again and sometimes we had to go to her office.

'She's a clever lady that is helping us to sort out some things to do with when you were born and the doctors made the silly mistake, thinking you were a boy,' Mum would tell me.

I didn't think any more of it. I know I went to Dianne's office a couple of times but all I really remember is her smart suits and her short hair, which was always dyed different colours.

I realise now that Dianne was very unique. She didn't seem to care about money, she just wanted to make things right, which is why she was spending so much time on my case that she wasn't even getting paid for. She'd successfully applied for legal aid to cover some things, like the barrister's opinion and the fee she had expected Mr Ransley to request for his report, but it did not extend to all the hours she was putting in drafting letters and making follow-up calls.

By the summer of 1992, Great Ormond Street Hospital had still not sent Dianne a report she felt was sufficient for our case and Mum was extremely frustrated with the whole issue of my birth certificate. She thought it was just so stupid and that anyone with any compassion could see that I shouldn't be condemned to all the problems transsexuals had to live with. She'd done some research and understood that many transsexuals felt traumatised by never being able to fully change their 'legal' identity. Gender dysphoria – where someone feels there is a mismatch between their biological sex and gender identity – is recognised now, but was not then.

Mum had grown very sympathetic to the transsexual cause, but though she understood their fight, she did not feel our battle was the same. I had never 'felt' I had been assigned to the wrong sex. When my sex was 'changed' I wasn't old enough to even have thoughts about my gender. As a four-year-old, I was living in the sex that doctors had said I should live in just as every other person does. My problem was that whereas most babies are immediately labelled male or female based on their external genitalia, when I was born I didn't have any genitalia so it wasn't obvious. It was only when I was 11 months old that doctors decided on the right sex for me.

'I think we should forget all this requesting reports and waiting around,' Mum told Dianne. 'I should just go to the newspapers and let them shame the idiots into giving Joella her birth certificate. If this went public, they'd sort it straight away.'

Dianne feared the potential harm that dragging me through the media could have and talked Mum out of it. 'I think we should see that as an absolute last resort.'

CHAPTER NINE

'What do you think of your baby brother then?' a nurse asked me moments after I saw Jarred for the first time.

I didn't hesitate over my reply. 'He's ugly, but we're going to keep him.'

Jarred arrived on September 29, 1992 and we were all thrilled to have him around. I loved running around getting bottles for Mum and liked to help change and bath him. It felt like Farmer, Mum and I were a proper family.

It was a manic time because the wedding was only a few weeks off and there were all the preparations for that going on too. It was going to be a big occasion, with Mum in a proper huge white dress and the men in top hat and tails. Mum and I went across to Stamford, a beautiful nearby town where a lot of period dramas are recorded, for loads of fittings for her dress because her shape was obviously changing all the time in the run up to the wedding. I, along with Mum's niece and Farmer's sister, was a bridesmaid and Nan was making our dresses.

I was a scruffy kid and wasn't a big fan of dresses, partly for practical reasons because they left my colostomy feeling unsupported. I couldn't tolerate jeans either or anything else with rigid waistbands because there was so little space between my stoma and my hip when my body was little. The only thing I really felt comfortable in was leggings and tracksuit bottoms, but, for once, I didn't make a fuss over wearing a dress for that day. I was okay with the dress but a lot less okay with not going in the Rolls Royce that had been hired to collect Mum from home and take her to the church.

Mum and Farmer were married at St Mary's, in Pinchbeck, and afterwards we went on to a hall in Spalding, for the reception. Two boys of a similar age to me, who lived next to Grandad, came and we all ran around playing together and sneaking food under the table. The main memory I have of the day is that all the presents were stolen from a room at the hall. That's the typical kind of dramatic thing that happens to our family.

The biggest part of the whole wedding for me though was that it meant I got a new dad. My real dad had pretty much disappeared from my life altogether and although I didn't dwell on it, I was keen to have a replacement.

Farmer and I got on really well and he was a nice person to have around and made me feel like he wanted me. He had a little seat on the back of his pushbike for me with 'toe-rag' written on it. We'd get round the corner, out of Mum's sight, and I'd get him to pull wheelies on it. We just had a laugh. Sometimes my colostomy would make really loud noises as wind passed through and if it happened in a shop, I'd say: 'Farmer, you're so rude!'

My favourite toy was a Disney fire station and I had a fireman outfit and helmet that I wore all the time and

Farmer would play out in the garden with me, throwing buckets of water around, pretending we were putting fires out. It was in the middle of one of those games just after the wedding that I asked him: 'Can I call you Dad?'

'Course you can,' he said and we carried on playing.

Ever since, whenever I have referred to Dad, Farmer is who I have meant.

I should really have started school that year, but Mum worried how I would get on managing my colostomy and everything without her there and delayed my entry. Living in Brownlow meant I didn't miss out on chances to interact with other kids. I was very close to the little boy next door, Ross, who had a climbing frame in his garden that, to us, was just about everything from a cave to a spaceship. I had another friend Semrah, who I'd played with since we were babies and there were tonnes of other kids about.

I was very small for my age, had a real pot-belly because of my lack of proper abdominal wall and, although it was presumably much less pronounced than it would have been if I hadn't had surgery, a waddle when I walked. I wasn't treated any differently by the other kids in the street because of it. It was a rough and tumble sort of area and I was quite able to hold my own with the others. When Daniel, a little boy from a couple of doors down, trod on the water snails I'd been keeping as pets in the garden then took my trike and started teasing me, I waited around the corner and bashed him with a bit of wood. His mum would have told him it was his own fault and, had it been the other way around, my mum would have told me the same. It didn't matter to the other kids that I had a medical condition any more than it did to me, but that was all different when I did start school.

The first day was the usual mixture of excitement and nerves. I had a little grey pinafore dress and felt all proud reaching up and holding Mum's hand on the five minute walk to the village school. The school wasn't quite as far as the shop we went to most days but it seemed further that day. Walking down the long drive, I felt out of my depth and everything seemed very big.

It was quite a large school, with around 250 pupils and had a typical 'school' look to it. It was a late 60s building with lots of brick and big square glass panel windows. My teacher was nice and fun and I had two nurses – one in the morning and one in the afternoon – to help me with my colostomy and things.

The other kids in my class seemed okay, but it was so obvious straight away that I was a bit different, particularly with the nurses being around. Everyone was okay with me in the classroom but no-one seemed to really want to be my friend. At break time everyone else formed into little groups and I was left alone.

Mum came to collect me all full of smiles and hugs. 'Hello! How was it? What did you do?'

'Not much' I replied, like little kids do and once home, I just wanted to play with my toys.

I wasn't so keen to go to school the next day or the one after that.

'Don't want to go,' I'd stubbornly tell Mum.

'Why not? It's fun there. You have lots of friends to play with.'

'I don't like it.'

'Why? What don't you like?'

'None of it.'

I was too little to explain the exclusion or to even understand it myself. Even at that age no-one wants to think, let alone have to say out loud, that nobody likes them and I became moody and angry. I tried so hard to join in with the games the other kids were playing and sometimes they'd let me, but I was never really wanted by anyone. On top of that, there were the inevitable remarks and teasing about the way I looked.

A group of kids in the upper school were my biggest problem. Mainly, I didn't have to mix with them because there were separate playgrounds for the younger and older kids but on occasion some of the bigger ones were allowed into our playground, supposedly to help look after us. They would follow me around mimicking my limp and making nasty comments. As my nappy and colostomy were common knowledge around the village, they were also common knowledge at school. My bag was even quite visible under my tight-fitting school uniform.

'Urgh, look at her, she's pregnant,' they'd say pointing out my tummy or 'Still wear a nappy don't you baby?'

I just wanted to disappear.

Apart from my condition, I'd always been quite 'well' until I started school. I never really got colds or bugs, but that started to change. I started to get terrible sickness bugs that would last ages and would mean me having to have a week or a fortnight off at a time. My stomach would cramp up horrendously and bloat and cripple me in pain.

On occasion, the sores I got from my nappy would also lead to time off. They'd be so bad at times that I'd have to strip off from the waist down and sit in my bedroom on a bag of frozen peas. When I was suffering from those things, even though it was incredibly uncomfortable, part of me was pleased that it meant I could stay home. On top of the illness, I'd get myself so worked up about going to school some days that often I'd be sick because of that. Other times, I'd fake illness to try to get the day off.

Staying home usually meant a day laying on the sofa, watching videos, but sometimes Mum would have something she needed to go out and do and I'd be allowed to go to Nan's. Those were my favourite days. She and I would play cards or Uncle John would get his beautiful fake ivory dominoes set out and we'd play that. I'd even be able to go outside and play in the garden because there I didn't have to keep up the pretence of being ill for the benefit of the neighbours.

I did eventually tell Mum and Nan that some of the kids said horrible things to me, but there wasn't a lot they could do about it. It was inevitable that I'd suffer a bit of name-calling and Mum knew I was going to have to find a way of dealing with it. Mum went into the school numerous times to talk to the teachers about how unhappy I seemed and they promised they were keeping an eye on me.

At the same time, the school was getting annoyed with Mum over the amount of time off I was having. A lot of it was genuine illness, but the school wasn't very accepting of it. Mum was warned that she would be reported over it and needed to get me into the classroom. Some mornings she would literally have to prise my fingers off the door frame and drag me to school.

'Jo, you can't stay home every day. You're not ill. You've got to go.'

'But I hate it.'

'But you have to go.'

One night, during my second year, Mum woke up to hear me crying out from my room.

'My back hurts,' I sobbed.

Mum looked and it was covered in bruises.

'What the hell are all these? How did you get them?'

'The boys at school have been Power Rangering me.'

The day before had been one of those few times I'd been allowed to join in with some of the other kids at playtime. They'd been chasing each other around playing Power Rangers, which was fine at first, but when I joined in, the game got more physical. Soon, all the boys were doing flying kicks and most of them were aimed at me.

Mum was horrified. It would have been a horrible thing for any kid but for me it was particularly dangerous as my organs were all still so vulnerable. Mum went to the school again and they said they'd speak to the boys to make sure they weren't playing too rough. I don't think it happened again. Instead, I went back to being ignored and teased.

I never minded the work and classroom stuff at school – I quite liked to learn, and got on okay with the others kids during lessons, but I never had friends outside of class. When the bell went, I'd find anything to do to cut down the time I had to spend outside. I would try to stick around the classroom, offering to help tidy up or I would hang around going through the stuff in my bag. I'd save up going to the toilet until playtime to waste time and once I was outside I'd be looking to see if the older boys were around.

There was a little row of trees on one side of the playground and a bench and I'd try to sneak behind there because I thought if I wasn't in sight they would leave me alone. Sadly, it didn't really work. I was in the corner of the playground one day, trying to stay out of sight near the fence, when the ringleader of the older kids, a boy with short, dark hair and a cocky face, spotted me and started leading the others my way. They were only very young themselves, eight or nine maybe, but they seemed like big kids to me.

'Let us have a look at this bag of yours then,' the cocky boy said. I tried to walk away.

'Oi, don't walk off, we only want to see.' The group had surrounded me and there was no way out.

'Come on, let's look!' The boy called it out like an order and the next thing I was on the floor. They pulled my skirt up and tried to have a look at my stomach. They were laughing and pointing and as I tried to hold onto my skirt, they were dragging my tights down. Over their shoulders I could see other kids running around, enjoying themselves and could even see a teacher. Once they'd exposed a bit of my nappy, the kids ran off cackling and I straightened myself up as quickly as I could. It felt terrible and demeaning. I was convinced the teacher had seen and just didn't care.

I was too ashamed to tell Mum or anyone else what had happened and I told myself I needed to toughen up. I even got Farmer to take me along to a kickboxing class, though I didn't really take to it.

Once I hit Year Three, I moved up into the bigger kids' playground where there was no avoiding the bullies, who started plaguing me every day. Half a dozen or so of them, boys and girls, would surround me and keep asking to see what I looked like under my clothes. I only remember one occasion where an older kid stepped in and told them to leave me alone. More than once, they got me to the ground and tugged at my clothes. I learned to curl up into a ball so they couldn't get my things off.

I'd got quite good at blocking out the other stuff – the name calling and isolation. I made myself numb to it, but the physical stuff was too much for me. I did everything in my power to try to stay at home each day and Mum would end up screaming at me in total desperation, trying to make me get ready. Usually I shouted back at her until she either gave in and let me stay home or hauled me out of the door. The day Mum knew things were really serious was the day that I burst into tears. I had never been the sort of kid to cry.

'Jo, talk to me. Tell me what's wrong,' Mum said. She walked me into the living room and sat me down on the sofa.

I grabbed a cushion and buried my face into it. 'They keep undressing me.'

'What? Who does? What do you mean?'

'The other kids. They get me behind the tree and they try to pull my clothes off.'

I have never seen Mum as angry as she was that day. 'Right, that's it. I've absolutely had enough of this.'

Mum grabbed Farmer and told him what was going on. They asked one of the neighbours to look after Jarred and the three of us marched up to the school and to the headteacher's office. Mum told me to sit and wait on a chair outside and she and Farmer stormed straight in.

Inside, the headteacher tried to get Mum and Farmer to sit and discuss things with him calmly, but they were way beyond that point. He tried to tell them that my differences were always going to attract attention and curiosity and he was sure that was all it was.

Mum went berserk. 'Curiosity? Are you fucking joking? This is sexual assault. Would you tell your wife to keep going to work if her colleagues were hauling her behind a tree each day and yanking her knickers off?'

'That's the end of it Ju,' Farmer said boiling with rage. 'I've got to get out of here before I knock this bloke's teeth out. Jo ain't staying here. That's the end of it. She won't be back.'

Mum and Farmer came rocketing out of the room, smashing the door back on its hinges.

Farmer took my hand. 'Come on, we're going to find you a different school. Let's get your stuff from your classroom.'

I was so happy. It was fantastic. Farmer walked me to my classroom and we walked in, right in the middle of the lesson.

'Where's your things?' Farmer said, looking at me. 'Go and get them sorted out.'

My teacher's jaw nearly hit the floor. 'Can I help you?'

All the other kids were dying to know what was happening as I cleared my pencil case and bits and pieces out of my tray. 'Jo, Jo, what's going on?'

Once I'd got everything we walked back into the corridor where Mum was waiting for us and I almost skipped out of the school entrance between them. Mum was already worrying about what she was going to do next, but I could not have been happier. Walking out of that school, knowing it was for the last time, was the best thing that had ever happened to me.

CHAPTER TEN

The closest school outside of Pinchbeck was Surfleet Seas End and it had the most crazy, eccentric and wonderful headmistress anyone could ever imagine. Mum phoned there as soon as we got back from the showdown at Pinchbeck Primary because she was terrified about what the authorities would do if I had any more time off. She made the phone call in private, but has told me since that she was in tears as she told Mrs Wakefield what had happened to me and Mrs Wakefield had cried too. She told Mum to bring me in that afternoon.

Surfleet Seas End was a tiny little Victorian school, which only had two classrooms and a hall. There were only 66 pupils in the entire school and each class had two year groups in it. Each day, the oldest kids had to help pull their desks into the middle of the hall to make it into their classroom.

Mrs Wakefield was in her late 50s or early 60s and had masses and masses of crazy, grey hair that looked like it hadn't seen a pair of scissors in years. She was so warm and welcoming, like a nan that everyone respected and wanted to be good for. As pupils walked past she'd talk to them all and they'd smile up at her.

'Hello sweetheart. How are you today? That's it, just walk nicely please.'

She told Mum there and then that she would find a way to squeeze me into the school, but there were two problems. One was that it would take some time to go through the process of recruiting a nurse to help look after me, but they could get around that temporarily if Mum was prepared to come in and help. The second was that the school was a 50 minute walk away and there were no buses.

Farmer had an old battered car, but Mum didn't drive and even if she had have done, Farmer needed the car to get to work. He'd stopped working with his dad long before and had since picked up jobs maintaining the machinery at the local factories. On the spot, Mum and Farmer decided that Farmer would switch to night shifts so that they could get me to school. Farmer could look after Jarred in the day and Mum could come to school with me until they got another nurse sorted.

On my first day, Mrs Wakefield called the whole school together and explained who I was and that I had moved from another school. She told everyone that I had a few health problems and might have to leave class occasionally to deal with things, but that it should not be an issue.

Surfleet was just the best school and there was no bad behaviour because Mrs Wakefield had a good imagination when it came to punishments. One day soon after I started, one lad kicked another so she took his shoes and threw them on the roof. He had to walk round without his shoes all day and when his dad came to collect him, the boy had to explain what he'd done and his dad had to get a ladder to get his shoes back!

Assemblies at that school were also a bit unique because Mrs Wakefield liked to play the drums. The vicar of Surfleet would come in each morning, but we never just sang hymns normally, we rocked out to them. Mrs Wakefield up on the stage thrashing the hell out of the drums as accompaniment.

The school's reception teacher, Mrs Robinson, was a lovely woman too, a real Mother Goose with a soft Mrs Doubtfire-type voice. Then there was my class teacher who was a bit more stern and strict but fine as long as you got on with your work, which I was happy to.

Similarly to at Pinchbeck, I got on quite well with the other kids in the classroom and would chat to the others on my table, but the playground was a bit quiet. I used to try to play football with the boys and sometimes they would let me but no-one really wanted a lot to do with me. I still had to have quite a bit of time off through illness, which didn't help.

Throughout those years I'd been at school, Dianne had continued to work away in the background trying to get my birth certificate sorted. She had given up on trying to get the report she wanted from Great Ormond Street Hospital and came up with the idea of applying for another lot of legal aid to commission a report from an independent paediatric urologist. She hoped to find someone who would be able to take the place of my own specialist to write a detailed report to explain to the General Register Office why I should never have been registered as a boy. Every few months, she would call Mum with an update – she'd got the legal aid, she was researching appropriate specialists to write the report, she'd found someone, she was writing to them.

Mum and Dianne waited so long for the urologist's report and then when it came back, not only did it not offer any hope of getting my birth certificate changed, it also raised a whole load of other issues. The urologist acknowledged that because of cloacal exstrophy my body had been badly malformed, but said that all the indications were that I had been a boy and, once again, stated that I was therefore essentially in the same boat as transsexuals. He did say it was normal practice to raise children in my position as female, but then said no-one really knew whether that was for the best of the children. Despite the removal of my 'gonads', the urologist said it was possible I might grow up feeling male. He even referred to a case where a boy who was born with no penis had been successfully brought up as a male. Mum had been told it would make me suicidal to grow up as a man with no penis. It became Mum's greatest fear that one day it might turn out she'd done the wrong thing in agreeing to make me a girl.

Dianne began to wonder whether my doctors had done enough to explain all the options and potential consequences to Mum. She wanted the opinion of a barrister again, this time not only to see how he thought we might be able to get my birth certificate changed, but also to advise if there were any case against the doctors who had treated me.

At the end of 1995, the new barrister sent his opinion and he was of the view that the doctors involved in my care had acted properly. He absolutely did not believe there was any foundation for a negligence case. He also thought, much like the first barrister, that, without a change in the law, there was no hope of me getting a new birth certificate. He did, however, agree with Mum that going to The Press might make a difference. To begin with, Dianne still tried to talk Mum out of going to the newspapers. She desperately wanted to find another way and convinced Mum to let her write directly to the General Register Office just in case she could say something to change their minds.

In July 1996, a few months after I'd started at Surfleet school, someone from the General Register Office wrote back and said there was nothing they could do. As far as my medical records showed, I was born a boy and therefore my birth certificate was correct. Dianne agreed that going public was the only other option and she and Mum decided that is what they'd do – once Mum had explained everything to me fully.

It had come round to summer holiday time and I was excited to have six weeks off. The holidays meant time to just be myself and play out in the street with kids who I felt comfortable around. Most of my friends from Brownlow were a year or so younger than me and we'd go and play in a den we had in the bushes at the back of a garage block down by the river, knock a football around and just hang about in the cul-de-sac. Ross was still around for make-believe games and I got along with Daniel most of the time. I was also still close to Semrah and then there was Laura, who had just moved into the street.

The holidays started just how I'd intended, with every day spent outside getting covered in mud and it was while I was having a bath after one of those days that everything changed.

Mum watched me climb into the water, then folded down the toilet seat so she could sit and chat to me while I washed, as normal.

'There's something I need to tell you about,' she said.

I was only eight, but I knew that what she was going to say was important and it made me feel a bit scared. I looked at her.

'You know your baby photo album with pictures of you when you had your other name, Joel?'

I nodded.

'Well, it's to do with that,' Mum continued. 'Everyone is given a piece of paper when they're born and on it, it says your name and whether you are a boy or a girl. Because we called you Joel to start with, your piece of paper – your birth certificate – still says Joel.'

'Why?' It was a frightening thing to hear.

'Well because although we know you are a girl, some people are still saying that you were once a boy and because of that, we haven't been allowed to get you a new birth certificate, but we really need to. It's what I have been talking to Dianne about all of this time. She has been trying to get it for you too.'

'But I wasn't a boy, was I?'

'I'm going to say 'no', Jo, but the doctors might say they don't know.'

I was having to stop myself from crying.

'What you need to remember is that nothing has changed,' Mum said. 'You are still you and this is just a piece of paper that we are arguing about, but we've tried everything to get it changed and no-one is listening to us, so what we need to do now is go public with it and tell a newspaper about it all and they'll want to talk to you and take your picture.'

'So I'll be in the newspaper?' I asked.

'That's right. It'll be exciting, won't it?'

I don't think I could take it all in really and tried to just think about the newspaper bit. That did sound quite good, but the rest of it didn't make a lot of sense. I couldn't believe that anyone would still think I was a boy or understand why they would. I kept saying to myself, 'I feel like a girl. They'll get this sorted.'

I could tell Mum had been worried about telling me and I didn't want her to be upset so I just did my best to not make a big thing of it. As I got dried and walked around upstairs after my bath, getting ready for bed, it was all going round in my head and it just felt horrible. I couldn't help but think how I'd always been a tomboy and wonder if that meant I could be a boy, but I'd never felt like one of the boys. I felt like a girl doing boyish things. Every time a bit of doubt went through my mind, I stamped on it. 'I'm not a boy, I'm not a boy, I'm not a boy.'

Mum and Dianne got in contact with the News of the World and they were interested in the story straight away. We thought it was going to be really simple. We'd speak to the newspaper, they'd print the story and the government would be shamed into giving me my birth certificate.

Mum must have done the interview over the phone at some point because I wasn't involved in that at all but I do remember the photo shoot. We got up that morning and I was a little bit nervous and a little bit excited. My dark hair had been cut into a short bob and it was usually really scruffy because it's naturally curly and I hated sitting and having it done, but, that day, Mum did a full sleek blow-dry. She sorted me out a pretty awful black and white checked short T-shirt dress thing to wear over black cycling shorts and took her time getting ready too. Mum has always taken trouble over her appearance – I don't think I've ever seen her without her nails done – and she put her full face on that day. Her hair was short and blonde and she used to back comb it all on top of her head and put on a tonne of spray.

Once we were sorted, I plonked myself in front of the TV downstairs and Mum rushed around washing up and tidying. Jarred and Farmer must have been around, but I don't really remember their presence much as we waited. It seemed like ages before the photographer finally pulled up outside and we watched him get out of his car and walk up to the door with a huge bag full of cameras and lenses. I'd never seen a camera like that before and was quite impressed.

The photographer was a tall, imposing guy and wasn't warm and friendly like most of the photographers I've met since. He was very much there to get the job done and didn't seem to want to chat with us much, though Mum was her usual self and was comfortable and chatty towards him. They decided we should go up to the riverbank because our garden had a couple of tall trees that caused a lot of it to be in shade. On the walk to the riverbank, the photographer was telling us that we needed to try to have serious faces in the photos and to look a bit miserable to match in with the story.

The photo shoot seemed to take ages and there was just a lot of posing while the photographer called out instructions to Mum and I.

'Put your arm up a bit, turn your head this way, put your faces closer together.'

I can't say it was much fun. I'd never had a massive attention span and it just all seemed to take so long.

We expected the story to go in that Sunday and Mum went off to the shop to get the paper, but it wasn't there. She rang up and they said it'd got bumped out by some other news story but they planned to use it the next week. The next week there was a story about a woman having seven babies and we weren't in again. I was quite disappointed because I'd been looking forward to seeing us in there. For quite a few weeks, we got the paper each Sunday and the story never went in and Mum started to wonder if they weren't going to use it, which would obviously have been a problem because we wanted the exposure. Mum rang again and was told the story about a four-year-old being addicted to smoking had come in late and had to go in.

It was the beginning of October when the story did finally appear and it wasn't in the main newspaper like we'd expected, but in the magazine instead. There was a nice, big picture of Mum and I in the middle of the page with our faces pushed close together under the headline: 'I had to tell my daughter: 'You're a Boy'

I didn't take too much notice of the words and was just quite excited to be in the magazine, while Mum was worried that the story wouldn't have enough impact there and might not do the job we needed it to. It wasn't something we had to be concerned about for long.

The phone rang and it was a reporter from the Peterborough Evening Telegraph, one of our local papers. They'd seen the piece in the News of the World magazine and wanted to come out that day to do a similar story on me and get their own pictures. Mum agreed to it, had a chat with the reporter on the phone and arranged for their photographer to come out.

Paul Franks, the Peterborough Evening Telegraph photographer, was such a nice guy and looked just like Woody from Toy Story to me. He put Mum and I completely at ease and the photo shoot with him was a lot of fun. I nicknamed him Woody that day and we all had a good laugh. We went across to Nan's garden for the pictures and it was all done quite quickly. It was much more enjoyable than the News of the World had been. Mum had done my hair half up and half down with a red ribbon tied in it and I was wearing a baggy sand-washed denim blouse and leggings.

The next day, Mum and I went into the village newsagent's where we knew the owner Keith and, on the counter, was the Peterborough Evening Telegraph with me splashed all over the front page. There was a huge photograph of me alongside the words: 'Pretty Joella wears a bow in her hair and loves playing with dolls but officials insist...SHE'S A BOY'

Everyone in the village pretty much knew the problems I'd had at birth and Mum was always stopping to have a natter with someone or other so it wasn't a shock to anyone.

'Look at you on the front page, Joella,' Keith said. 'A little superstar. It must be exciting?'

I smiled and nodded. It was sort of exciting, but it also felt weird to have the newspaper saying that about me. Mum was pretty furious about the headline.

'They're going for the shock factor Jo,' she told me. 'Don't let it get to you. It's just the way they do things.'

I was a bit confused about what they'd put, thinking that if that was what they were reporting perhaps I was a boy, but Mum told me that wasn't the case and I felt sure it wasn't. They'd said I liked playing with dolls and I wasn't sure where they'd got that from because I never had, but I did have pink in my bedroom and I wore girl's clothes. I began my mantra in my head again: 'I'm not a boy, I'm not a boy.'

When we got home from the paper shop, the phone was ringing and it was another reporter. They'd seen the story and they wanted to come out and talk to us too. Mum agreed and when she hung up, the phone began ringing again. It was the local TV news and they were asking if they'd be able to come out and do some filming with us because they wanted to feature our story too. As soon as Mum put the phone down, it was ringing again. This time, it was the Daily Mail and they wanted to come out and see us as well.

'Well, do you need Jo because obviously she's at school in the morning?' I heard Mum ask. 'Oh right, okay. Well, this is important to us so I'll keep her home. I've had the TV on the phone and another local reporter so I'll ring them back and tell them they can come in the day too because it doesn't seem fair otherwise. Okay, see you in the morning.'

That evening, the phone did not stop and it seemed like every reporter in the country wanted to come and see us.

I could feel my stomach churning with nerves as the realisation hit me that this was really important to my future. I was starting to understand that it was my only hope of getting my birth certificate changed so that I didn't have to spend the rest of my life feeling as if it wasn't certain who I was. I was still only little but everything suddenly seemed very important and very serious.

I didn't sleep a lot that night, thinking about how I'd have to try to make sure I said the right things the next day to make a good impression so that the reporters would write about me and help me get my birth certificate.

CHAPTER ELEVEN

The next day, we opened the curtains and there was a satellite truck pulling up outside our house. I found it all pretty nerve-racking and could tell Mum was a bit stressed too, but she had her usual big smile as she opened the door wide to the first reporter and invited them in. The reporters came one after the other and Mum told them to set up their equipment wherever was best. At some stages we had TV crews in the living room, radio in the dining room and newspaper reporters standing around chatting in the kitchen. My baby photo albums were all laid out on the dining room table and the photographers were taking photos of the photos. Someone set up one of those big light reflecting silver discs for their pictures and all the time the phone never stopped ringing with more requests to see us.

Mum and I sat next to one another in the living room in front of one of the reporters who had a notepad on her lap and a dictaphone on the arm of Mum's chair. Luckily Mum did most of the talking and the reporter spoke mainly to her, asking her to tell her what had happened when I'd been born and how I'd come to be called Joel. I sat and listened, already knowing the story off by heart.

'And what kind of girl is Joella? I expect she likes princesses and things?'

'She's just an ordinary little girl, she likes playing outside and mothering her little brother.'

'Dolls and fairies? That sort of thing.'

'A bit of everything really. She loves football more than anything.'

Mum never felt I had anything to hide, but I was already worried about the reporters making assumptions about me and was happy to let them try to make me seem girly. It started to play on my mind that I wasn't interested in dolls but did love football. I had to tell myself that it didn't mean anything.

'And what will it mean to Joella if you can't get her a new birth certificate?' the reporter asked. 'What sort of repercussions could that have?'

I hadn't really considered that I might not get the new birth certificate and Mum and I definitely hadn't talked about it.

Mum was quite matter of fact in her reply. 'She won't be able to marry, she might not be able to go to a girls' school, if she has a passport it will be in the name of Joel.'

It was frightening to realise those things could really happen to me. That could be my life. I wondered, with a pounding heart, if the Government could actually force me to become a boy.

The reporter turned to me. 'And I should think you really want your birth certificate so you can get married one day?'

I nodded.

As soon as the reporter was finished with us, someone else was at the door.

'Can we have you next?' they asked.

That day, it felt like Mum and I were on some kind of media conveyor belt, answering the same questions over and over again and posing for the same photos. It all felt a bit surreal, like being on a film set. It became quite obvious that the reporters and photographers all wanted me to be as 'female' as humanly possible and some of them even wanted to put lipstick on me. I could see what they were doing and was prepared to do whatever it took to get my birth certificate, but it all added to that nagging doubt inside that made me wonder why I didn't actually want to put make-up on and what that meant about me.

In the morning, we knew we were facing another similarly hectic day and got up to find the cul-de-sac full of reporters and photographers. Mum pulled the curtains so that we could have breakfast without feeling like everyone was looking at us. It was quite intimidating and made me feel like we were trapped.

The entire week ended up being much the same and my story and picture went everywhere. We were in all the national newspapers, on TV and radio news. Some of the reporters had asked to look through the letters that had been written by doctors and Dianne in the pursuit of my birth certificate and in some of them it referred to my having had 'hemi-phallus.' Some of the reports took that to mean, I'd had a penis of sorts and they had reported that. Mum had to reassure me that it wasn't the case. Other reports referred to the 'gonads' I'd had and Mum told me gonads could be testicles or they could be ovaries. I couldn't even bear to contemplate the fact that they could have been testicles.

Everyone carried the same quote from me: 'I just want to be able to get married one day.'

I'm not sure I'd ever actually said it as such, but I didn't mind, though really I was a lot more bothered about being able to go to the right secondary school. All the secondary schools near us were single sex and I was terrified at the thought of being made to attend a boys' school.

For one of the TV news crews, I had to do a mini bit of acting because they wanted footage to splice in between the interview they'd done with Mum and I. They shot some footage of me walking along the cul-de-sac, eating my breakfast and pretending to write something. It was quite exciting to be around a professional TV crew and everyone came round to watch it that night – Nan, Grandad, even Ross and his mum. Us kids all sat on the floor waiting for it to come on and the adults were sitting on the sofas. Afterwards, Ross and I went off to play outside and I was all overexcited and giddy.

The story wasn't just being aired in Britain, but abroad as well and we started getting letters and cards through from people as far away as Australia wishing me luck. Most of the letters were really nice and very supportive, from people who'd seen us and wanted to say how much they hoped we'd get justice. Some of them were from other mums who had ill children and felt they understood what Mum was going through. We had letters from people who said they'd never contacted someone they'd seen from a news item before but just felt they had to write to us.

I used to collect the post and stand in the dining room and read the letters people had sent, until we got a really spiteful one.

'Your child is nothing but a disgusting freak and you should be ashamed of yourself for inflicting it on the world,' this idiot had written. 'You should have locked it away in the attic at birth and forgotten all about it.'

I went through to Mum in the kitchen and handed the letter to her.

She glanced over it. 'There are some really vile people in the world Jo, who do not know what they are talking about,' Mum said and tore the letter in two.

I totally agreed with her. I wasn't particularly upset by the letter because I couldn't imagine what sort of person would say that about a baby, but Mum used to read all the post first after that.

Mum also got quite a few phone calls from transsexuals, who wanted to tell her about their own battles to have their identity recognised. She would always make time to listen and talk to them, sympathising with their problems even though she felt my situation was different. She also thought it was kind of them to take the time to call and tell us they hoped I got my new birth certificate.

One or two of the callers started ringing up quite regularly and Mum got quite friendly with some of them. One lady, from Yorkshire, rang originally just to urge Mum to make sure she kept fighting. She never would tell Mum her name, but eventually revealed that she had been born with physical deformities a lot like mine. She'd been registered as a boy but always felt like a girl and in puberty she'd developed breasts. She said she'd spent her childhood being treated like a freak and had been given a terrible time by some of her teachers in particular. Eventually she'd had an operation to create a vagina but she still had some internal vestiges of male. She'd met a man and fallen in love but when he asked her to marry him, she'd had to explain that it would never be possible because she had a male birth certificate. His response had been to beat her almost to death. She'd had to move away and start her life again, living almost as a recluse through fear of anyone finding out about her.

Another of the callers was not so nice and called himself Sarah Jayne.

'Do you think I'm a woman?' he asked Mum in his first call. 'Actually I have male tackle!'

'Oh right,' Mum said, not sure how to respond.

'I think you are a wonderful mother and what you are doing for your daughter is incredible.'

'Thanks,' Mum said cautiously.

'I imagine it's all very stressful. Have you ever tried yoga? It's a wonderful way of releasing tension.'

'Oh, okay,' Mum replied.

'Ballet is lovely too, don't you think? Keeps the body supple. Does Joella do ballet? You really ought to get her signed up for classes.'

Mum was uncomfortable with the conversation and wrapped the call up. Sarah Jayne had sounded a bit unhinged and Mum was very uncomfortable when he rang back a few days later.

'I love watching you on television,' he told Mum. 'You're wonderful. I feel we have a connection – like sisters – do you know what I mean? If we went out for a night we'd go to the toilet together and share a cubicle, wouldn't we?'

'I'm not really sure about that,' Mum said with a nervous laugh.

'Some people mock me, you know,' Sarah Jayne said, sounding angry. 'You won't mock me will you?'

'Of course not,' Mum replied. 'But, I am a bit busy, I'd better get off the phone.'

'I think I'd better come over to Spalding to see you and Joella in the flesh soon,' Sarah Jayne replied. 'Tell me, exactly what does Joella look like down below?'

Mum slammed the phone down and reported Sarah Jayne to the police, who tried to trace the calls but without success. Mum started to become concerned that Sarah Jayne or anyone like him could easily come to the house – our address had been widely publicised.

The media interest in us didn't seem to be dying down at all, in fact, if anything, it was gathering pace. Some friends from the village had suggested starting a petition and it reached 1,000 signatures within a week or so. Someone else came up with the idea of Mum writing to celebrities and officials to request their support for my campaign and one of Mum's letters went to Princess Diana. We were amazed when we got a reply from her personal secretary a few days later.

'The Princess read your letter with great concern,' the letter said. 'She has asked me to say how touched she was to receive your letter and to thank you for taking the trouble to write as you did.

'The Princess of Wales will have you in her thoughts and sends you and Joella all her love and very best wishes.'

To think that Princess Diana knew about me and our campaign made me feel as if our message was really starting to get across to people.

I couldn't keep having time off school for interviews so we had to try to fit the ongoing requests around the school day. None of my classmates seemed to be aware of what was going on and no-one ever mentioned it to me, but I was getting home some days and then having to go out again to be filmed or recorded. One evening I got home and we had to get straight on a train to go to ITV studios in Leeds for Calendar News. It took forever to get there, then we had to find a taxi in the rain to get to the studio. It was cold and dark and we only just got there in time for the show. The only plus side was that we met Nan's favourite local newscasters and she was thrilled with the autographed photographs I got for her.

It didn't take long for any excitement I'd had about doing the interviews to wear off. The whole thing got very old, very quickly. At the weekend, when I wanted to be playing outside, Mum kept telling me I couldn't because I needed to stay tidy because a photographer was coming round. I think she was also concerned for my safety after the Sarah Jayne calls and looked for excuses to keep me inside with her.

A few of the TV interviews we did were still quite fun, probably because there weren't so many of those. Mum, Farmer, Jarred and I were all asked onto the One to Three show, a Sky talk show with Paul Ross and Sarah Greene. When we got there Paul came to see us in make-up and we had a good bit of banter with him and he covered Farmer in loads of lipstick, which made us all laugh and broke the ice. The show was the first substantial live thing we did and I was very nervous in case I made a mistake. An assistant walked us onto the set past lots of very big cameras and got us sat down in the sofa area to talk us through what was going to happen. The interview didn't take very long and followed the standard format. Mum was asked to outline what had happened when I was born and how she'd been advised to raise me as a girl and then we got a chance to say we just wanted the Government to recognise me for who I was.

In early November, we were invited onto ITV's This Morning, which we thought would be great for us because of how popular it was, but for some reason they cancelled at the last minute. We were very disappointed, then, a week or so later, we got a call to say we were wanted on The Big Breakfast the next morning. Everyone I knew watched the programme on Channel 4 and we couldn't believe we were going to be on it. The only problem was that it was filmed in London, started at 6am and they needed us to be there at 4am.

Mum put Jarred and I to bed as normal then scooped us up in our pyjamas in the middle of the night and loaded us into the car for the journey. Our car was a total banger – our cars always were, they changed from one colour to another as various parts got replaced – and we never knew if it would hold up to a long journey. I slept most of the way, which was good as I used to get pretty travel sick. When I opened my eyes, we'd come off the motorway and Farmer was very flustered trying to find the studio. We were very lost and didn't have much time and the atmosphere in the car was getting pretty heated. It was before everyone had mobile phones so it wasn't like we could have just rung up and told them we were on our way.

Farmer pulled off the road for a second, trying to get his bearings and the next thing a couple of coppers pulled up alongside us.

One of the officers got out and Farmer wound down his window. 'You do realise you can't stop here, Sir?'

'I'm sorry, we're a bit lost,' Farmer began explaining.

Then the police officer spotted me in the back and recognised me from the newspapers!

'We're trying to get to the Big Breakfast and we're late,' Mum told him.

'Don't worry,' he said. 'We know where it is. Just follow us.'

Knowing time was getting on for us, the coppers flicked the blues and twos on and led us right up to where we needed to be. I was still pretty tired and bleary eyed, but thought that was pretty cool. I already quite liked the idea of joining the police force and that made me want to even more.

The Big Breakfast was filmed in an old lock keeper's cottage and at the start of the programme the camera panned round to show it in what looked like huge grounds. It was no surprise that Farmer had struggled to find the entrance because, bizarrely, it was in the middle of an industrial estate. Jarred and I got changed quickly in the car then we all walked through some trees and there were the grounds from the opening scene. It was all a bit strange. You couldn't see it from the road and there were no signs. In front of the studio was a big canal and a little footbridge across it.

We walked over to the Big Breakfast house and were met by a stage-hand who ushered us into the green room, which was in an outbuilding at the back. They put a quick bit of make-up on us all and gave us all name badges. Then we were taken into the main house and through to a seating area made to look like a living room, where they sat us down. All the cameramen were buzzing around us trying to get their equipment through with wires everywhere. We'd been on a few TV sets by then, but the Big Breakfast house was totally different and a bit weird. The walls all turned around to change the appearance of the rooms so the room we started off in didn't look anything like that by the end of the show. It was all a bit mind-bending.

Sharron Davies was presenting the show that day and she came across and had a chat with us, putting us at ease. She was lovely and really down to earth. They were going to do our little bit quite early on and it was the same standard kind of interview we had become used to. We were used to leaving the studio as soon as they were done with us, often before the show had finished, but on the Big Breakfast it was different and they wanted all the guests to hang around. After the interview, they took us through to another seating area where we were on the sofa next to Vanessa Feltz and Shaun Williamson, Barry from EastEnders. They were getting Shaun to do all sorts of jokey stuff and say loads of things in a broad Cockney accent. During one of the breaks he taught Jarred to say: 'Go away you slaaaag,' which had everyone laughing.

Vanessa Feltz wasn't very nice at all and is the only person I have ever met on one of these things that I felt that way about.

She came across as really up herself and was, I guess, what you'd call a diva. We'd taken our petition along to the show and everyone signed it for us. One of the production assistants asked Vanessa if she'd done it and she bit their head off.

'Of course I have, who do you think I am?' she snarled.

The show always ended on everyone looking like they were having a really good time and we were a part of that too. Shaun was singing and everyone else was up on their feet dancing. It was all really a lot of fun.

After we'd been on the Big Breakfast we actually got recognised in the supermarket back in Spalding. People stopped us to tell us they'd seen us on there and wish us good luck. We were really shocked by the level of interest in the story, but Mum was always really polite and took the time to stand and chat.

The other person who obviously suddenly started to see my face everywhere was my biological father, who I'd had little contact with since Farmer had been around. My dad's mother Barbara still lived in our street and I had a little bit of contact with her. I'd go down some days and do a bit of baking with her, that sort of thing and we still saw Aunty Di, in Kent, a bit. One year Barbara had handed me an Easter egg and said it was from my dad, which had just made me feel quite angry at the time. What was the point of an Easter egg when I never saw him?

I had very little memory of my dad and did my best not to think about him, but every now and again I couldn't help but wonder what he was like. Sometimes I'd do something a certain way or pull a particular expression and Mum would say: 'God, you're like your dad.'

My dad was a quiet and reserved type and I don't think he was happy that his name had appeared in a couple of the articles. He rang Mum to ask her to keep him out of the stories and the conversation developed into an agreement between them that he ought to see me. Mum sat me down and asked if I wanted to see my dad and, although I'd always told myself I didn't need him, I felt quite excited at the prospect of it.

CHAPTER TWELVE

I knew my dad would have changed a bit from my baby photos and was worried I wouldn't recognise him. It had been agreed that he'd come and pick me up from home and take me out for a bit. As I waited for him to arrive, I was very excited, but quite nervous. When he knocked at the door, Mum came with me to answer it. She pulled the door open and started chatting with him very civilly while I stood silently at her side. I looked up at my dad and it was a bit like meeting a stranger. Though I could see it was the man from the photographs, he'd put on about 30lb and had a lot less hair. We didn't hug or anything – I can't remember ever having hugged him – and it was all a bit awkward.

After a few moments on the doorstep with Mum, my dad and I went and got in his car. He had a brand new blue Peugeot 306 – he always has new cars, I discovered, usually sticking to the same make and just getting the updated model. He also always wore a shirt and jeans and that day the shirt was blue and stripy.

As we drove off, I glanced across and noticed that we looked quite alike. Our conversation was careful but not as stilted as I'd feared and we hit upon some subjects we had in common. We both still loved cars and, like me, my dad was a fan of The Simpsons.

We went to Ayscoughfee, a big and beautiful park in Spalding and had a bit of a walk around. We chatted all the time but never about anything too deep and after an hour or so, he said he'd drop me back home. As I got out of the car, he said he'd come to see me again and I felt good about that.

My dad still lived with Shirley in Peterborough and a few weeks later he offered to pick me up and take me back to their house. Mum had sent him one of the pictures the News of the World had taken of me and it felt nice when I saw he had put it on the wall. My dad had a computer, which we didn't at home and the highlight of the visit for me was playing an aviation game he had on it.

After that my dad would come and see me every few months and maybe take me to the cinema or bowling. We never became very close and he never felt like my dad, more a friend or distant relative, but it was good to feel we had some kind of relationship and I felt I knew where I came from a bit more. My dad and I are both much quieter than Mum and probably aren't that dissimilar in nature in a lot of ways. At Christmas and birthdays, I'd get a card from him, often with a cheque inside. I wasn't bothered by the money but liked being able to stand his card beside my others.

By December 1996, the petition had reached 3,000 signatures and the local papers rang all the time to ask if there was any update. At Christmas, one of the Spalding weekly papers asked if they could take a picture of me writing a letter to Santa asking for a birth certificate. We were happy to do almost anything to keep the battle in the public eye.

Dianne had decided to apply for legal aid in preparation for my case having to go to the European Court of Human Rights because she believed that was the only way it would ever get resolved legally. In January, the legal aid was turned down and Mum was furious. She had a habit of getting the vacuum cleaner out when she was angry about something and crashing around with it.

'Even murderers get legal aid, but Jo can't have it to get her birth certificate. How is that right?'

She made those comments to one of the local newspapers and the Daily Mail, Express and all the rest were soon on the phone again.

'Betrayal of the girl born a boy,' was one of the headlines.

Friends decided we should launch a fighting fund to appeal against the decision to deny me legal aid and we all started thinking of fundraising ideas. Farmer and some of our friends from the village decided to do a walk from the clocktower in Skegness to The Bull, in Pinchbeck. It was more than 30 miles and I don't think any of them really realised what they were taking on. Someone took them all up there in a van in the early hours and acted as a support vehicle. We waited at home with a load of the local photographers, including Woody, who had become like a friend. I walked the last mile or so with them along the main road in Pinchbeck from Nan's to The Bull. Farmer's feet were in shreds and I felt really proud that he had done all that for me.

A complete stranger got in touch with the Spalding paper and did a sponsored cycle for us and I had my picture taken with him. It was really touching that someone we didn't even know wanted to help that much. Mum and Nan also organised a big Joella Appeal party at the village hall and everyone we knew paid to come along.

It was all a lot of pressure for Mum who seemed to spend all of her time on the phone to journalists, Dianne and the various well-wishers. It was an additional stress that added to the financial pressures she and Farmer were always under. He was always having to swap jobs because some of the factories were seasonal and others relied on one or two contracts that, if they lost, meant they'd dramatically reduce staff. Around the time we were turned down for legal aid, Farmer lost his job again. He and Mum wondered if it might be a positive in terms of our legal aid application, but it also meant things were very tight. As it was we never had a lot of money and clothes were always bought through the catalogue. Getting a new coat was a big event and would be something to go and knock up the neighbours to show them.

A friend of Mum's fostered children to bring in some extra money and Mum, who because of me had extra sympathy for kids who'd had a rough time, was so moved by some of the stories her friend told, decided it might be something she could do too. Even with everything she already had going on, she started looking into it as well as taking on some shifts at the social club.

Mum was starting to get frustrated with a transsexual organisation called Press for Change, who had taken to ringing and writing to her all the time, thinking that if I won my case it would help their members get new birth certificates and identities. In one of their first letters they'd referred to me as the youngest transsexual in the country, which hadn't gone down too well with Mum. They were also pushing for her to drop Dianne and allow them to take on my case, presumably wanting to use me as some sort of figurehead for their fight. Mum didn't want to make an enemy of anyone, but she didn't like the way the organisation went about things and wanted them to leave her alone.

Sarah Jayne also hadn't given up and would still call every now and again and threaten that if Mum didn't agree to meet up with him, he'd find me instead. The police didn't seem to be getting anywhere with finding out who the caller was and Mum was tempted to meet him just to prevent him coming for me, but Farmer wouldn't allow it. Then, when Mum was at the social club one day, she got a call from someone claiming to be from my school. They said I'd run out of my prescription items and asked if she could drop some off. Mum thought it was all a bit strange because she knew there was plenty at the school and before she set off to bring the stuff in, she called the school just to check. They said no-one had rung her and Mum is convinced it was Sarah Jayne. Freaked out by it, Mum asked Farmer to come and walk her home from the club that night and when he got around the corner he saw someone hanging around in the shadows. He chased the guy, but he got away. Sarah Jayne went very quiet for a long time after that, but the fear he had caused did not go away.

Mum and Farmer were also really wound up after they set up a meeting with an MP, who they'd thought might help lobby for my birth certificate in Parliament. The meeting didn't go to plan and, although I don't know exactly what was said, Mum had to pull Farmer out of there because he was so angry with the bloke. Then, on top of everything, Grandad was diagnosed with cancer. He'd had bronchitis and a patch had been found on his lung. The doctors reckoned he only had six months to live.

Mum was so close to Grandad that his diagnosis just pushed her over the edge. I walked into the kitchen one morning in February 1997 to find her sitting at the kitchen table, looking in the mirror, her head almost completely bald.

'What's wrong? Are you ill?' I panicked.

'No, no darling. Nothing like that. I'm just very stressed with everything and I think this is my body's way of reacting to it.'

Mum was very calm about it, but I could see she was upset and I felt terrible. I knew most of her stress was down to me and my stupid birth certificate. Within a couple of days she had no hair at all – not even eyebrows.

Grandad magicked up some money from somewhere and sent Mum off to Lincoln to get the best wig she could find. Mum had always changed her hairstyle so regularly that, once she had the wig, most people didn't even know what had happened and, bravely, she barely mentioned her alopecia again, but it worried me. Everything worried me at that time – Grandad's illness, Mum's health, my birth certificate, what would happen if I never got a new one, who I really was. I still didn't tend to dwell too much on the male/female thing, but it was difficult not to let it cross my mind sometimes.

Whenever I walked into the local shop there was my petition on the counter and newspapers saying I was a boy. Occasionally I'd find myself having to repeat that old mantra 'I'm not a boy, I'm not a boy.' I knew I wasn't because I felt like a girl, but I felt like I needed to assert it more than I ever had before. I know I asked for a doll as a present around that time, not wanting it, but thinking it was what I ought to want. In some of the interviews we did, reporters would ask who I liked off the TV and I'd say 'Leonardo Di Caprio' because some of my friends liked him, but really I didn't like anyone. In squabbles, kids in the street sometimes made comments about me 'being a boy'. It didn't really get to me – I was seeing it in the papers so them saying it made no difference – but it was annoying.

I'd lay awake for hours at night with everything going round and round in my head and would feel so anxious it made it difficult to breathe. Some days I felt shaky and my heart would race for no apparent reason, I'd find it difficult to concentrate on anything or I'd just feel completely miserable, but I couldn't pinpoint why. I didn't want to let on to anyone that I felt that way because I didn't want them to think I was weird. I didn't even tell Mum or Nan, I was a big enough problem to them already without admitting I had head issues too.

I thought a lot about what might happen if we never managed to get my birth certificate. We'd initially thought it would be sorted out quite quickly once we went to The Press but nothing seemed to be happening. I was very aware of the single-sex secondary school issue and worried all the time what would happen if I didn't have my new birth certificate by the time I needed to move up. I used to visualise being made to go to the boys' school and walking in on the first day with everyone pointing and laughing at me.

'What if I end up having to go to the boys' school?' I asked Mum once.

'I'd never let that happen. We'd home-school you rather than let you be forced to go to a boys' school. Don't even think about it.'

It became another concern that I buried and tried not to let out, but like the other thoughts it was always there. I just bottled everything up. I rarely cried or got angry, I just focused everything inward and tried to get on with things. Everyone was always saying how well I coped with everything and they seemed more concerned about the potential impact of it all on Jarred because the attention was always on me.

Before each interview we did, I was starting to feel more and more responsibility for making sure we got our message across to get things changed. There's a tape somewhere of me on one programme where I turned and looked straight into the camera.

'I want the Government to know I am a girl and that I deserve to have my identity,' I said.

It looked like I'd been coached in what to say and I was so little that it's kind of ridiculous but no-one had told me what to say. I'd just listened to Mum talking about the Government in interviews and can remember coming up with that little speech that morning.

I continued to have a constant trickle of health problems with the sores and my stomach blocking up. I took a lot of laxatives to try to keep things moving but still had a reasonable amount of time off school. School was nowhere near as bad as it had been at Pinchbeck but I still didn't like it and the days off were always a relief.

Nan's was still my favourite escape and being at her house was the only time I really felt at ease. At home everything always seemed so stressful and busy, whereas at Nan's I just felt free. My mind felt at peace there and I could go outside and play without worrying what anyone thought of me or what I thought of myself. I could pass hours just sitting up in one of the trees in her garden. When I was at Nan's and when I was allowed to play out in the street at home with my friends, I could switch off and be a kid again. The rest of the time it felt like I needed to be thinking and acting like an adult.

I spent too much time contemplating the legal stuff, the Press coverage, the gender stuff and I felt like I spent my life thinking and talking about my condition and the legal consequences of it. I was being pulled towards all these big issues and felt I had to sort of sit and judge them properly so I had a better understanding of what was going on.

A few big things happened in the first few months of 1997 that gave us all a bit of a lift. Firstly, Mum got her first foster child – a Jamaican baby girl who needed somewhere to stay for a few weeks. She was so, so cute and I was really excited to have 'a baby sister' to help out with like I had done with Jarred when he was born.

Secondly, the doctors appeared to have got it very wrong as far as Grandad's lifespan was concerned. Mum helped him move into some retirement flats in Spalding where there was a warden to keep an eye on him and, although he wasn't keen on it there, his health seemed unbelievably good. He was still riding his bike, still sneaking off to the pub, eating stew and dumplings even though Mum had been told he'd have no appetite and he revelled in winding up the nosy old dears who lived alongside him. He did become a bit less mobile towards the middle of the year and ultimately moved in with us, but things weren't nearly as bad as we'd originally feared.

In addition, a barrister called Robert Hill got in touch and said he'd seen us on the television and in the newspapers and wondered if he could do anything to help. Mum put him in contact with Dianne and she agreed to share all the details of my case with him. Just like Dianne, Robert was not interested in payment, he just wanted to make things right for me.

Lastly, someone from the BBC's QED programme called us and said they were interested in making a documentary about me. The producers explained that they would want to do quite a lot of filming over a number of weeks and they'd really want to try to have something exclusive. I liked the sound of it – having a programme just about me was exciting. As well as that, QED wouldn't want us doing loads of other interviews while they were involved so it would put an end to all the other media for a while, which sounded great.

CHAPTER THIRTEEN

The moment Mum and I met the QED producer and researcher, we got on with them so well that we knew we wanted to go ahead with the documentary. Gail and Veronica were so easy to talk to and made everything seem easy and casual. Mum felt QED would give us the right kind of in-depth exposure and I was star-struck because Veronica had also worked on Animal Hospital. She wowed me with all her stories from the show as she and Gail explained what taking part in QED would be like.

We were told that QED would be very different from anything we'd already done because the filming would be built up over a period of time. They said they'd want to film me at school, having days out, would interview family and friends and perhaps join me for hospital appointments.

Mum confided in Gail and Veronica that I'd barely had any contact with Great Ormond Street Hospital since she decided not to allow the Mitrofanoff to go ahead, but she had been wondering recently if the time might now be right for that procedure. Gail and Veronica said they'd be keen to explore that in the documentary. They could even film the operation if I went ahead with it. That made Mum even more keen to take part in the programme because she wanted a record of exactly what organs I had. She wanted to know if there was any Fallopian tube, which would obviously have helped our case.

We were both really happy to get involved with the programme and signed up there and then. They even offered to pay us a few hundred pounds to be a part of the programme which was an unexpected bonus.

It wasn't long after we started working with QED that Mum went with Dianne to meet Robert Hill, the barrister, in his London chambers. He'd spent some months looking over all the documents in my case and was convinced he had found a new way forward. Mum, wearing her smartest outfit, was nervous about meeting him, but needn't have been. Robert was such a kind man. He had a birth mark across half of his face but it didn't stop him being strangely good looking. He wore a serious and expensive navy pinstripe suit and tucked under his desk was a pink My Little Pony lunch box.

'My daughter insists on packing my lunch every day,' he explained with a smile.

When Robert started explaining his ideas about my birth certificate, Mum listened closely.

'As yet, Joella's birth certificate has remained unchanged as the vast majority of the paperwork refers to her having undergone a sex change operation. I believe that the key to this case is in demonstrating that no such change ever happened. I think it is possible for us to prove that, at birth, Joella could just as easily have been assigned to female as male.

'On the day of birth, Joella's admission sheet said: 'Ambiguous genitalia. Chromosomal abnormality?' The more I have looked at her records, the more I have come to realise that was probably the most credible record of her actual sex. I believe it could be said that Joella was either of 'no sex' or was 'intersex'.

'The law says that sex is determined by testing of chromosomes, genitals and gonads. In Joella's medical records there is no recorded result of a chromosome test so that test was clearly not used to decide which sex to assign her to. She had no genitalia at all so that test also becomes inconclusive, which leaves us with the gonadal test. While Joella did have gonads, which were labelled 'testicles', they were not testicles in the sense that they were recognisable as such or capable of one day functioning as male genitalia and they were not where testicles should have been. They were, in reality, nothing more than intersex tissue and, I believe, the operation Joella underwent in 1989 would have been the same operation had she gone into it a girl or a boy.'

The argument hit a chord with Mum, who had felt so sure that I'd always been destined to be a girl as soon as I'd made the switch from Joel to Joella.

'So you think Joella was always a girl?' Mum asked.

'From the evidence, I believe it would have been equally logical to regard Joella as female as it was to class her as male,' Robert replied. 'I would be seeking to show that in being registered as Joel, of the male sex, an error of fact or substance could well have been said to have been made and, as such, a change on the birth certificate to Joella, of female sex, could be made within the context of the law.

'Rather than staging the big fight and crusading in The Press, I believe we need something of a change of tack. We should seek to lodge another application for an amendment to Joella's birth certificate as if it is not in any way controversial. We shall support the application with a detailed legal argument setting out why an error was made in the original record.

'We should view the exercise of applying for Joella's birth certificate an extremely difficult challenge, but not a hopeless one. We must still expect that the application will be turned down and should always consider that we may still have to resort to the European Court in Strasbourg, but that should be our last resort. We should know that if we go there, while the outcome would hopefully be favourable, it would take a vast amount of time and inevitably mean many more years of uncertainty.'

Robert explained that two people would need to make a sworn declaration that a mistake had been made on my original birth certificate. The rules stated that those people had to be either 'qualified informants' or 'credible persons having knowledge of the truth of the case'. There was no more detailed explanation of who was classified as 'qualified' or 'credible'.

'But who will we get to make the statements?' Mum asked. 'Joella's specialists don't seem to want to help.'

Robert had thought of a way around it. 'Looked at one way, yes it is true that if Joella's specialist refused to support the application it is doomed to failure, but there could be an alternative view. It might be said that Joella's specialist, who advised that Joella should be raised as male and performed

surgery on her, had a vested interest in vigorously supporting her application to avoid allegations of professional
negligence. If we could find another specialist, of similar or
higher standing, the suggestion could be made that they
were being relied upon because they were independent.

'In addition, I believe it would be difficult for anyone to
argue that the hospital chaplain, who helped you conclude
to christen your baby Joel purely on the basis that you did
not have a girl's name, is not a 'credible person' in this case.
If we can find him and he can remember Joella's arrival into
the world, I believe he too could help.'

Mum left that meeting feeling that her decision to raise
me as a girl had been validated in some way. She also had a
renewed confidence that my birth certificate case could be
won. I was still only nine years old and the detail of the meeting was obviously too complicated for me to understand, but
Mum told me that the barrister had said we might not have
to go to court after all. In my mind, 'might not', meant we
still 'might' have to go to court and images of wigs, gowns
and judges continued to trouble me. However, I was reassured by the feeling that we would eventually win.

'When this is all sorted, we'll have a big christening to
celebrate you having your proper identity,' Mum promised.

That was something I really looked forward to.

Robert said it was fine to continue with QED, both
because we had already agreed to it and because we could
use it as an excuse not to talk to newspapers. Robert reiter-
ated to Mum that whenever she did talk to anyone about
my case, she needed to focus on the fact that I was born of
indiscriminate sex – 'intersex' – and try to get them away

from reporting that I was a boy turned girl. I became aware of the term 'intersex' and of Mum telling people that I was 'intersex'. I wasn't completely comfortable with it, but it felt much better than them saying I was once male.

Meanwhile, the QED team got me a set of appointments lined up at Great Ormond Street in May, a couple of months after we'd first met them. The deal was that Mum and I would have a chat with the doctors initially and then we'd do it again for the cameras. Mum was keen for the appointments to be about trying to help me with my condition and knew it wouldn't be useful to raise the legal case. Veronica and Gail, a cameraman, a sound guy and another chap came down to the hospital with us and it was really quite exciting and good fun.

The first appointment was with Mr Ransley and we talked about operations I could have to create a more normal external appearance as well as the Mitrofanoff to get rid of pads. I really wanted to be more normal and it all sounded very exciting to me. Mr Ransley even said he could make me a belly button, which probably excited me more than anything. It had always bothered me that I hadn't got one!

After seeing Mr Ransley, I had an appointment with an endocrinologist, a hormone specialist, who talked to me about the large amount of growth that took place in the teenage years. Professor Brookes was really, really nice – a real proper professor, complete with dicky bow – and said I'd need daily medication to induce puberty, ensure I grew breasts, got taller and grew adult hair. He said they'd need to X-ray my hands and measure me regularly to document how things were going.

I was sent home with all these tiny pills and a little pill cutter because I only needed a quarter of one a day to start with. I'd sit at nights and cut them down and after the initial novelty it was really quite tedious. When they eventually upped the dose to one full pill it was quite a relief.

Professor Brookes seemed to really know his stuff when it came to my condition and Mum mentioned him to Robert afterwards, wondering if he could be the expert we needed. She was also putting a lot of time into trying to track down the vicar who had christened me in hospital, the Rev John Read. After many months she eventually traced him to a retirement home and he remembered clearly what had happened when I was born. He agreed to make a statutory declaration about it as part of my application and Robert organised it all.

QED had a string of things they wanted to film me doing and the same team of five started coming along to spend a day or two with us every couple of months and then disappearing for a while. We got to know them all very well and became really comfortable around them. Their visits were always fun and it was like acting really because we'd have to do around half a dozen takes of each scene.

One day, they took us to Skegness with the idea of getting some footage of us having a fun family day out at the seaside, but the day they picked for it was absolutely foul. We would occasionally have a family day at the beach but we'd choose a sunny day. The day we went with QED, it was windy, cold and wet. We were supposed to pretend to be having fun on the beach but the wind was so strong that just trying to walk along it was almost impossible. They gave Mum an umbrella to hold over us and she put it down for a second then lifted it up and found it was covered in dog poo, which pretty much summed up what the day was. We all laughed about what a disaster it was and unsurprisingly none of what they filmed that day made it into the programme.

The team also wanted to film me having a typical 'girly' day out with a school friend and suggested I pick someone to take shopping and for a haircut. It wasn't the sort of thing I'd ever do normally but I didn't mind.

I still didn't really have friends at school, but I asked a girl who I sometimes sat with in lessons and she was very excited at the thought of being on TV. The QED team took us to Queensgate, the indoor shopping centre in Peterborough, and filmed as we picked out some clothes in the shops, which we were allowed to buy and keep. Mum wasn't in the shots for any of that day but she was there all the time watching. Other shoppers kept looking across at what was going on and a little crowd gathered a couple of times. People always like to have a little look when you're doing something like that. They usually look for a minute and then walk away. The attention didn't bother me that day. It was all quite enjoyable.

The crew also wanted to come into school and film me a bit there to create footage of 'an ordinary day in the life of Joella'. They decided to come in September, on the first day of Year Six, and it was one of the last times I found school bearable. I had a new headteacher and I didn't like her anywhere near as much as Mrs Wakefield.

We did some filming at home first, of me pretending to have just got out of bed, eating my breakfast, watching a bit of TV and walking down the road. Then the crew came into school for the morning and everyone was quite excited about having them in assembly. I don't think the other kids were that bothered about exactly why they were there. They just liked the idea of being on television. The team filmed us in an art lesson, a bit of me walking around the school and then came with us onto the huge back field where we played some football.

Things were moving towards me having the Mitrofanoff and a date in December was being talked about, but Mum and I were still cautious about it. Mum had been told that, with only one good kidney, there was added risk for me and any complications could lead to kidney failure. We also still worried whether I'd be able to carry on playing football.

QED suggested introducing me to a girl of a similar age who had already had a Mitrofanoff to talk about what it was like. I agreed to it and we went down to Great Ormond Street and into a park where I talked to the girl about the operations we'd both had and compared scars. It was nice to meet her, but in reality, her case was quite different to mine and Mum and I wanted more reassurance.

A few weeks before the operation was due, we went up to Great Ormond Street without the QED team to discuss it further. We went to have a look around the ward where I'd be recovering and talked to some of the nurses who would help me learn to adjust to self-catheterisation. They confirmed that there was every chance I'd have to have a string of operations to get it right.

Mum wanted a second opinion before we agreed to go ahead and asked to speak to one of the other consultants.

'I'm concerned about the pressure a Mitrofanoff could put on Joella's kidney if we go ahead,' Mum told him. 'Do you think it's risky?'

'With Joella only having one viable kidney, I would have to say that it would be of concern to me. I obviously don't know Joella's history in as much detail as her own specialist, but certainly a Mitrofanoff is very invasive surgery and it isn't impossible to see an ultimate outcome where she might have to look toward a transplant. I have to say, I think you would be very wise to give it careful consideration before going ahead.'

Mum called the operation off there and then, fearing the risks were too great. She came out of the room and told me what had been said and my overriding feeling was relief that I hadn't gone through with surgery that could have changed my life for the worse. I felt I'd had a lucky escape especially if there was still any doubt about whether I'd still be able to play football. I thought I could put the operation off until I was older when I wasn't running around and climbing trees any more and medicine may have advanced to make it all safer. It meant that again nothing was done to create any kind of 'normality' to my physical appearance. My undercarriage was still just stitched up with nothing like genitalia of one kind or another.

The QED team were very understanding of my decision and said they'd come up with something to round off the film instead of the expected surgery scenes. They ended up waiting until early summer 1998 to do the final filming. They asked me to write a letter to the girl they'd introduced me to that had undergone the Mitrofanoff and took me across to the river bank at the back of the house to wistfully read it out. I wrote that I'd decided it wasn't the right time for the operation for me but it had been good to meet her.

Afterwards, all the crew came back to our house for coffee and biscuits and, after more than a year of working with them, it was quite sad knowing we weren't going to be seeing them again. We took some pictures of me with everyone, holding all the filming and sound equipment and Veronica made my day by presenting me with an Animal Hospital badge. I had a denim jacket that I'd attached loads of badges to and was really pleased to add that one.

The documentary had still not aired by November 19, when Mum walked into the kitchen and tore open one of the letters that had arrived in that day's post. She read the contents and sat down silently.

'What's up?' Farmer asked. 'Who do we owe now?'

'We've won,' Mum said. 'They've given us Jo's certificate.'

Mum handed the envelope to Farmer, unable to believe what she was reading and he looked it over. 'You're right! This is it. They've given it to you!'

CHAPTER FOURTEEN

The Registrar General had sent a simple letter saying the request for my birth certificate to be amended had been granted. Enclosed was a short-form version of a birth certificate that listed me as Joella Holliday, sex: female. It had been nine years since Mum had first applied for my birth certificate to be amended and almost two years since Robert Hill had first got in contact. Mum did not dare to believe we had really won until she had spoken to Dianne.

The reaction of Dianne's secretary when Mum phoned the office turned out to be enough.

'Julia! Congratulations! We have been trying to ring you. Dianne has been notified too. It's amazing!' Everyone in Dianne's office knew us and our case well.

Mum was still in a bit of a daze when she called me downstairs and, with a shaky hand, passed me the letter.

'It's your new birth certificate,' she said. 'They've given it to us.'

I don't think any of us could quite believe it but as it soaked in, we all felt relief more than excitement to start with. I'd had it in my mind for so long that we'd have to go through this big court case and all that fear and worry just ebbed away.

'I've got to go to school to tell everyone!' I said. I don't think Mum could believe that either. She'd fully expected me to use it as a reason to stay home. It was probably the first and last time I ever actually wanted to go to school. We started talking about the christening straight away and began planning the huge party we were going to have.

When I got home that night, Mum and Farmer had hung a great big congratulations banner up and filled the house with helium balloons. We all wanted to shout the news from the rooftops.

It had seemed as if the letter had come completely out of the blue, but it actually followed all the hard work Robert, Dianne and Mum had put in since the first meeting the three of them had. It turned out that Mum's idea that Professor Brookes might be able to help my case had been spot on. Robert had made contact with him soon after Mum and I met him at the hospital and discovered he was very renowned in the field of gender assignment.

It became apparent that very many babies – up to one in 1,000 according to some researchers – is born with an 'intersex' characteristic. People can be born with the internal workings of one sex and the external appearance of another or with the genitals of a man but the chromosomes of a woman. Often people live much or all of their lives without even knowing that they have those idiosyncrasies. Sometimes they only discover a problem when they want to have children of their own. For others, like me, the problems are more obvious.

Professor Brookes was able to agree with the conclusion Robert had formed that children born with conditions like mine were basically assigned a 'sex of rearing'. A large part of which sex was chosen was based on what physical attributes a child had and what could be created for them. Professor Brookes said it was quite usual for babies with male chromosomes to be assigned to the female sex and vice versa.

Professor Brookes was also happy to categorically state that had I have been in his care when I was born, he would have assigned me to the female sex and I would have been registered as a girl. He, therefore, agreed that it could be viewed as a mistake that I had been registered as male and said he would be happy to sign a statutory declaration to that effect.

Robert knew that to have any chance of success, the documents submitted with my renewed request for an amendment to my birth certificate needed to contradict some of the previous statements made about me by physicians. Professor Brookes was happy to agree that it was wrong to state that I'd undergone 'sex reassignment' surgery, as had been stated by some doctors. The basis of that argument was that had I have been in the care of Professor Brookes, I would have gone into the 1989 surgery a girl, but had exactly the same operation.

Professor Brookes was also prepared to challenge documentation that said I'd had 'hemi-phallus'. He stated that terminology was misleading as I'd never had a penis. He was also happy to state that while there was no record of my having ever had a chromosome test, it was irrelevant because even if I had XY chromosomes – those of a man – it would not have affected the fact that he would have decreed me to be a girl.

The final statutory declaration, which Robert drafted and Professor Brookes signed, was 46 pages long. In the summer of 1998, Dianne and Robert had submitted it to the Registrar General's office, along with the statutory dec-laration of the Rev John Read, who'd christened me. The Registrar General must have spent a few months mulling it over and then decided it was enough to base an amendment on.

All of that detail is something I have only become aware of in the process of writing this book. At the time of the 'win' it seemed much more simple to me. I'd always felt like a girl, Mum had told me she believed I was a girl and now I *was* a girl because my birth certificate said so. I knew we'd won through arguing I was 'intersex', but the point was we had won so I shouldn't have to think about it anymore. In my mind, I felt that if the Government was prepared to acknowledge I was a girl, there should be no more doubt about it.

Mum rang the QED team to tell them the update and they were really pleased for us, but asked if we could keep it quiet so they could amend the footage and use the exclusive line for their documentary. We were happy to do whatever we could to help them. A fortnight later though, a reporter from the Peterborough Evening Telegraph phoned up and said they'd heard a rumour that I'd got my new birth cer-tificate. Everyone in the village knew about it – Mum and Nan knew so many people and had shared the news with their friends and I'd obviously told people at school – and we'd also met with the vicar to talk about the christening so I guess it was inevitable it would get out. We had always been grateful to the Peterborough paper for supporting our case initially and Mum wanted to do the right thing by them. She asked them to give her a few minutes to speak to QED and promised to get back to them. QED agreed that we couldn't contain the story any longer and, instead, they helped manage its release.

On December 1, the story of my birth certificate success appeared on the front page of the Peterborough Evening Telegraph and, somehow, the London Evening Standard. The Peterborough paper's headline mirrored its first ever headline about me. This time, instead of 'She's A Boy,' it read 'She's A Girl.'

The next day, I was in every national newspaper in the country, including the front pages of The Times and The Daily Telegraph and page leads in The Daily Mail, The Mirror, The Independent and The Guardian. Mum and I walked into the Spar and all we could see was our faces on everything.

All the papers wanted to come out to see us again to do in-depth features and interviews and the cul-de-sac filled up with journalists and satellite trucks again. Mum tried not to let it completely disrupt my life and sent me to school as usual, but then she got a phone call from them asking to arrange for me to be picked up because some photographers were hanging around the school gates. Farmer came and picked me up and took me to Nan's for a bit of peace. It was insane and we have heard since that some of the photographers were making hundreds of pounds out of their pictures of me. It never occurred to us to ask for any money for the interviews we gave or pictures we posed for. For us, it wasn't about money as we felt we owed it to The Press to help them after the coverage they'd given our campaign, but in hindsight it's annoying to know others were profiting from it.

We had phone calls from media and well-wishers in Australia, Asia, even an English doctor, who was living in Pakistan, wrote to congratulate us so we knew the story had gone pretty much everywhere. A week after the story was in all the nationals, we were booked to appear on This Morning with Richard and Judy and that night QED was going out. Everyone in the neighbourhood was quite excited about This Morning and they all said they'd watch it. Nan thought it was great too and even came down with Mum, Farmer, Jarred and I to the studio, which was the first time she'd ever come with us to anything like that.

Farmer drove us all down to London and it was a case of having to leave quite early again to be there for 8am. I still suffered quite badly with travel sickness so hated the journey as always. We arrived at the studios on the South Bank and were taken through all these side doors and corridors up to the green room, which was quite large with a few grey sofas and a little kitchen area. There were quite a few people hanging around and others rushing about collecting guests for make-up and their appearances. Mum, Farmer and Nan kept slipping out onto the little balcony area for a smoke.

Paul O'Grady was in the green room with his dog, who kept having a go at the sandwiches that had been laid out on a tray for guests. It was one of the early times that he was appearing on TV as himself and not Lily Savage and Nan really hit it off with him. I knew Lily Savage was a man, but it was a shock to see he looked so normal. He was a lovely bloke and he and Nan were chatting for ages.

I went off to the toilet, which seemed to be miles away through all of these corridors, like a maze and on the way back bumped into a presenter I'd seen on children's TV. It was a bit weird just bumping into people off the television in the corridors. Lesley Joseph, who I recognised from Birds of a Feather, was also appearing on This Morning and when Mum and I went off to make-up she kept Jarred busy messing about with him.

I never liked having to have make-up on, but they always wanted you to wear it so you didn't look too washed out on screen. Mum and I sat next to each other in the little make-up room that you sometimes see on TV, with all the lights around the mirror and the make-up girl chatted to us about some of the other shows she had worked on.

We were on towards the middle of the show and as they went to an ad break one of the stage hands came through to get us. We were led down a corridor, through some double doors and out into the big This Morning studio. We could see all the areas we were used to seeing on TV all laid out in the one big room – the kitchen area, the sofas in front of the window where they do the interviews and, that day there was a little Christmas set-up with fake snow and a snowman for something they were doing.

Richard and Judy came across to shake our hands and led us over to the interview area where I was most interested in the view over the Thames, which I'd always thought was lovely on television and enjoyed seeing in real life. Richard and Judy seemed a nice pair and ran through a few of the questions they were going to ask. I was quite used to being interviewed and was quite comfortable with it all by that time though I guess I was a bit more nervous knowing so many people we knew were watching. Quite soon the ad break was coming to an end and it was a case of all in positions and a guy with headphones started counting down, then Richard and Judy did their bit to camera before turning to us and doing a fairly straightforward interview.

Quite a few people we knew said they'd seen it and told me I'd done well, but I never actually saw it myself. We'd asked someone to tape it for us but they forgot or it broke or something. I'd never been overly bothered about having to see myself on TV so I wasn't too upset, but I guess it would have been quite nice to see that one with it being a programme we knew so well.

That night we all sat down and watched QED together. I was on the floor beside the wall-mounted gas fire where I always tended to sit and Nan was on the sofa with Mum, Farmer, Jarred and Grandad. We were all really pleased with the programme, which they'd added a final written information page to saying that I'd now got my birth certificate.

We'd mentioned the christening we were planning on This Morning and in a lot of the newspaper interviews and everyone seemed quite interested in coming along. We got a date organised for the week before Christmas and a lot of the papers used the line that my birth certificate was the best present I could have wished for, which it was really. We went to Matchmakers of Stamford, who had done Mum's bridal gown, to get me an outfit and while we were there Mum was getting calls asking what my outfit would be like, which was weird. We chose a white dress, with a Christmassy red sash around the middle and a green jacket. It was £60 to hire or £500 to buy and when Mum handed the shop owner £60, she told us we could keep the outfit as her treat. Everyone around us seemed kind of euphoric on our behalf. I was so excited about the christening and finally knowing my name was really properly mine and even quite liked the dress.

My story seemed to be quite big all across Europe, especially in Germany, where a production company asked if they could do a kind of fly-on-the-wall documentary about the christening. Mum didn't see any harm and agreed to them coming across. Loads of photographers and reporters had also asked to come along and Mum had a bit of a the-more-the-merrier attitude to it.

We had a bit of a scare when Sarah Jayne got back in contact to 'offer his congratulations' and said he was going to come along. Mum told the police and I think they actually came on the day and issued the legitimate Press with badges or numbers or something to make sure no-one sneaked in.

RTL arrived a couple of days before the christening and did a bit of filming with us out and about around the village very much like we'd done with QED. The cameraman was a big South African guy who was good fun and did silly things like dancing about the kitchen. The night before the christening we had a big rehearsal, which ITV and some others came to so they could plan where they needed their cameras to be. The rehearsal started early evening and went on until gone 10pm and I was shattered. I remember feeling a bit annoyed that the day was being hijacked by the media and their requirements.

RTL were back the next morning before I was even dressed and started filming as we were all getting ready. Mum had ordered a big cake and made dozens of sandwiches for everyone to have back at our house afterwards and it was all really hectic. The atmosphere was a bit frantic but the RTL guy was there to lighten the mood doing the YMCA in the kitchen. Grandad was getting quite frail by then and decided he wasn't up to coming, which was especially hard for Mum who thought she would have been able to convince him if she'd had more time to help him get ready.

Mel and Dianne had agreed to be my godparents, which seemed right as they had both been so important in my life. Mel had been my godparent first time around anyway and Dianne had more than proven that she was prepared to always look out for me. Dianne insisted on buying Mum an outfit to wear for the christening even after all she'd already done for us. Mum got a long red dress with a full-length black coat and trendy black hat, which looked great on her. Nan also looked really lovely on the day in a new dress and hat, though she always did look nice. Farmer was so smart he looked like my bodyguard and Jarred, who was six, looked lovely in his little suit.

At the church there were dozens and dozens of Press and barely enough space for our guests between them. I sat at the front between Dianne and Mel and wasn't really aware of the cameras during the service. Mum, who was on the other side of Dianne, joked they were like the angel and the devil in my life. Throughout the service Mum and Dianne laughed and cried in equal amounts. Getting to the christening had been such a long fight for them both.

The vicar was quite hilarious in the ceremony and seemed to quite enjoy his period in the spotlight. He even stopped the first hymn after a line or two, shouting: 'Cut! That was nowhere near loud enough.'

As we left the ceremony the reporters and photographers all wanted a moment with us and it felt great to finally be able to smile for the pictures!

CHAPTER FIFTEEN

Getting my new birth certificate had been such a battle, over so many years, that once we'd won, it felt like a chance to relax a bit. It felt like the pressure was finally off and though the media attention kept up, the things we agreed to do felt like part of the celebration.

Early in the New Year, we were asked to appear on a chat show that Julie Goodyear, the Coronation Street actress, was doing on Sky. The show was filmed in Manchester, right next to the Coronation Street set and, as a huge Manchester United fan, I was very excited just at the thought of going to the city.

Farmer, Mum, Jarred and I all went along to the studio and we parked our car right near 'Coronation Street'. We had a bit of time in the green room and then we were taken on to the Julie Goodyear Show set, which was a bit like the This Morning set really – a sort of mock living room. We sat next to a big window and did the interview, which was all pretty standard until the last moment.

'Actually, Joella,' Julie Goodyear said. 'We have a present for you.'

Then, this guy came on carrying one of Gary Pallister's old Man Utd shirts signed by all the players as well as a letter from Alex Ferguson! I wasn't expecting it at all and was quite amazed. Julie read the letter out and it apologised that David Beckham couldn't be there, but said he was off training somewhere with the rest of the team. The letter went on to invite us to go along to a home game a few weeks later. I couldn't believe it.

Afterwards, I got to have a look around the studios where they film player interviews and stuff for MUTV. I'd been fairly unmoved by being on TV again and meeting a Coronation Street actress, but was over the moon at being at MUTV. Jarred was just getting into football at that age and had sort of adopted United like me so he was pretty pleased to get to see it all as well.

What I didn't realise was that an even bigger surprise was just around the corner and it was delivered to us a couple of days later by our vicar. He came to the house and told Mum an American TV station was trying to get in contact with us.

'They want you and Joella to go on the Maury Povich Show,' he said. 'It's filmed in New York.'

I don't know why but New York was the only place I'd ever really wanted to go and Mum knew it. Maybe it was because I was such a big fan of the Friends series, which was set there. Whatever it was about the place I'd dreamed of going there for as long as I could remember and although neither Mum nor I had ever heard of the Maury Povich Show, she knew I'd want to do it. She called me through to the kitchen and told me what the vicar had said and, although, as always, my emotions were very moderated, I did have a big grin on my face.

Mum made contact with the show and they explained that Maury Povich was an extremely popular chat show host in America, watched by about three million people. They just wanted us to go along and tell our story and they would pay for our flights and our stay.

'So would you want just Jo and I or my husband and son too?' Mum asked the production assistant.

'Oh, I'm sure we could arrange for you all to come across. We'll organise a bit of spending money for you too. Don't you worry, we'll take care of you.'

A few of the neighbours knew of the show and kept saying 'They'll want you on Jerry Springer next.' That show I did know and thought 'I hope not!'

The trip was arranged for February and we'd be getting back just a couple of days before we were due to go to the United match. My two biggest dreams – seeing United at Old Trafford and going to New York – were going to happen in the same week. It felt like it was my reward for everything that had gone on. The only worry was what we'd do about Grandad, but Nan said she'd make sure he was looked after and told us to enjoy ourselves.

The passport I got for America was the first one I'd had and it was great to see 'Joella' written on it. Going to an airport was another new experience. We drove down to Gatwick in the old brown Cavalier we had at the time. When we arrived in the car park, the planes were flying really low overhead and it was like a scene from a comedy as little Jarred – six at the time – looked up at one as it came in and just kept looking at it and kept looking at it until he fell backwards and hit the floor.

Mum had been to Spain a couple of times, but wasn't a fan of flying or low-flying aircraft and was a bit freaked out by it all, whereas I was quite amazed by the whole thing. I couldn't believe how big and busy it all was. Once we got checked in, we had a little time to waste and sat in a restaurant area looking out at the planes. I loved planes and couldn't wait to get on one.

At the boarding area, the nose of the plane we were going on was right up to the window and I couldn't believe the size of it. It was an old DC 10 and I was a little bit more nervous than I liked to let on. We boarded it and got sat down. Mum and I were sitting next to each other with Jarred and Farmer in front.

Mum's nerves weren't helped when the first take off went a bit wrong. We were hurtling down the runway and there was this almighty bang. It turned out a cover had fallen off one of the engines and we sat looking out of the window while a guy came along and screwed it all back on. We were later informed it was the plane's last flight, which I was glad they didn't tell us beforehand!

When we landed it was dark and late in the day New York time and there weren't many people in the airport as we lined up at passport control. My two overriding memories are the extremely over-happy guy who stamped our passports and welcomed us to America and the police with big guns, who were patrolling all around. I'd watched so many action movies that I found the sight of real guns fascinating. It was all quite a novelty!

We got though the airport pretty quickly and came down some really long escalators to the exit where there was a guy with a board that said 'Holliday'. He walked us out the front where all the yellow taxis were lined up and and told us to wait while he went to the car. As we stood there, this brand new huge, white limousine pulled up and we thought 'God, I wonder who's in that,' then this guy got out and came round and opened the door for us. I was just 'Wow!' We'd been expecting to get in one of the cabs.

Inside the limo it was all leather seats, the ceiling was covered in tiny spotlights and there were individual little TVs and fridges. As tourists, we obviously got our camera out! It was incredible. We went through the Hudson tunnel, which seemed to take ages and when we came out it was the most amazing sight. There was all of the huge New York buildings lit up and just to see it all up close and for real was mind blowing. I looked out the window to the right and there was the Statue of Liberty all lit up green and purple.

Driving through Manhattan everything looked so huge. On the veranda of one building we passed there was a huge lorry. It was massive with a trailer and everything, dozens of floors up. It was just unbelievable.

We were driven up Broadway and it was all lights and glam, right up to this posh hotel and theatre combined. A bellboy in a suit came out the front with a big trolley to put our bags on and we were booked in. We were taken up to our room in a lift and it was like a little apartment, with a kitchen, lovely bathroom with a huge bath, a living room with a giant TV and a bedroom with two beds in it.

We were all quite tired and went to bed fairly soon – Mum and I in one of the beds, Farmer and Jarred in the other. At about 5am, which would have been 10am for us at home, we all got up. I looked out the window and thought the building opposite looked like something out of Ghostbusters. Even though it was so early, there were already loads of people around. Over the road there was a huge Fairways supermarket and it was full of people. We learned later that the store only ever closed for an hour or something once every couple of days for restocking. When you come from a little country village, it was all pretty amazing. We went across to do a little bit of shopping in there later and the bread aisle was huge, cheese seemed almost to have its own shop, there were live lobsters and upstairs was this huge room full of different types of coffee.

I remember Farmer going up to an assistant to ask: 'Do you sell instant coffee?' They looked very confused.

The Maury Povich producers came to our hotel room at some point on that morning to explain how things were going to work. I fell asleep during it, but they told Mum and Farmer, we'd be collected in the limo on day three and taken to the studio before being returned to the airport for our flight home. In the meantime, we were free to do whatever we wanted and they gave Mum and Farmer a few hundred dollars as spending money.

When I woke up, we went out and found a little coffee shop near the hotel to have lunch. Farmer ordered a ham sandwich and chips, forgetting that in America that meant crisps, which made us laugh. While we were sitting there some fire engines went by on a shout and I was quite amazed again by how huge they were. We went for a walk and everything around us looked like a movie set. Just around the corner from our hotel, we found Central Park and the Strawberry Fields memorial to John Lennon. Mum picked that moment to announce, quite loudly, that she never really liked John Lennon, then she decided to start singing Strawberry Fields Forever. She was still singing it when we noticed there seemed to be some sort of memorial going on and no-one taking part looked that impressed with us. We ran away, quite quickly!

The old buildings and the skyline were absolutely gorgeous and we took loads of photos. When we saw a hot dog seller, we felt we had to have one and that was about a foot long. From there, we took a yellow cab to the Empire State Building. We went in one of the little gift shops there and had a look at all the clocks and things they were selling in the shape of the building and Statue of Liberty before deciding to go up. We walked into the huge lobby area that was about three floors high, up some stairs and went through metal detectors and things a bit like being back at airport security before getting into a lift. It went up so quickly that the display didn't even register each floor, it just went '10, 20..' That was quite an experience. Then we got out at the gift shop full of more tacky T-shirts and things, before going out onto the balcony area, which seemed unbelievable.

Although it was very cold, it was also very clear and you could see for miles and miles. Mum was desperate to get a really good picture and was standing on the little perimeter wall and dangling her hand outside of the fencing to take a picture looking down at the ground. I was just over-awed to be at the top of such an iconic building, the whole magnificence of it and the view, which back then included the Twin Towers. It's a bit of a regret that we didn't get time to go to the top of those in light of the horrendous terrorist attack that destroyed them two years later.

The next day we went shopping to a huge mall and that's when it started snowing. Farmer wanted to go to the Harley Davidson shop, which we did and bought some jackets. In there we were accosted by some guy who started chatting to us until a heavily armed security guard came over and ushered him away. The guard warned us that the guy had a mate outside and they were probably planning to mug us. I guess we were obvious tourists and the guard had decided we needed a little bit of advice. I think Mum was pretty good at making us stand out!

Later that day, we caught one of the open-top Circle Line tours and stayed on the top deck for as long as we could stand it, given the cold. We knew we weren't going to have time to actually go to the Statue of Liberty, but got quite close on that tour. The whole experience was just excellent. We all had such a good time.

The next morning was the day of the show, which I hadn't really given much thought to at all. I guess, in my mind, I just thought it was going to be like all the things we'd done before. We got all packed up and the limo came to collect us as planned.

At the studio, we were all taken through an office area where people were sitting working at desks and into a green room, which all seemed fairly standard. We sat there alone, had a drink and waited. Then we were taken through to another holding area where there was a woman who we discovered had been born with nothing below the hips. She was there with her husband and baby and was telling us how she'd managed to get pregnant. It was a really interesting story. In the corner of the room was a TV and on it we got to see some of the filming the show had done with the woman at home where she was talking about how she got around on a skateboard and that sort of thing. Then Mum got called by one of the production assistants and went through to do her bit, leaving me with Farmer and Jarred.

It was five or so minutes before I got my call. 'Just walk out there, there are a few steps down, you'll see where to go,' a production assistant told me.

I got to the top of the steps and was, completely unexpectedly, faced with an audience of what seemed like a couple of hundred people cheering, clapping and generally being loud. I'd still never seen the show and had no idea it was filmed in front of an audience. It turned out that Mum had been quite terrified by how I was going to cope with it, but I wasn't really fazed. I just kind of thought 'okay, this is what they do here then'.

I walked down the steps and Maury Povich greeted me and showed me to my seat and made me feel really welcome. Having the audience there made the atmosphere so different to when you've just got a couple of cameras on you. People were reacting to questions and answers and there was a bit of a buzz in the room. It was almost like being egged on. I felt as much like myself as I had during the QED interviews and enjoyed the whole thing.

Maury Povich had introduced me by saying I was the youngest sex change in history, which felt a bit weird, but as everyone was smiling, it didn't bother me. Mum had already outlined the story of my birth and why she'd changed me from Joel to Joella.

Maury's first question to me was: 'So, what's it like growing up with a history like that?'

'It's strange really,' I replied, grinning, and there was a little ripple of laughter in the audience.

He asked if I ever got teased at school and I told him I was badly bullied in my first school.

Maury then said to Mum: 'There are realities of life, you have to tell your daughter about aren't there? Can she have children?'

'No, never,' Mum replied. 'She knows this. I've never hidden anything.'

Maury turned to me. 'So are you okay with this?'

'Yes, I'll adopt,' I said, still smiling, believing it was all very simple. The audience gave me a big round of applause. Mum told me later she spotted one or two people wiping away tears.

'This is one brave family,' Maury said. 'A brave mother and a brave daughter.'

He then spoke to us about the hormone treatment I'd had to have and the battle to get my birth certificate. 'So, there's this word people use,' Maury said. 'Transsexual. Do we like this word?'

'No, we don't like that word.' I replied, but I wasn't bothered that he'd said it. I'd heard it all before and didn't think it applied to me.

Mum explained that while we had nothing at all against transsexuals, she just did not believe I was one and that was why she had fought so hard for my birth certificate.

Maury wrapped up the section with the words: 'You're all girl to me.'

While we'd been in New York, a few people had asked about our plans and when we'd told them we were there to appear on the Maury Povich Show, they'd all been quite impressed. It had been clear he was quite a star so even though I didn't really know anything about him, I felt quite privileged meeting him and being on the show.

It was dark as we left the studio and climbed in the limo to go straight off to the airport where we boarded a much more modern 777 for the return flight. It was all state-of-the-art with little individual TV screens in the back of each seat with electronic games and things. Ironically, I missed out on most of it because I fell asleep quite quickly. Mum got chatting to one of the stewardesses who sat with us for ages and listened to everything we'd been up to.

A couple of days later, Farmer drove Jarred and I up to Old Trafford for the match we'd been invited to and I was absolutely buzzing when we got outside the stadium I'd seen so many times on TV. We got there really early, when there weren't many people about and a steward showed us to our seats, overlooking the tunnel. The steward led us along next to the pitch and I actually got to touch it which was pretty special.

When the players came on, we got to see them really close up, including Peter Schmichel, who was my idol because I played in goal. We were playing Southampton, so our 2 – 1 victory was no surprise, but it was still fantastic to see my team win and all my heroes in the flesh. Everything was so perfect, it felt like I was living in a dream, but, sadly, reality was about to catch up with us.

CHAPTER SIXTEEN

A few days after our trip to Manchester, Grandad had a really unpleasant fall. Mum had seen him start to topple as he got up from the dining room table but although she screamed out to Farmer, who tried to catch him, it was too late and Grandad's head smacked on the floor, leaving his face badly cut.

Grandad was taken into hospital and had to have his face stitched and when he came home it was as if he was a different man. It had seemed like one minute he was quite good and then suddenly we all knew he didn't have long left. Within days, Mum was gathering his family to say goodbye.

The night before Grandad died, there were lots of nurses there and Mum got her brother down from Middlesbrough. We all knew, we were just waiting for him to go and none of us even went to bed that night. I eventually fell asleep on a duvet on the floor and woke up at 7 o'clock in the morning. As soon as I opened my eyes, I thought 'he's gone'. There was still a lot of family in the living room, but it was so quiet you could just tell, there was this feeling in the house. Because we'd all known this moment was coming, I'd had time to wonder how I'd react and I'd expected to be really over emotional, but the tears just did not come. All I felt was a sense of deflation deep inside.

As the day went on, there was all this emotion around me as everyone remembered Grandad and laughed and cried, but I just felt almost empty, like it hadn't registered. I kept thinking, 'my grandad has just died. I should be in floods of tears. What's wrong with me?'

It took a few days for Mum and the family to organise the funeral and Mum didn't want Jarred and I to go, so we stayed home with Uncle John. The hearse arrived at our house and I saw the coffin, but it was still as if I was on autopilot. I still didn't react and my lack of response worried me a lot. I started to wonder whether it was just my body that was different to everybody else's or whether perhaps it was my mind as well. It was a thought I'd had previously when I'd been really anxious about my birth certificate, but I'd never allowed it to linger before. Now it stuck in my head and kept going round and round in it.

Getting back into the routine of school did nothing to help my mindset either. The flurry of Press and TV stuff after I got my birth certificate had broken the weeks up a bit, but I no longer had that respite. I still got on okay with the children on my table in lessons, but at break times I continued to feel excluded. I used to try to play football with the lads, but it wasn't very often I'd feel welcome. I'd befriended a boy in the year below who had some special needs and would look out for him and tell anyone who picked on him to leave him alone, but on the whole I was pretty isolated.

The thought of school had always made me anxious and the feeling started to become more and more overwhelming.

I could never eat in the mornings and once I got to school, I felt constantly uncomfortable and unsettled. It all added to my growing certainty that there was something wrong with me mentally.

Because of all the time I'd missed, I was kept in class at break times to do extra work, which made me feel even more different. I'd always been quite an avid reader, but I used to be sent to get reading books from the lower classes and I felt so embarrassed parading through to get them.

One particularly awful incident happened on a school trip to Rutland Water – a nearby reservoir where they had a butterfly and reptile house. The trip was something related to school that I'd actually looked forward to, but it went horribly wrong. In the butterfly house there was a cave full of spiders, scorpions and snakes. I'd always hated spiders and couldn't stand the thought of going in there.

'Oh for goodness sake, you are just being silly,' I was told.

I was shepherded up to one of the glass tanks where one of the spiders was right in front of me. I was petrified and the incident left a psychological scar that came back to haunt me at a later date in a really awful way.

I counted down the days until I could leave Surfleet Primary School and move on to secondary, where I was convinced everything would be so much better. In Lincolnshire, there's still a two-tier school system, with the 11 plus exam and those who pass the exam go to grammar school and those who fail go to secondary school. Taking the exam is optional and somewhere along the line, it was decided that I wouldn't take it. It wasn't an issue to me because everyone I knew from the village went to the secondary – the Gleed Girls' School, in Spalding – and I was quite happy to go there too. When my last day finally came at Surfleet, I couldn't have been happier and left there believing my problems were behind me. I also discovered there was another big thing to look forward to, as my youngest brother Chris was on his way. His arrival filled our house with giggles and a bit more chaos and I was just as pleased as I had been when Jarred was born.

I felt really positive on my first day at the Gleed and, surrounded by quite a few familiar faces, I caught the bus in the village to head off there. I'd never been to the school – I wasn't even sure exactly where it was – and when I arrived, I was a bit taken aback by how big it was. My primary school only had 70 pupils, two classrooms and a mobile outside and this school had 700 pupils and dozens of classrooms and teachers.

As soon as I got off the bus, some girl came up and told me I was wearing my rucksack too high on my back and it wasn't cool.

'You don't wanna get beat up,' she said.

The day was mainly taken up with sitting around and waiting for books to be given out. I couldn't help but notice the classrooms smelled the same as the classrooms at my previous school. All classrooms, to me, had a 'classroom' smell, a bit like hospitals smell of hospitals and the smell made me feel a little anxious, but I wouldn't allow myself to dwell on it.

In each new class I arrived at throughout the day, I tried to make conversation with the other kids, but could feel that familiar sensation of them not really wanting to talk to me. I still walked funny, my stomach poked out, I was small for my age and was just generally different. When everyone is doing all they can to try to fit in, nobody wants to be friends with the 'different' kid. When the bell went for break time, everyone split off into their own groups and headed outside. I was on my own. Again.

I was more quiet on the bus ride home than I had been in the morning, feeling all the old anxieties starting to bubble up. I tried to tell myself that it was just the first day and this school still could be different, but I was already beginning to doubt it.

'How was it?' Mum said when I got in.

'Fine,' I said, as I went to get changed out of my uniform, already dreading the thought of putting it back on in the morning.

I really tried to stay positive over the next few days, but things just seemed to go from bad to worse. The teachers decided I needed extra help with lessons so I had to go to a mobile classroom in the playground at break times. I was different again. I wasn't allowed to do cross country so the teacher asked me to mark a point on the course to make sure no-one cut any corners. Did they seriously think I was going to tell all the other girls what to do? I was already enough of a target and felt singled out as it was. I took no notice as dozens of girls took a short cut across the area of the course I was supposed to be watching.

As I walked around the school, there was the odd comment about my appearance and snigger behind my back but nothing too bad and I just tried to ignore it, though I was always on guard expecting someone at some stage would mention the stuff that had been in The Press. It finally happened about two weeks into my time at the school and it was far worse than I'd ever expected.

I was standing in line waiting to go into a history lesson when a group of older girls walked by. It was quite quiet and I was standing with all my new classmates who I was desperately trying to fit in with.

One of the older girls pointed at me. 'You should be next door at the boys' school. You've got a cock.'

After weeks of suppressing my fear and anxiety, I saw red and was overwhelmed by an anger I'd never experienced before.

'Fuck off,' I spat and stepped towards her. She was far taller than me but I didn't even care.

The girl looked shocked that I'd dare to speak back to her and screamed at me. 'Don't you fucking speak to me like that, you little tranny, you shouldn't even be here.'

Everyone was listening to what she was saying and I felt totally humiliated and just lost it. I went to hit her, but someone grabbed hold of my jumper. Then there were two or three of them on me, holding me back.

The older girl's friends looked a bit shocked, embarrassed even, by the way she was. I'd done nothing at all to provoke it. They started dragging her away in the other direction.

'Stop, stop, you can't hit her, the teacher's coming,' I heard one of my classmates saying. I couldn't have cared less.

I was struggling to try to get free, to get at the older girl, but her friends got her through some double doors and away. The teacher arrived and unlocked the classroom door without seeming to notice any atmosphere at all. Everyone started filing into the class and I was kind of bundled along with them.

I sat at the desk unable to focus on anything that was going on around me. The lesson began and everyone else seemed to just forget about it, but I couldn't think of anything else. I was so ashamed that the girl had said those things in front of everyone and was just so angry. This school wasn't going to be any different, I realised. It was all just a waste of time.

As soon as I got home that night, I felt sick at the thought of going back to school the next day. I hardly slept and when I got up, I couldn't eat. When I got on the bus, I sat alone at the front and didn't even bother to try to talk to anyone. At school, my heart started racing and wouldn't stop. I went into registration, trying to hide the panic I felt inside. The feeling stayed with me all day and the next day was the same and so was the one after that.

I never saw that girl again and there were no other memorable moments of anyone saying anything nasty to me, but the damage was done. There no longer seemed to be any rational reason to my fear, it was just a total dread of school, a phobia. The anxiety never left me. Even at the weekends I'd spend the whole time fearing going back to school.

I got to the point where I'd try anything to get out of going. I'd miss the bus, deliberately not do my homework and tell Mum I'd get into trouble if I hadn't done it, fake illness.

'Are you being bullied?' she asked. 'Is there something going on that I need to know about?'

Her questions just made me angry. 'No, I'm not being bullied. I just hate school!'

'But you can't just not go! It's not optional!' she'd shout back.

How could I explain how I was feeling? There didn't seem to be any logical reason behind it. Everyone else managed to go to school and make friends and get on with it, but I just couldn't. Mum and I rowed over it most mornings. Some days, I'd angrily give in and go and get the bus, but a lot of times, I just couldn't. It was like being in a cage. I was so scared every day that I'd have to go to school.

'I don't feel well!' I'd scream at Mum.

'You're fine! You have to go to school! It's illegal for you to just not go!'

Mum would be furious, but on my worst days even her anger wasn't enough to force me out the door. Going to school literally felt like the most terrifying anyone could ask me to do and I was having to face it every day. Sometimes, I'd get so worked up that I was actually ill. I'd vomit and my stomach would cramp up. On those days, Mum would cool down a bit but other times, I knew she was still boiling. On the days I didn't go in, I'd sit and watch videos or whenever I could I'd go round to Nan's. Nan would never make me explain or feel bad about any of it. She seemed to just understand.

I'd been at The Gleed for about two months when things came to a head. It was one of my bad days and I knew there was no way I could face going, but Mum was having none of it.

'Right, that's it. We'll take you in the bloody car,' she said. I was terrified. I knew I could not face walking into that building that day.

Mum and Farmer physically hauled me out of the house – I was actually clinging to the door frames – and bundled me into the back of the car.

'If you're going to act like a toddler, Jo, we're going to have to treat you like one,' Mum said. 'You have to go to school.' I know she was desperate.

'I'm not going,' I was screaming. 'I won't get out of the car.'

'You bloody well will. Dad is going to be late for work because of this, you do realise that do you? Just because you won't get yourself on the bloody bus!'

Mum and I screamed at each other for the entire 15 minute journey. To begin with, I was just adamant I wouldn't get out, but the closer we got to the school the more I feared they'd somehow force me into the building and I couldn't stand the thought of it. When we pulled up outside school, I was holding on so tight to the headrests of the front seats that my knuckles were white. I was determined they wouldn't pull me out of the car.

'Get out,' Mum screamed from the front.

'No! Mum, no, I can't.'

'You have to! Jo there is no choice in this!'

All rational thought was out the window. My fear wasn't rational. I knew Mum and Farmer didn't understand it, I didn't understand it. As it dawned on me that Mum wasn't going to back down, I just crumbled. Through all of the turmoil of the previous years, I'd barely shed a tear, but in that car that day, the floodgates opened. I curled into a ball on the back seat and began to sob hysterically.

I don't know at what point Mum and Farmer decided to give up on trying to get me out of the car, but I remember the sense of utter relief as we turned around and started heading for home. I felt myself beginning to calm down immediately. I knew Mum and Farmer were angry but all I cared about was that I didn't have to go to school.

After that there seemed to be a sort of acceptance that I wouldn't be going back to The Gleed. It was clear there was a big problem and Mum said she'd look into other schools or home tutoring. I was relieved, but felt really guilty for being the cause of yet another problem. I was embarrassed and ashamed and didn't want to think about any of it let alone talk about it so I don't remember any great heart-to-heart. I wondered what was missing in me that meant I found it so difficult to do what every other kid did every day.

Over the following few weeks I slipped more and more into myself. I'd get up in the mornings and just sit and watch videos. Nan's was still my salvation and I went there whenever I could. It was always so loud and busy at home, but at Nan's I could just help shell peas for dinner, sit and watch murder mysteries and chat about normal stuff.

By Christmas time, I'd been off school a good six weeks and nothing was yet in place for me. I felt a little bit of excitement over Christmas, but had started living a sort of half-life where I was so trapped in all the thoughts in my head that I didn't quite have the energy to fully concentrate on real life as well.

We always had people round for a few drinks on Christmas Eve and that year was no different. It was a bit of a tradition and everyone around me was enjoying themselves while I just sat quietly.

'I'm going to go up to bed,' I said around midnight.

'Okay darling, I'll come up in a minute to say goodnight,' Mum called across the room.

As I climbed the stairs I could hear Mum and Farmer, Nan and the one or two other family friends who were still there, chatting and laughing. I walked into my bedroom and sat down on the edge of my double bed. The room had looked the same for as long as I could remember, filled with cuddly toys that I'd been bought when I was tiny and poorly and everyone spoiled me because they didn't know how long I'd be around for.

It was while I was sitting there that I saw the first spider.

I yanked my legs up on to the bed and felt every muscle in my body clench as I drew in a shuddering, petrified breath. This thing was huge and fast and had run across the floor so quickly that I was only just able to see that it wasn't a normal house spider. It had looked just like the North American mouse-eating thing I'd been forced to look at on that primary school trip. Its eight chunky legs had propelled a thick fury, black and orange body towards my bed.

Before even a moment had passed I caught another movement out of the corner of my eye and suddenly realised this thing was not alone. All of a sudden there were dozens of spiders running into the room, each with a big bulbous head and discernible fangs.

I became aware that these things were now growing in size. The ones reaching the top of the stairs were the size of small dogs. A few steps from the top, a monstrous thing the size of a small pony was flailing and slipping, struggling to get a grip to haul its great bulk up on to the landing.

The smaller ones were on the bed now, crawling all over me. It seemed totally real.

I screamed and covered my eyes.

I can't remember who came to get me or what I said to them, but I know they had to drag me to get me out of the room. I was petrified going towards the stairs because we were going towards the huge spider that was struggling to get up. When we got to it, we sort of went through it.

In the dining room everyone was sat around and I was still screaming and still seeing spiders everywhere. Mum came towards me and reached out to grab me, but as she did it, she started turning into a spider. Her arms turned to legs, her eyes went black and she had fangs. I looked around and everyone else was turning too.

I was hysterical, kicking and screaming, trying to get away. Mum tried to slap me out of it, but to me it just looked like I was being attacked by a spider. I tried to get to the kitchen, but no-one would let me go. They all started clinging on to me, sitting on me, trying to hold me still so I didn't hurt myself or them. I don't know how long they held me before the real world started to morph back in. Eventually, the spiders started to recede and I could see people again. They got me to the sofa and I curled into a ball, terrified and exhausted. When I looked at the clock it was 3am. It had only felt as if I'd gone up to bed a quarter or half an hour before, but three hours had passed.

Mum phoned the out-of-hours doctor and asked for him to come out. Our friends all went home and I remember seeing Nan crying on the doorstep as Mum convinced her to go and get some rest too.

When the doctor arrived I was still shaking, still having the physical effects of being hysterical. All I'd managed to tell Mum was that there had been things attacking me. She and the doctor had a whispered conversation before he came to sit next to me.

'Can you tell me your name?' He asked.

'Joella'

'And your birthday?'

'January 24.'

'Do you know what day it is today?'

There was a Christmas tree in the corner of the room but I had no idea what day it was.

The doctor checked my blood pressure, which, unsurprisingly, was very high, but he said everything else seemed okay. He left, telling Mum he thought I'd had a night terror, but to go to the surgery after the holidays if she was still concerned.

I could barely talk and couldn't sleep. I was far too terrified to go back upstairs and Mum and I ended up spending a lot of the rest of the night walking around outside. It was cold out there but I felt a bit safer because I could run away if the spiders appeared again. I did eventually fall asleep cuddled up with Mum on the pull-out sofa in the dining room, but when I woke the next day something had shifted in me. I felt like a total wreck, completely emotionally empty. I felt destroyed.

CHAPTER SEVENTEEN

Christmas passed in a blur that year and I don't think I even opened anything on the day. I think I just put a video on and stared at it. Everyone kept telling me that whatever I'd seen wasn't real but it had felt real to me.

I was too terrified to go upstairs because that is where the spiders had been. Whenever I needed to go to the bathroom, Mum or Farmer would have to go with me and I'd rush to get up the stairs past the point where the biggest spider had been as quickly as I could. I spent a lot of time just sleeping on the pull-out sofa and at night Mum would sleep there with me.

I started having panic attacks where I felt like I couldn't breathe. I'd hyperventilate and sweat and be overcome by fear. I'd feel enclosed in the house and would just have to get outside. I think I was just constantly frightened that the hallucinations would happen again.

I managed to tell Mum roughly what I'd seen, but even thinking the word 'spider' could trigger a panic attack and God forbid if there was a real spider around. I saw one on the television one day and ended up curled up in a ball on the sofa screaming.

Then I started having these incidents where I'd just black out and lose time. I'd lose an hour and be told afterwards that I cried and kicked about during it, but I didn't remember. I started keeping an eye on the clock on the mantlepiece, checking to make sure it hadn't happened again. Inbetween times I was like a sort of zombie. I didn't really feel anything and would just stare into space. It was like I had a trigger in my head and all the emotion came out in these little bursts that I couldn't remember.

Mum took me to the doctor's and he said my symptoms could be caused by a tumour. He sent me to have scans on my brain at my local hospital. I had various probes put on my head, flashing lights played at me and had to go through all sorts of weird scanning equipment I'd never seen before. I was so withdrawn that I don't remember feeling anything about any of it. The results all came back clear and it was decided my problems must be emotional.

To this day, no-one knows what caused it, but I think it must have been an emotional breakdown of some sort. None of it made any sense, but it just scrambled up my head. I was having trouble sleeping at night and didn't like being on my own at all. They said they'd refer me to a psychiatrist and Mum explained that he would help me through the problems I was having. I was excited to think someone could make me better and on the day of my first appointment I felt a bit better just at the thought of going. Mum and I got the bus into Boston and walked the few yards from the station to the medical centre where the psychiatrist was based. He was a Russian man in his late 40s with a little beard and glasses and a thick accent. Mum and I sat down in his office and after a brief chat with Mum, he asked me to tell him about Christmas Eve – the night that had started everything off.

'I can't,' I said, looking at Mum, wanting her to do it for me.

'It will really help, if you can tell me yourself what happened,' the psychiatrist said, but I just couldn't get the words out. I could feel the panic rising just thinking about it again.

'Could you draw it, do you think?' he asked.

I said I'd give it a go.

He sat me alone in a playroom just off his office, which had a mirror all along one wall. I knew he was watching me on the other side but it didn't bother me because I just desperately wanted him to be able to help me. In the middle of the room was a little table with a piece of paper and some colouring pencils.

I picked up a brown pencil and made a mark on the paper but the moment I'd done it, the visions of the spiders started filling my head and I couldn't bear it. Trying to make me talk about it and draw it was just making it worse. Tears started streaming down my face. Even the little mark I'd made on the paper had started representing spiders to me and I turned the paper over so I couldn't see it. I sat crying with my head in my hands until the doctor and Mum came back in to get me.

Mum and I were taken back into the office and there was a lot more talking between them. Although I was aware of the talking, I wasn't taking a lot of notice of what was being said. All I was thinking was 'So, this isn't going to help either'.

When we caught the bus back home, I felt worse than ever. To me, it felt that my mind was so broken even a psychiatrist wasn't going to be able to fix it.

I hit a real low after that and just did not want to get up in the mornings. It seemed like everyone else was normal and healthy and I was different and it made me feel very alone.

Mum and I went back to the psychiatrist three or four times over the following weeks but every time it was the same thing. We'd chat for a while and then he'd want me to talk about Christmas Eve and I just couldn't. Eventually the appointments fizzled out because it was obvious we weren't advancing at all.

After that, I did my best not to think of that night at all and that seemed to work much better. The further away from it I got, the better I was. Mum decorated my bedroom and moved all the furniture around to try to make it feel different in there and after a few weeks, I started sleeping in there again. I still didn't really feel comfortable in there, but it was all about little steps.

I still struggled to go upstairs alone and to start with Mum and Farmer were very patient with me but after a while they did start getting to the end of their tether with it and would push me to go alone. I always used have to close my eyes and run to get past the point where the spiders had been. The memory was so real and so deep, I couldn't get rid of it. If I was on my own during the day, I'd have the front door unlocked so there was a way to get out. If I had to go upstairs, I'd run down afterwards and go straight outside to get some fresh air.

One good thing about going to the psychiatrist was the tips he gave us about dealing with the panic attacks. I was having them quite regularly and he'd taught Mum how to talk me down from them. I'd have to sit down and take deep breaths and over time I got used to them and they became more manageable and less frightening. He'd told us that some of my problems were caused by me not dealing with things. He felt that I buried all my emotions and he said I needed to make sure I didn't keep bottling everything up.

I still didn't want to do a lot apart from watch videos, but Nan would come round and try to get me to go with her to the shops or the social club. I started doing that and went back to spending a lot of time at her house.

By the time the summer holidays were approaching again, I'd been off school nearly a year and Mum was under pressure to get something sorted for me. She found out about a school in Boston, St Bede's, that had a good reputation at the time for dealing with children with disabilities and health issues. They had a policy that meant you could leave lessons when you needed to for health reasons and would not tolerate any bullying.

I was nervous when Mum suggested we go and have a look but knew I had to go somewhere. We went and had a meeting with the headteacher and her deputy. They were both very nice and it was clear they both really wanted to make me feel comfortable. The deputy head was a mumsy sort with short dark hair and glasses. She was in her 40s and wore a skirt and cardy and she was very easy to get on with. The headteacher was a bit more formal but still nice.

They took us on a tour of the school and it wasn't very big and the kids seemed very different to ones at The Gleed. They all said 'hello', they weren't rowdy or rough and tough and everyone seemed quite friendly. I noticed that the classrooms still smelled of classrooms, but I told myself I was okay with it.

A plan was drawn up for me to start at the school in September, at the beginning of Year Eight. I was going to do just half days to start with to give me a chance to settle in. Mum and I went out to get my new uniform and I was nervous but excited at the idea of going there. It felt a little bit different to all the other schools and I was convinced it would be the one where I would be okay.

A few other kids from my village went to St Bede's for one reason or another and there was a special taxi laid on to pick us up from our houses and take us there. On my first day, the taxi arrived at 7.30am and a girl I knew a little bit from the village was already in there. I can't remember if we chatted but I know I felt okay. I got to school, got on all right with the teachers and I got through it quite well.

While I was still on half days it was possible to ignore the fear that was still there in the back of my mind. I'd wake up and dread going to school and it was still quite a struggle to get into a classroom but I did it and was getting on better. But, once I was having to do full days, the old feelings started to take hold again. Each day, there was a little bit more fear and it was a little bit more difficult to ignore.

I kept telling myself 'there's nothing to be frightened of' and didn't understand why my stomach was churning. I didn't really understand exactly what I was so scared of, but the dread was consuming me again. Whenever I get nervous my stomach problems start and I could feel that all flaring up again too.

Within six weeks, I was waking up in the morning and dreading the taxi pulling up. Then it started to get difficult to walk through the school gates. I'd get there and feel sick and frightened. Then it became difficult to even get into the taxi. It was almost made worse because I didn't understand it at all. I didn't say anything to Mum until the day when I just couldn't bring myself to leave the house.

I could feel a panic attack beginning to rise up and looked across at Mum.

'I can't do it, Mum. I can't go.'

I hadn't told her, I'd been finding it tough, but she must have known.

'It's fine Jo, let's leave it.'

There was no big scene. The decision that I would not return to school was made there and then with barely any conversation. It was clear to both of us that there was no point in continuing to pursue something that was just going to make me worse and it was decided it would be better if I was home tutored. From that moment, without daily fear of returning to school, I seemed to start moving on a bit. It felt as if, before then, I had always been overwhelmed with crushing worry and all of a sudden it had lifted.

Over the following months, I was still having panic attacks, but was able to cope much better with them and was just generally happier. I was much more stable and whereas little things would have set me off before, like if I saw a spider I'd freak out, suddenly I could deal with it.

I was still good friends with Semrah and Laura and they'd come round the house and we'd sit and chat. They were starting to get into boys and would talk about the crushes they had. I tended just to listen partly because I was beginning to realise that no-one would ever be interested in me and partly because there was no-one I was interested in anyway. Even at 13, I knew that with no vagina I didn't have anything to offer anyone sexually. I was actually more preoccupied wondering what exactly I was supposed to look like than I was in caring about what men looked like. If anything, the curiosity made me a bit infatuated with other girls. There had been one girl in particular at St Bede's who was really pretty and popular who I thought about all the time.

Nan was still the person who I felt most comfortable with and I went to her house a lot. It wasn't that we did anything special but we just seemed to be on the same wavelength. I even started to stay at her house most nights, which is why I still find it difficult to accept that the night she needed me most I was not there.

It had been a normal day, we'd been out in the garden for most of it and Nan had turned all the soil on the borders and trimmed all the roses, then we'd played cards and dominoes as usual. I know I'd planned to stay but for some reason I changed my mind at the last minute and went home, which I'd never done before.

The next morning, I was shaken awake by Mum in the early hours.

'It's your Nan, she's been taken ill.'

I was immediately alert. 'What?'

'She's in hospital. I've got to go.'

When Mum came home she was in a total state and it turned out Nan had had a heart attack in her sleep. She hadn't been able to wake Uncle John and had to crawl downstairs and drag herself to her brother's house, four doors away, to get help. All I could think was that I should have been there. When I stayed at Nan's I slept on the floor beside her bed and I would have been able to help her.

'The doctors say there's no chance of survival,' Mum said through tears. 'You all need to come up there with me to see her.'

I couldn't really believe what was happening. We'd had such a normal day the day before. Mum was so emotional and I did cry, but I was still able to deal with it somehow. We all got dressed quickly and I sat in the hall hating myself for not having been there when it happened.

Nan was in intensive care at Pilgrim Hospital in Boston and we all trooped up there and into this little waiting room. My uncles and Nan's other grandkids were all there too so it was packed out with people, but it was very quiet. Intensive care has a different feel to other hospital wards, everything about it is very serious. We were only allowed to go through to see Nan two at a time.

I went through with Mum and we knew one of the nurses, who lived in Brownlow and she gave me a sympathetic smile as I walked past. We walked past an old man who was all piped up and so completely pale he looked dead. Then we came to Nan, who was on a life support machine and looked almost as terrible.

I stood next to Nan and talked to her, almost trying to say goodbye, but I was in disbelief that it was really her because she looked so weak. Nan was such a larger than life person, but it looked as if that had all been sucked out of her. She was full of drips and pipes and although I'd watched Grandad change as he got ill, this was so sudden and different. It didn't look like Nan could possibly survive, but I don't think I could really believe she was going to die either.

That night Nan had another heart attack and had to be resuscitated. One of the nurses had to punch her in the chest to shock her heart back into action, which saved her but also broke her ribs. I think they put her into a drug-induced coma after that and the next few weeks are a bit of a blur.

Nan looked even worse after the second attack because her eyes were all black. When I went to see her, a lady in the next bed had died moments before – the poor woman's bed hadn't even been made yet. There was a trolley with a box underneath it, which I knew the woman's body was in and I kept looking at the box thinking that if Nan died that is where she would go.

Day in, day out we went to the hospital and each day we were expecting to lose Nan, but the longer it went on, the more I thought, at the back of my mind, that she would be okay and I knew Mum was thinking the same. Each day at the hospital was so stressful and I'd go with Mum down to the smoking area every now and again while she had a cigarette.

Everyone in my family smoked and I suspected Mum knew I'd started having the odd one on the quiet. At the hospital, I asked to have a few drags of her cigarette and she let me. I found it really helped to ease my mind and started smoking quite regularly from then on, not because it was 'cool', but because it seemed to help me cope with things.

It was while Mum and I were down in the smoking area at the hospital having a cigarette one day that a pigeon started hanging around us. We had a bit of a thing about birds in our family and when Nan's sister had died, a robin suddenly appeared in Nan's garden every day. Nan always used to say it was her sister and Grandad would joke that he'd come back as a pigeon and would poop in our drinks. When the pigeon out the front of the hospital pooped in Mum's tea it was pretty funny and it was sort of our sign. From that moment on there was always a pigeon on the windowsill of Nan's room and Mum and I felt it was just a matter of time before she opened her eyes again.

CHAPTER EIGHTEEN

The doctors didn't share the optimism Mum and I had over Nan's recovery and when she did wake up they were amazed, especially as all she seemed bothered about was that her hair was a mess. Her eyes were still so dark, her skin so pale and she had lost so much weight, but once she'd woken up, I knew she wouldn't die.

Nan was in hospital for quite a few weeks before they said she could go home and when the time did come it was clear that although she'd survived, she would never be the same again. The hospital supplied a proper hospital bed for her to go home with, which we had to put in her living room and Nan was barely able to leave it. She was on oxygen permanently and Farmer had to load all the huge tanks into the shed, which Mum and I would go and get as Nan needed replacements. Even though Mum already had a lot on her plate with me and the boys, neither she nor I would leave Nan's side and both of us slept on the floor next to her bed.

Initially, Nan could barely move, had no energy and was always cold so even though it was coming into summer we always had to have the fire on permanently, which was uncomfortable for us. Nan found it all very frustrating and although she'd do quite a good job of not taking it out on us, Uncle John would sometimes bear the brunt of her anger. Because of his own difficulties he didn't always think and would do things like make a cup of tea and not think to offer her one and she'd get so cross with him. She was so used to being active and out in the garden all day and now she couldn't even leave the living room. Even talking would take so much out of her.

It was both physically and emotionally draining for Mum and I too. Just dealing with the oxygen tanks, which were so big and heavy and had to be dragged into the kitchen and through to the living room from the garden shed – sometimes in the middle of the night – was a big job. As was sorting out all the medication Nan needed. There was a huge box of it and Nan had to have what seemed like dozens of tablets a day. I fell into a routine of spending one evening a week setting out a pill box with them all to make sure nothing was forgotten or duplicated. I was keen to do as much of Nan's care as I could.

'Aren't there other things you'd rather do than look after me Bella?' she'd ask me sometimes. She'd called me Bella, or Bell, for as long as I could remember. I think it was just because it rhymed with Joella.

'You've done so much for me, I'm just repaying a bit of it,' I'd respond.

'I never did anything!'

'But you did,' I'd tell her, really meaning it. She really never did understand how much it had helped me just to have her in my life.

It was at the height of Nan's illness that the house next to hers came on the market and Mum and Farmer realised it would be perfect if they could buy it. Mum's brother said he'd lend them some money towards it so they could be close to Nan.

I was sad at the thought of leaving my friends in Brownlow, but very excited to be going to the new house. It was so big! It had a huge corner bath with a shower over it and Mum's room had all these fitted wardrobes. The garden was massive just like Nan's with a huge pond in the first section and a second pond further down. Right down the end of the garden there was a huge outbuilding, the size of a bungalow.

I had my own bedroom at the new house, but I never did sleep in it. I made the decision that I should continue to stay with Nan, while I thought Mum ought to be able to get back to being at home where the rest of the family needed her. Quite soon after we moved in she had even more reason to be at home because she was asked to take another foster baby.

The little African girl – Tamsin – was one and very cute. I was 13 and just at the stage where I was very maternal and because Chris was still young and in need of a lot of Mum's attention too, I started to take on a lot of Tamsin's care. I loved to dress her, wash her, change and feed her and she always chose either me or Farmer to put her to bed.

'Lella' or 'Baldy,' she'd say, which would always make us laugh.

I fell into a routine of sleeping at Nan's house, waking at 6.30am so I could get up and dressed before Nan needed me to help her get ready. Then once Nan was up and I'd sorted her breakfast out, I'd go across to Mum's and help out with the kids. I'd flit between the two houses during the day, before helping put the kids to bed and going back across to Nan's. Gradually Nan started to get a bit stronger and Farmer made a ramp at the back door so I could take her down to the supermarket in a wheelchair to do her weekly shop. At home, she could get around a little bit on her own using a stick and didn't have to use her oxygen full-time. Then, after a time, we were even able to get her a mobility scooter and she could take herself out a bit.

Mum had been trying to get the local authority to provide a home tutor for me since I'd left St Bede's and it was finally organised soon after we moved house. In the meantime, I'd become so concerned about all the work I was missing that I'd gone out and bought myself some books to try to teach myself, but I knew it hadn't been enough. It was never the education I didn't like, it was the school environment I was afraid of.

I was allocated the tutor for two to three hours, three days a week, but any hopes I had of catching up on what I'd missed were soon forgotten. The tutor was in her 50s with curly greyish hair and looked and dressed like a teacher, but seemed to spend more time talking about herself than anything else. I quickly knew everything about her family and not a lot about maths. It worried me a lot that I was falling further and further behind my peers and I wondered what future I could hope for.

Whether the worry over that contributed, I don't know, but I started to get a lot of stomach problems again. It got so bad that I had to go to my GP and get a horrible, thick, sticky medicine, to try to get things moving. I'd been taking it for about a week, with very little effect on my bowel when things started to get very uncomfortable. One evening, I was across at Nan's and the pain in my stomach became close to unbearable and I realised I needed to get home. I made my way back to Mum's and got as far as the dining room, before hitting the floor and being sick.

The next thing I knew, I was in an ambulance with Mum beside me and a paramedic giving me gas and air. The gas was making me a bit out of it, but I knew things were pretty serious because the blue light and siren was going. My stomach had stretched to 40 inches and I was in so much pain that I didn't know what to do with myself. I focused on a spot on the ceiling of the ambulance and just told myself to block everything else out. My stomach was so big, I looked like I was heavily pregnant and I was aware of conversations between Mum and the paramedics about fears I could rupture. I was aware of Mum at my side, could hear the conversations and the sirens and see the flash of the blue light, but I just focused on the spot on the ceiling.

We got to the hospital very quickly and they carried me out of the ambulance, which made the pain a million times worse. It felt like someone had hold of all of my organs and was just squeezing and pulling them. The skin over my stomach was so, so tight, I was sure it was going to tear and the pressure was continually building. My lungs must have been being crushed because I couldn't breathe properly. I was screaming and screaming and just wanted something to happen to get me away from the pain.

They pulled me straight through the main building, onto the children's ward and into a side room. I was aware of lots of people around me - doctors, nurses, Mum – and they were worried because my heart was racing so fast they feared I could go into cardiac arrest. There was talk of a helicopter being on the roof ready to transfer me, but everything was becoming a blur. The pain was so horrendous I couldn't think about anything else. A nurse who was trying to comfort me left the room in tears.

They put a large dose of morphine through me but it didn't have any effect so they put another in and it didn't either. I knew they thought my stomach was going to split and poison me and I just assumed I was going to die. The pain was that bad that I was almost looking forward to it and if someone had handed me a lethal injection I know I wouldn't have hesitated to use it.

The maximum amount of morphine I could have was a third dose, which would normally completely knock someone out and once they injected that, I finally couldn't feel the pain any more. My head started swimming and all I could hear was the beeps of the machines. The morphine turned out to be more than just a painkiller because the relaxant effect of it seemed to get my system moving again. My blood pressure came down, my heart stopped racing and my stomach gradually started to soften. The doctors were still very concerned about me and no-one was sure exactly what had happened but the immediate emergency had passed. A weird and horrible night followed where, although I was exhausted, I just could not sleep. I think my body was so hyped up with adrenaline that even the morphine wasn't a match for it.

The next morning Farmer arrived with a teddy bear, which wasn't very like him and then my dad came to see me, which made it obvious how concerned everyone had been. I'd continued to have some contact with my dad, but it had slipped to us only really seeing each other at birthdays and Christmas and to see him there meant Mum had been worried enough to feel she needed to inform him.

My recovery was actually very quick and after a couple of days and a few inconclusive X-rays, I was discharged. The problem appeared to have been more trapped wind than anything but no-one could figure out what had caused it. Emotionally, it was very difficult to recover from because it had been such an ordeal and no-one could tell me how to prevent it. It was like going through an incredibly traumatic, horrendous car crash, but one that's very likely to happen again. I became very cautious over what I ate and what I took for my stomach. I knew from past experience that potatoes with their skins on, tomatoes, fruit with the skin on and anything too fleshy fruit and vegetables wise could cause me a problem and whereas before I was quite relaxed about eating it, I didn't take any chances any more.

I was distracted from my troubles when something unexpected happened with one of the lads I'd known forever from Brownlow Crescent. Farmer had put a pool table in the garage and some of the kids from Brownlow used to come down from time-to-time to play on it with Jarred and I. Danny, who was a year or so older than me, was one of them. Danny was seen as quite desirable among the other girls and one day while we were playing pool, Jarred went into the house to get a drink and while he was gone Danny leaned across the table and kissed me.

I'd never considered whether I found Danny attractive or not – thoughts like that about the lads never really entered my head – and my immediate reaction to his kiss was embarrassment, but then I considered what it meant that he was kissing me. Danny was someone who knew all about my past, all about the birth certificate stuff and he was still interested in me. I kissed him back and felt a rush of adrenaline and excitement not because I wanted to kiss him but because he wanted to kiss me.

When Jarred came back, Danny and I flew apart but a few days later he came round to play pool again and when we were left on our own for a few minutes the same thing happened.

'Are we boyfriend and girlfriend now then?' I asked.

'Yes, but let's not tell anyone,' Danny replied. 'It'll be better if we just keep it to our ourselves.'

I was happy to go along with that, being a bit prudish I didn't want the embarrassment of everyone else knowing about us, but I liked the thought of having a boyfriend and how normal it made me. Danny started coming round to see me every few days and we'd go and sit and snog in the garden shed. To start with, I felt that same adrenaline rush each time and it was exciting, but the novelty did not last.

When I looked at Danny, I didn't feel anything at all and I didn't think of him any differently to any of the lads I'd grown up playing football with. When I thought back to the girl I'd been infatuated with at St Bede's, my stomach flipped and I knew now that I lusted after her. I'd spent so long trying to rationalise my thoughts about other women, telling myself that it was just a curiosity or jealousy of what they had and I didn't, but I started to accept it was attraction. I'd suppressed the knowledge of it for so long, but my experience with Danny made me realise, I was gay.

In my own head, I was quite comfortable with the realisation of being gay but I didn't like the idea of telling anybody else. It was impossible, even for me, not to think, at least for a second, 'am I really a gay woman or am I actually a straight man?' While I did not let that thought linger in my mind, I didn't want anyone else to be thinking it. I was particularly worried that it would trigger doubts for Mum and I definitely did not want that. I told Danny that I wasn't interested in carrying things on with him and kept everything else to myself.

Tamsin was still living at Mum's house but had regular trips home to her family. We'd got to know her mum quite well and she was warm and loving and we knew that as soon as she'd got on her feet she'd want Tamsin back.

In early 2003, Tamsin's mum arranged to have her for one of her weekend visits and somehow I just knew she wouldn't be coming back again. As we loaded Tamsin into her mum's car, like we had dozens of times in the year we'd had her, I felt really choked. Everyone was smiling and saying 'see you in a few days' like we did every other time, but before they left I leant back into the car and gave Tamsin a second kiss. They drove away and I felt a very big, very empty void. A few hours later Tamsin's mum rang and said she'd be able to look after her from then on.

I missed changing Tamsin, feeding her and just generally having her around and losing her became like a grieving process. For months after she'd gone, I slept with one of her T-shirts bundled in my hand. It dawned on me that having Tamsin was probably the only time I was going to get to nurture a baby in that way. I would never be able to foster myself – I got far too attached, adoption was out of the question with my poor health and I couldn't have children of my own. Having Tamsin was probably the closest I'd ever come to being a mum and it was over. I felt like I'd lost a child.

Around the same time, a girl I knew in the village got pregnant and it really highlighted how I was feeling. We were both 15 and I should probably have pitied her, but I was jealous. Looking back, it sounds ridiculous, but I just wanted a baby. My desire for a child, combined with my realisation over my sexuality, started to eat away at me and Mum seemed to have a sixth sense about both things.

'Is there anything you want to tell me?' she asked me one night.

I looked at her unable to find the words.

'You're gay, aren't you?' she said.

I nodded.

'Jo, it's fine,' Mum responded. 'I've suspected it for a while. So long as you are happy, I'm happy too.' She paused for a moment. 'The only thing that does worry me is if you think I made the wrong decisions when you were little?'

'No,' I told her, meaning it. 'Of course not.'

Mum and I talked about my desire for children too and she tried to tell me there would be options in the future for adopting or having a surrogate baby. I didn't think either of those things could ever realistically happen but talking about it did help a bit and I tried to concentrate on other things.

I'd never lost my ambition to be in the police force and when I spoke to my tutor about it, she mentioned a Uniformed Services course that was available at Boston College. I wasn't sure, but she seemed quite keen on the idea and brought a prospectus to show me. The course, which involved training with the army and marines, sounded great and when I spoke to a police officer we knew, he said it would help me get into the force.

I was very nervous but filled in the application and, after an interview, was offered a place starting in the September before my 16th birthday. I was nervous about going back into a 'classroom,' but was assured college would be different to school. My faith was a little shaken when after signing up only for Uniformed Services, I was sent a timetable that included English and sports, with sessions dotted throughout the week. I decided to try not to dwell on it and just to give it a go.

On the first day, I found my way to the room I was supposed to be in, expecting it to be full of college students, but when I got there, instead of all being older as I'd expected, some of the kids were younger than me. I sat down already fearing the worst.

The teacher stood at the front and called everyone to order.

'Okay, everyone. Welcome to Boston College. Good to see you all. I thought we'd start out by going around the room, introducing ourselves and telling everyone why we are here.' She gestured for one of the other kids to go first.

All the kids were so giggly and stupid and it soon became clear that I'd been signed on to a part-time course for people from the Boston secondary schools, designed to let them get used to college. They'd all been given the choice of either hairdressing or uniformed services and most of them weren't even interested in it at all.

When I spoke about wanting to get into the police force, I could sense the others taking the mick out of me. I was an obvious target because I was probably the only sensible one there. I was already having trouble with the environment and the nerves were kicking in. Perhaps if I'd have been sharing the class with older people who really wanted to be there I'd have been okay, but I knew this wasn't looking good.

After the first session, I went out for a cigarette to try to calm myself down and while I smoked, I made conversation with one of the lads from the course. He seemed okay but it was clear we had little in common. Once I'd finished I walked into the canteen and all the kids from my course were sitting together. I could feel them looking across at me and laughing. I stuck with it until the end of the day but by then I was in a knot. I went off to find my bus and discovered the last one back to Pinchbeck had already gone.

Farmer, who had started working as a builder and tiler by then, was thankfully working nearby that day and was able to pick me up. I could feel all the old nerves and anxieties taking over me and within five minutes of getting in his car, I was being sick out of the window. At home, as I realised I couldn't return to college, I was very emotional and tearful. I felt deflated and as if I would never get anywhere

JOE HOLLIDAY WITH LOUISE CHAPMAN

or be anything, but tried to just accept that education was a minefield for me and would never work however much I wanted it to. It was difficult though as there were already so many things I couldn't do. I decided I just needed to put it behind me.

I had to keep having home-tutoring until I turned 16 but it was just a box-ticking exercise and everyone knew I'd drop out as soon as I could. I knew I hadn't learned anywhere near enough to pass any exams and didn't even contemplate going in for any of them. Mum suggested asking in the Spar shop in the village to see if they'd have any work for me. They were looking for someone for Saturday nights, which suited me fine and after a bit of training on the tills and the National Lottery machine, I had my first proper shift there on my 16th birthday.

Not wanting to attract attention, I didn't tell anyone it was my birthday. I was nervous enough about sitting behind the till, which felt like a little platform where everyone was looking at me. I struggled to talk to customers and panicked if I made a mistake, but everyone was friendly and understanding and I soon found my feet. Among the staff was a girl called Sam who was about 18 and I got on with instantly. Then there was Dawn, who was tiny and timid and Daryl, who was loud and silly and loved to play jokes on everyone. All the customers were local so I knew most of them already and a lot of them asked after Mum and Nan, which made me feel much more comfortable.

I ended up having a great time and feeling really good and happy for the first time in ages. Farmer came to pick me up at 9pm and as we got back home, I noticed what I thought was my dad's car outside. We walked in the house and a couple of dozen people leapt out shouting 'Surprise!'

That night everyone got quite drunk, including me, which gave me the courage to tell everyone that I was gay. I knew Mum had already spoken to Farmer and Jarred about it so they were already used to the idea, while Chris was still a bit young. Daniel, Laura and Semrah didn't seem at all surprised or bothered and from what I can remember my dad took it fine as well. He got me interested in golf not long after my birthday and we'd go up to the driving range together every now and again. He never brought up my sexuality again so I assume he was all right with it.

The day after my party I woke up feeling good that I didn't have a big secret any more. The only person I never did speak to about it was Nan and I didn't ever want Mum to talk to her about it either. If she had been well, I think I would have told her, but as it was, I felt it was unnecessary. She was from a different generation when homosexuality was much less accepted and I never wanted her to feel awkward about who I was. Although she was never told, I think she may have known anyway.

'I hope Bella finds someone to make her happy one day,' she told Mum some time later. 'Whoever that person might be.'

CHAPTER NINETEEN

A rite of passage at 16 was receiving your National Insurance card through the post and I was a bit confused when, instead of a card, I got a letter detailing a temporary National Insurance number. It wasn't something I thought too much about until years later when the significance of it became more obvious.

At the time, all I was really interested in was that, because I was registered disabled, I could start learning to drive a year sooner than everyone else. With my first wage packet from the Spar I bought a battered old Nissan Micra for £150 and used to spend every spare second driving it up and down the very short driveway in between Mum and Nan's houses. I must have spent hours just moving those few metres backwards and forwards and started proper lessons as soon as I'd saved up again. Nan insisted on paying towards my lessons too and I couldn't wait to be able to take her out for days.

I worked at the Spar every Saturday night and when-ever they needed me in the week too and continued to really enjoy it. I soon got to know what the customers smoked, drank and read and enjoyed having a bit of banter with them. Outside of work, there was also plenty to keep me busy with looking after Nan and, once they were on study leave, hanging around with Laura and Semrah. Mum got a huge blow-up swimming pool for the garden and the three of us spent no end of time in it that summer.

Everything felt good so when someone from our local ITV news channel Calendar called out-of-the-blue and asked if they could do a catch-up piece on me and how my life was going, I didn't see the harm. I guess it felt a bit like things had worked themselves out and it would be nice to show everyone I was doing okay.

ITV brought their cameras down and did an interview with me, one with Mum and filmed me at Nan's, helping out there. They interviewed Nan and she got quite emotional telling them how I looked after her and saying how proud of me she was. I was sitting beside her as they filmed and it was quite touching. I was careful in everything I said not to allude to my sexuality because although I was all right with it and I knew those close to me were, I didn't feel ready for the whole world to start commenting on what it did or didn't mean about me.

The crew also wanted to film me at work and Daryl – the practical joker of the team – was so excited at the thought of being on TV. They filmed us stacking some shelves together then did a little bit to camera with Daryl, which was like all his dreams come true. On the evening the piece was airing, I was at work, which didn't bother me at all, but Daryl could not wait to see himself on screen. He took the night off, ordered a Chinese and got all his family round to watch his TV debut. He was gutted when it turned out his part had been cut and when he came to work the next day we ribbed him relentlessly.

I think I would have stayed at the Spar for a long time had it not been for Nan's health starting to deteriorate. She was finding it more and more difficult to get about even in the house and it became clear that she couldn't really be alone. She was so limited in what she could do and it was very frustrating for her. Sometimes she didn't make it to the toilet in time and had to wear pads, which she found quite degrading, though we'd always do our best to make a joke of it.

'Come on now Jean, time to change your pad,' I'd say as if I were some patronising care home worker. It would make her laugh, but there was always a sadness in her eyes.

I decided to leave the Spar and move the remaining things I had at Mum's across to Nan's so that I could look after her full-time. Nan was always very conscious of the fact that I was young and spending all of my time with her, but being with her was still the thing that made me happiest. She'd often need me to help change her oxygen or help her to the toilet in the night and although it was tiring, I wouldn't have let anyone else do it. Nan was always so grateful, but determined that I shouldn't sacrifice my whole life for her so she bought me a caravan to put on the driveway at her house as a bit of space of my own. It had a fridge, cooker and some storage space and was a bit like my first home. It was excellent and I loved it, but I still slept in the house so I was close when she needed me.

Nan was no longer able to get about on her mobility scooter and that proved even more of an incentive for me to pass my driving test. I was very nervous about the theory test especially as I'd never sat any kind of exam before and went to the library to get myself some books and mock tests. I did hours and hours of revision and took it so seriously that I wouldn't allow myself a break until I passed three tests in a row, that sort of thing. I was terrified of failing after all the work I'd put in, but it all paid off and I passed first time. I couldn't quite believe it when I did the same with the practical test, even after getting the examiner everyone dreaded. My driving instructor drove me back to Mum's and pulled up outside beeping her horn. Mum knew it was good news and came running down the path with a bottle of Champagne.

As I wanted to be able to take Nan out in comfort and be sure we wouldn't break down, I decided to give Mum the Micra I'd bought and invest in a Zafira from the mobility scheme instead. It meant I could easily get Nan, her oxygen tanks and wheelchair in, which was worth every penny. I was very proud the first day I was able to take Nan out to Spalding with her wheelchair for a walk around the market and a bit of fresh air. For a number of months, the trips out Nan and I had in my car were the highlight of the week for both of us and they helped distract me from just how frail she was getting.

During that time, Farmer had a major development in his life that none of us had seen coming. He had a dream one night where he'd walked to the door of a house and a priest had opened it and when he woke up he felt like he knew where it was and drove there.

He knocked on the door and a vicar opened it.

'I don't know why I'm here,' Farmer told him.

'I do,' the vicar said. 'You've had a calling.'

Farmer was a big biker and builder, who I rarely saw out of his work clothes, but he gathered us all around and told us he wanted to study to be a minister. We'd always gone to church now-and-again and we'd pray when something bad happened but we weren't overly religious. Regardless, Farmer told us he was going to start going to church every week and intended to study theology.

We all had a lot of respect for Farmer's wishes and it was really inspiring to see him follow it through. He signed up to an evening theology course with Lincoln University, which involved him driving 40 miles across there a couple of times a week. He could barely type a word when he started, but stuck with it and learned how to use a computer. When he told us the next step would be for him to get confirmed, Jarred, Mum and I said we'd do it with him to show our support. Later, Farmer and Mum also decided they wanted to renew their wedding vows.

Mum and Farmer planned the renewal of their vows for September 2005 and decided to make it a huge ceremony and party. Mum had a dress made, I was to be maid of honour and Jarred best man. Nan was desperate to be at the blessing, but I knew she had started to really believe she might not make it. She needed oxygen more and more and was so weak that if she woke in the night needing the toilet, I'd have to almost lift her to the commode.

I'd worry about Nan's health constantly and my biggest fear was that she would die in the night alone. Every morning I would lay in bed and dread going downstairs in case she'd passed without me being there. Each day I'd have to build myself up to get out of bed and I'd go down with my breath held until I saw Nan was okay. I couldn't even bear to begin to think about what my life would be like without her.

The day of the ceremony came round and the excitement seemed to give Nan such a boost. She was so much stronger that day than she had been in months. I helped her dress in a beautiful grey suit and got her into her wheelchair and she looked just lovely. Mum and I had a very busy morning with all sorts of people running in and out doing hair and make up and things. Mum's dress had lilac flowers embroidered down the front and her hair was all curled. I was wearing a matching lilac strappy dress, which wasn't my style at all but I knew it made Mum happy to see me in it. Jarred and I ordered her a limo as a surprise to take her up to the church and he, Chris and I stood either side of Mum and Farmer as they exchanged their vows. We had quite a lot of family and friends there and Nan particularly found it very emotional. Mum's friend Rose sang Ave Maria, Mum's favourite song and later Jarred did a little speech.

Farmer had worked hard in the run-up to the ceremony to do up the bungalow in their garden and we held the after-party in it. We hired a load of tables and chairs for the do and pulled together a buffet for 100 people. The first thing I did when we got back was to change out of the lilac dress and into a suit, which felt much more comfortable.

The night turned into a pretty heavy one and everyone got very drunk – including Nan! We had a big karaoke and there's a video of Nan singing on it, which was incredible considering she could barely breathe much of the rest of the time. She even fell out of her wheelchair at one point and laid on the floor with her legs in the air laughing her head off. She was battling an infection on her lung a few days later and looked as frail as she ever had, but that night had meant so much to her.

In the run-up to Christmas, both Nan and I were struggling with our health – her with recurrent lung infections that meant she was in and out of hospital – and me with my stomach again. I was having days where I'd drink a litre and a half of prune juice just to keep my system moving, but there didn't seem to be anything my GP could do.

In the three or four days leading up to Christmas Day, my stomach was particularly bad but I was determined not to let it ruin what I feared could be my last Christmas with her. On Christmas morning, it was even sensitive to touch, but I wheeled Nan round to Mum's and did not mention it to anyone.

At lunchtime, I sat at the table barely daring to move, wanting so much to enjoy the time with the family, but at the same time desperate to just go and be on my own and try to deal with my discomfort. As the meal went on, I couldn't eat a thing and was starting to get quite worried about how bad it was. The last thing I wanted to do was ruin Christmas for everyone so I made an excuse and went off to my caravan for a bit. I started setting up a new TV Mum had bought me, but as I fiddled with the plugs and switches, the pain in my stomach started to come in waves like contractions and when it was bad, I could barely cope. Eventually I was sick and woke on the floor of the caravan in agony more than an hour later.

I had to almost crawl to Mum's and could feel myself slipping out of consciousness. Mum took one look at me and dialled 999. The paramedics arrived and put me in a wheelchair to lift me into the back of the ambulance. As Mum climbed in beside me, all I could think was that I'd ruined everybody's Christmas. There was very little traffic around so we went through to Boston with the blue lights flashing but no siren. We were almost there when there was an almighty crash and some drunk had driven straight into the side of the ambulance then sped off. One of the paramedics got out to check the damage and I could hear all this conversation about whether anyone got the registration of the car, while all the time, I struggled to manage my pain.

Luckily it was only really the bumper of the ambulance that was affected in the crash and we set off for the hospital where I was wheeled into A&E and put onto a bed in a side room. Whereas last time I'd been taken to hospital, I'd been screaming in pain, this time my body was just shutting down because of it. I was slipping in and out of consciousness and whenever I came round, I'd throw up masses of green bile.

A doctor examined me and told Mum he feared my liver had ruptured, which would almost certainly be fatal. He sent me down for an X-ray and told Mum she needed to get the family in to say their goodbyes. Initially Mum called Farmer, getting hysterical, but the more she considered things the more she felt the doctors had got it wrong. As far she could see, we'd been here before and I came through it last time.

The pain that I feel when my stomach goes is indescribable and a large part of me just wanted to die. You don't only have to deal with the pain itself, but in the rare moments where it eases off very slightly, you are dealing with the fear and knowledge it is about to come back. When it was at its worst I was unable to breathe, unable even to see and then I'd pass out again.

Mum began to realise that the doctors drafted in to cover Christmas Day in A&E were more than likely young and fairly inexperienced, expecting to have to deal with a few drunks and suicide attempts. I was a case most experienced doctors had never seen before and if I was going to recover she was going to have to convince them to pump me up with morphine. All the doctors had to go on was an X-ray and Mum's say-so, but eventually they listened to her and started injecting me. As the morphine hit, the tiredness took over me and I fell into a sort of sleep, the pain instantly beginning to ease.

I spent Boxing Day laid in bed reading magazines and was discharged the following day, physically on the mend, but very drained. It takes more time to heal your mind than your body after something like that. I was reasonably okay, but needed some rest. I went to see my GP afterwards to ask for some investigation into what had gone wrong but as I was almost 18, it wasn't clear which hospital I needed to be referred to as clearly I'd outgrown Great Ormond Street. My GP said he'd write and ask for my notes and I followed it up a few times with him, but each time he said he hadn't managed to get my notes back and in the end it was another worry that I just put to the back of my mind.

The same day I got home from hospital, Nan was taken back in with breathing difficulties caused by the recurring lung infection. A part of me was relieved Nan had gone in because I knew if she was home I wouldn't have been able to help myself from insisting that I should continue looking after her, but I knew I needed to recover myself. Another part of me never really relaxed when she was in hospital as I didn't trust them to ensure she got everything she needed. They were always good at treating the infection, but often seemed to overlook the other tablets she took on a permanent basis. There had been times when I'd gone in and she was filling up with fluid and I discovered she hadn't been given her water tablets.

Nan was home again in time for my 18th birthday and although neither of us was up to much, it was lovely just to have her there for it. Without thinking much about it, Mum put an announcement in the local newspaper, the Spalding Guardian, which triggered a call from one of their reporters, who wanted to write an update piece. Mum had a quick chat with them and they ran something fairly innocuous.

The day after the paper came out, I was round at Mum's sitting with her in the dining room when Pick Me Up magazine rang and asked if they could do something on me too and offered £500. Apart from the few hundreds pounds given to us by QED that ended up helping towards the extra costs of the New York trip, we'd never been paid for any of the stories about me and £500 was a lot of money to us. We were quite excited and I told Mum we'd split it 50/50.

Almost as soon as we put the phone down, there was another call from someone who said they worked for a news agency and were interested in doing a story on me for Reveal.

'Sorry, we've just agreed to do something with Pick Me Up,' Mum said.

'Have you signed anything?'

'Well, no, not yet. We've just put the phone down to them.'

'Great, look there's a chance to get a bit more out of this then. If you agree to do the story with me, I'll play the magazines off against each other a bit and see if we can get your fee up. What do you think?'

Mum told me what was happening and we thought, why not? It sounds awful but I think we just felt a lot of people had earned a lot of money out of my story and photographs in the past, so why shouldn't we? It was different when we'd needed the media to help with the birth certificate and we always felt we owed the locals something but these were national magazines, who could afford it.

A few minutes later the agent called back.

'Reveal is offering £1,000, but Pick Me Up is coming back to me. I'll let you know.'

For the next couple of hours we were getting calls every half hour, the fee going up a bit each time, until Reveal offered £3,000!

I rushed back to tell Nan what had happened and she couldn't believe it any more than Mum or I could. It was a shard of light in an otherwise very difficult time where Nan was going downhill so fast that we knew, each day, she was the best she was ever going to be and the next she was only likely to be worse. Looking forward to seeing the Reveal article in print became the next thing to aim for and she was determined not to go anywhere before it happened.

CHAPTER TWENTY

Reveal sent a package of clothing a few days before the photo shoot containing things they wanted me to wear and inside were a mass of miniskirts and crop tops. It was completely inappropriate with my colostomy and scars and, while I wasn't really bothered by it, Mum was furious that they'd been so stupid. I put on some nice jeans, a white shirt and brown cord jacket instead and thought no more about it.

Steve Hill, a local freelance photographer, who we'd got to know quite well over the years, was drafted in to do the shoot, which made it all more comfortable – until he told us he wanted to do it at Ayscoughfee, the Spalding park. Mum and I were both needed for the pictures and we were in the park for well over two hours in the end, with Steve getting us to do all sorts of poses. On one he wanted me to sit with my arms on a tree branch, but as the only one we could find was about 6ft in the air, I was just sort of dangling. In another he got me to climb on a sort of stone plinth thing and, although we were having quite a laugh, quite a few people were stopping to have a look what we were up to and it was quite mortifying.

The interviews were done over the phone on another day and weren't particularly taxing. They wanted all the back story from Mum and then the usual quotes from me about how excited I was about being able to get married one day. I was a bit concerned they'd start delving into my sexuality, but they didn't probe me on it and I was happy not to go into it. I didn't really want that all over The Press and for someone to start saying it was proof that I was a boy.

Nan was really looking forward to seeing Reveal in print, but apart from that life was becoming quite unbearable for her. She was battling one painful chest infection after another and was just drained with it all. I was pushing her through town in her wheelchair one day when a hearse went by.

'Lucky bugger,' she said, looking across at it.

In March, she was admitted to hospital again and filled with antibiotics and steroids yet again. We were all quite surprised and pleased when they started taking effect and Nan appeared brighter than she had in ages.

'I'm sick of sitting around doing nothing all the time,' she told Mum, me and her son Terry on one visit. 'When we get home, you can get me out in that garden and we'll get it sorted.'

The doctor put his head around the door and asked for a quick word with us outside.

'I'm sorry to say that in one of the X-rays we have found a shadow on Mrs Ives' lung,' he told us. 'I'm afraid it's cancer.'

Mum was disbelieving. We all were.

'Cancer? No, this is the infection you've been treating for months,' Mum said. 'That shadow keeps returning and then going again.'

'I'm sorry Mrs Baker, but I'm quite certain. This is a dark patch typical of cancer and we think it best to break the news while you are all here.'

'What? You can't tell her she has cancer, it'll finish her,' Mum said. 'Can't you do a biopsy first to be sure?'

The doctor was young and cocky and seemed sure he knew best. We all felt sure he'd got it wrong, but he assumed we just didn't want to believe it.

'I'm afraid I have a duty to tell a patient the truth,' he informed us as he lead us all back into Nan's room.

Mum, Terry and I watched as the doctor told Nan she'd got lung cancer and we saw her deflate before us. She nodded and laid down on her pillow, defeated. Mum tried to tell her that she thought there may be a mistake but Nan was from a generation that believed doctors were always right and we couldn't get through to her.

We never saw Nan being her chirpy self again and instead she went downhill very fast. Within a week she was being released from hospital on a die-at-home package. We'd been struggling to keep her weight up for a long time, but in hospital it had dropped to 5st. She was back on the oxygen constantly and couldn't get out of bed at all. While I still couldn't think about life without Nan, I wanted a release for her. She wasn't really talking and it was as if she had already partly gone.

Nan came home on the Monday and various family members were in and out from then on to see her and say their goodbyes. Her breathing was very laboured and it was difficult to see her struggling as she was so we agreed to allow a nurse to come in to give her an injection to make her unconscious and help her be more peaceful. On the day the nurse was due, Reveal came out and we were able to show it to her.

Nan looked at Mum in the photos, all made up and with her dark hair curled at the ends and we could see she was trying to say something.

'You look like a bleedin' madam!' she told Mum

We all laughed and it was one of the last things Nan ever said.

The nurse came that afternoon and administered the injection that allowed Nan to slip into a coma. By the evening, Nan's breathing had slowed right down and all that was left to do for her was to swap her oxygen between a nasal tube and mask every couple of hours to stop it irritating her.

Terry and his wife and my uncle Kevin and his daughter Katie, came to sit with Mum and I at Nan's bedside and we ended up getting a bottle of whiskey out to share while we chatted.

Kevin started telling us a funny story about a little boy we all knew.

'Poor little bugger, got hold of an ice bucket the other day and thought it was a football. He only went and headed it!'

I was holding Nan's hand and, as we all erupted into laughter, I felt her twitch and I just know she took her last breath at the moment – to the sound of her family gathered around, having a drink and a laugh together.

'I think she has gone,' I said.

Terry jumped up. 'No, quick, we need to put her mask back on.'

'Okay,' I said. 'I'll get it,' but I knew.

A weird calm and purpose took over for the next few hours as we called the doctor to tell them it had happened and waited for Nan to be taken. I sat for ages just holding her hand and Farmer came and did a prayer with everyone. One of Mum's brothers on Grandad's side, Steve, rang within an hour of her passing, just knowing something was wrong.

Before the funeral directors carried her away, I tucked Nan's hand back under her blanket and gave her a kiss. I went off down to the bottom of the garden and the tears came, then I had to run to Mum's house to be sick in her bathroom.

I went to see Uncle John, who was upstairs at Nan's and checked he was okay then went to bed. I woke in the morning just not knowing what to do. I ended up spending most of the day sat at Mum's dining room table talking about Nan. We all agreed that if she'd been able to choose how to go, that was the way she would have wanted it.

I made a couple of calls to friends to tell them Nan had gone and the day just chugged by very slowly. It was a relief that she wasn't in so much pain any more and I didn't really think about the impact on my life at that point. I had a few tears every now and again when I was on my own, but we had the funeral to organise and all the paperwork and stuff to sort out so I was able to keep myself busy.

Mum had promised Nan that she'd make sure she looked true to herself at the chapel of rest and didn't feel the funeral directors had managed to achieve it with their attempt. In the end, she said she'd go in and do Nan's hair and make-up herself. Strangely, I think having that last bit of time with Nan, just the two of them together, doing something like that for her, turned into something quite special for Mum. Mum chatted to Nan throughout and every now and again Nan's eyes would fall open and Mum would joke with her about it, telling her to stop it.

When Nan had died she'd looked so terrible, drawn and fragile, but when I went to see her after Mum had made her up she just looked fantastic. She looked so well that if she'd have got up and walked out I wouldn't have been surprised. Seeing her like that again was such a precious thing.

The family all decided we should write something or take something for Nan to take with her. No-one knew what anyone else had written – it was just between Nan and each of us and we each put our own words in sealed envelopes. Writing my letter was one of the hardest things I've ever had to do. I shut myself in my caravan and wouldn't allow myself out until I'd finished and it was very emotional.

I told Nan how important she was during my child-hood, how she had helped bring me up and that she was more like a second mother than a grandparent. I said it had been an honour to help care for her and do something to pay her back for all she had done for me, told her how much I'd miss her and how much she meant to me, which was pretty much everything.

I didn't tell Nan anything in the letter that I hadn't told her before, but it meant a lot to know it was going with her. I also gave her a copy of Reveal magazine because seeing that article was the last thing she'd held on for and it was the last thing we'd talked about. Mum and I took our letters to Nan the day before her funeral and Mum had bought two necklaces with one half of a pendant on each. One piece of the pendant was inscribed with 'mum' and the other 'daughter' and Mum kept the 'daughter' and put the 'mum' around Nan's neck.

The funeral was held at St Mary's Church in Pinchbeck where Mum and Farmer's blessing had been a few months before. People came from all over to be there and there must have been at least 100 people there. I have never seen a funeral so big and everyone, even big blokes, were crying. The service passed in a blur for me and all I really recall is having to grab Mum as we walked out to one of Nan's favourite songs and her legs almost buckled.

The burial was a short drive away at the village cemetery and when we arrived the path was lined with people, so many of them that by the time I got to the plot, I couldn't see an end to the line. It was unbelievable.

Mum and I read a poem at the graveside, taking one sentence each and it was so emotional that I wasn't even really aware of what I was saying. Seeing Nan's name on the coffin as it was lowered, made it so real, but walking away from the grave was the most difficult bit, knowing that was it – I was leaving her behind.

Compared with the funeral, the wake was quite intimate, but the place was still packed. It was at the social club where they'd laid on food for free as a gesture for Nan. They had also had a frame made up of photos of Nan over the years – dozens of them in the club and a few dressed as a genie and nurse on the social club carnival float, which she used to make all the costumes for each year. For weeks before the carnival, you'd arrive at Nan's house and she'd have a line of people there all being fitted for togas or something or other. Then, on the day of the carnival she'd be up on the float with piles of sweets to throw to the kids on the route and a bottle filled with a sneaky drink for the adults to share on the way. The social club hung the frame of pictures of Nan up on the wall so she'd always be there.

Loads of people from the village, all our family and Semrah, Daniel and Laura were at the wake. Whiskey and lemonade was the family drink and I went at it quite hard, which continued when we all went back to the bottom building at Mum's. I thought 'I'm just going to get as drunk as I possibly can' because whereas previously I'd always been quite sensible so I'd be coherent if Nan needed me, I didn't have that to think about any more.

The day after the funeral I woke up in my bedroom at Nan's and realised I just didn't have anything to do. I used to get up and get showered early every day so I was ready for Nan when she wanted to get up. I laid in bed and felt absolutely devoid of everything. I had no reason to get up, no reason to do anything. The thing I did was no longer there. Realising that was as big a loss as actually not having Nan. I'd lost the person I loved most in the world and my reason for living.

I went downstairs and looked around. The hospital bed was gone from the living room, the vast array of drugs Nan had needed were all gone and so were the oxygen tanks. I was down and empty and totally lost. I went to the caravan and flicked the telly on and sat there looking at it. I didn't register what programme it was, I just needed something to help move my mind elsewhere.

John was still at Nan's house and I felt he didn't need me under his feet all the time. Without Nan there I felt awkward and like I was just in the way. I didn't feel like I belonged there any more but moving back into Mum's didn't feel like an option either. I'd given up my bedroom there so the boys could have it and Chris, aged seven, and Jarred, 13, were both fairly full on, which I found too much at that stage so I ended up spending more and more time alone in my caravan.

I tried so hard to give myself an aim each day and would go into town with Mum or take my golf clubs down to the driving range, but I felt I was just passing the time rather than using or enjoying it. Each day I was getting more down and feeling more hopeless. I was 18 and everything I'd been doing for the past few years had ended. I couldn't see a lot of point in anything any more. There was a good dose of just missing Nan and a good dose of missing the activity of looking after her.

I missed being able to talk to Nan and felt there was no-one left who really understood me. In Nan's company, I was easy and comfortable in myself and just felt happy. While I knew Mum was always there for me, our characters are so different. I'm a realist where Mum is more positive. I couldn't see an emotional way out, but I felt Mum couldn't really understand where I was coming from and just wanted me to be able to snap out of it. I found it was best to avoid her when I was feeling really low because otherwise it would just end in an argument.

One positive thing I did do in those days was to give up smoking, which is something Nan had pleaded with me to do. She blamed a lot of her illness on cigarettes and I had promised her I would quit. I'd tried before, using patches and gum, but the stress of being a carer for Nan always led me back to it. As soon as Nan died, I knew it was time to do it. I smoked a lot in the run-up to the funeral and the days after but then decided that was it. I went from a 10-20 a day habit to nothing and have never touched one since.

A few weeks after Nan had gone, the Mirror newspaper contacted us, offering to pay £500 for another catch-up type story. It sounded like an easy job – a photo shoot in the garden and another interview over the phone, so I agreed.

'With her long blonde hair, sparkling blue eyes and sunny smile, Joella Holliday exudes the carefree self-confidence of those who have just turned 18 and know the world is at their feet,' their story began. My eyes aren't blue but I had bleached my hair at that point so that was right I suppose.

'Her birthday celebrations fresh in her mind, Joella hopes the future will bring a successful career, a loving husband and the chance to become a mum,' it continued.

Most of the story wasn't exactly wrong, they had just taken everything I'd said and padded it out and adjusted it a bit to make my life sound like a happy-ever-after fairytale. It couldn't have been further from how I really felt.

The interviews and photos we'd done for Reveal appeared in the teen magazine It's Bliss and a few weeks later French Closer and the renewed fuss prompted This Morning to get back in touch and ask Mum and I to go back on. I was getting a bit sick of the intrusion by then and was very reluctant, but in the end, agreed with Mum that it would be a day of fun.

This time in the green room we met one of the dancers from Strictly Come Dancing and Denise Welch, the Coronation Street actress and Loose Women presenter. The Strictly dancer was extremely showy and danced about all over the place even though it was very early in the morning while Denise was very down to earth and lovely.

Phillip Schofield and Ruth Langsford were presenting the show at that stage and they really put us at ease. We were on for about five minutes and it all went really well. I told them about Nan and they asked about my plans for the future. I think I said I was keen to get a job, which was true, but I knew it wasn't going to happen because I couldn't stay well for long enough. My stomach was constantly up and down and one day I'd get up and be fine and the next I could barely move.

As if on cue, I was in agony with my stomach all the way back to Peterborough where Farmer was coming to collect us from the station. Mum and I stood outside waiting and I felt pretty shattered and low. Then a taxi driver pulled up in front of us and wound his window down.

'I saw you on This Morning!' he said. 'You're fantastic. You did so well!' And he started to clap!

It was funny and just so nice. I thought 'Wow, he saw us?' When you're doing things like that you almost forget people are actually watching it.

I got up the next day, feeling just as lonely and empty as I had every day since Nan had died. I slept at John's, got washed and cooked my meals there and spent the rest of the time in my caravan. I'd sit looking blankly at the TV for hours on end just wishing I didn't have to keep existing. I'd go through the motions of what was necessary to survive but there was no joy in anything. In hindsight I was severely depressed, but was about to discover that alcohol was the perfect escape. Or so I thought.

CHAPTER TWENTY-ONE

Mum had been trying to get me to go out with her and her friends on a Friday night, but I'd always refused in the past because of Nan. When she started going on about it again, I didn't have the energy to argue, found a pair of smart trousers and a nice jacket and did my best to smile. I'd known all of Mum's friends – Mel, Gary and a few others – forever and told myself it would be a chance to catch up with them.

The night started out – as it always did – in the Pied Calf, a quite lively but fairly traditional pub just off the market place in Spalding. I ordered a whiskey and lemonade and drank it down quickly. Once the drink was inside me I felt a bit better, a bit happier and a bit less out-of-place. The others were drinking fairly fast too and we ordered another.

Mum is very outgoing and so are a lot of her friends and whenever they were together things were always pretty loud and it soon felt like our little group was at the centre of things. We had quite a few drinks in the Pied Calf, then moved on to The Red Lion, a similar pub a few doors down. Mum, Mel and the others knew some of the staff and we burst in there and sort of took over there too. The more I drank the more confident and happy I felt and Mum and the others were pretty funny to be around. I realised I was actually having a really good time. We moved on to The Punchbowl, a late night party pub where the older crowd in Spalding generally ended the night. The pub was rammed with people, the music was loud, Mel and Mum were all over the dance floor, laughing their heads off as they wrapped themselves around a pole on a little stage and I was happy with another whiskey in my hand.

The night ended at about 1am when we all fell into a taxi and went home. I realised that it was the first time since Nan's death that I'd actually felt okay and decided going out and having a few drinks wasn't so bad after all.

I started going out with Mum every Friday and those nights were the only decent thing that happened all week. I was finding each day more and more difficult and looked forward to getting a whiskey in my hand and knowing everything would soon be softer and hazier and I'd feel happy for a little while. I never got completely out of it, always wanting to make sure everyone got home okay, but I had plenty. In the daytime, I still didn't know what to do with myself. Apart from cleaning the caravan and John's house, when my stomach wasn't causing me too many problems, there wasn't really anything else for me to do.

Gary, who was gay, convinced me to set up a profile on a gay dating website and I started going on there every now and again to see if there was anyone I found interesting. There were a few weirdos on there and I had the odd strange email, which I got rid of pretty quickly but mostly the profiles were fairly ordinary people. There were one or two I thought I could get on with and I exchanged a few messages with some of them but it didn't go any further than that. I was still fairly convinced that no-one would want to get involved with me with all my problems but it gave me a bit of hope.

Being on the website might have been what gave me a bit of extra confidence one night when we were in The Punchbowl and a woman made eye contact with me across the bar. I smiled at her and she smiled back. Moments later the woman came and tapped me on the shoulder and asked if she could buy me a drink.

We moved to the beer garden – a huge outdoor area with patio heaters and shelters where the music is still loud and people can have a smoke. The woman told me she was in her 30s, had a 12-year-old son and was in Spalding visiting her sister. The conversation flowed easily and she seemed really nice and before I knew it we were kissing. It felt totally different from the times I'd kissed Danny, was exciting and just felt right.

Mel came outside at some point and spotted us. Her jaw fell open and she went rushing back into Mum.

'Jo's out there kissing a woman. I didn't know she was gay!'

Mum was thrilled and the pair of them started peeking through a window at me and smirking like a couple of kids.

I exchanged numbers with the woman at the end of the night but I never heard from her. I wasn't really surprised. It had been a bit of fun anyway.

I was still searching for something to give me a bit of focus and Mum, who had a Yorkie Terrier, suggested that I get a dog. I gave it some thought and quite liked the idea.

I decided I wanted something quite small as it would be in the caravan with me most of the time and when I found an advert in the newspaper for some Parson's Russell puppies they sounded perfect. They were out in the Lincolnshire Wolds, which was a fair drive but I was pretty confident I'd be coming home with one. I went out and bought a basket and bowl and all the other bits and just doing that gave me a boost, then Mum and I set off to collect a puppy.

We found the house and walked in to see all these gorgeous little puppies running around. One came straight across and weed on Mum's shoe. He was so tiny he could have fitted in a mug and had this sense of mischief about him. He was clearly the naughty one and I was drawn to him immediately. I spent a few minutes sitting and playing with him then agreed to take him.

Ages before, Jarred and I had joked about the most silly name you could give a dog. We were watching the Friday Night Project with Alan Carr at the time and decided Alan would be pretty stupid. We'd laughed about it a lot and said if either of us ever got a dog that's what we'd call it, so Alan got his name right away. He's actually Alan Fitzgerald Colin Holliday in full.

Mum and I loaded Alan into the carrier I'd bought and as we left he started crying straight away. I felt awful both for taking him from his family and for leaving the others behind. In the car, Alan's crying continued until Mum and I couldn't take it any more, so we pulled over and got him out. He crawled into the nook of Mum's arm and happily settled down for the drive home. When we got back, Mum handed him to me and he crawled inside my cardigan and fell asleep. I zipped it up and cuddled him all evening and, that night, I even let him sleep in my bed.

I was a bit surprised when I woke up in the morning and still felt the emptiness. I'd sort of told myself that everything would be fine once I got a dog, but it wasn't. I still didn't know what to do with myself and still felt alone and miserable. I took Alan out to the caravan and clicked the telly on. I kept telling myself to get up and do something but whatever I thought about doing just didn't seem worth it. I thought I could go and do the Hoovering, but then thought 'What's the point?' The longer I sat doing nothing, the more annoyed I got with myself, but the more I tried to think of something to do, the more pointless it all seemed. I felt like I was going crazy. Often I'd think 'is it time to just get out of this? Is it time to just switch my life off?'

Not wanting to wait for Friday night to feel good again, I decided to go down to the shop and buy a cheap bottle of wine to drink in the caravan that evening while I watched a film. It numbed all the thoughts in my head and gave me that calm feeling I got when I went out with Mum and her friends. I realised I could drink at home and feel happier without having to make the effort to talk to anyone. That night, I dropped off to sleep almost as soon as I got in bed and it was a relief not to lie there thinking. The next Friday, when Mum asked me if I was going out, I said I was going to stay home and save some money. I bought a couple of bottles of wine and drank them in the caravan alone and it quickly became a habit to do that two or three nights a week.

Whenever I was with Mum, Farmer and the boys I was embarrassed that I was still feeling down because they'd lost

Nan too but they seemed okay. I knew I was hard work to be around and often couldn't be bothered with conversation and could be snappy and short-tempered. I'd always eaten Sunday lunch with Mum and the family, but even that became difficult. The boys liked to test and tease in the way brothers do but I was too fragile to take it. Obviously they didn't realise how much it was getting to me as I always seemed tough on the outside, but it would get to a point where I'd shout at them. Then Mum would get annoyed with me and little things would turn into a row. I decided it was easier to be alone and left my caravan even less.

It was after a family fall-out of that type that I reached my lowest point, shut the door of my caravan and fell to pieces. Without Nan I felt so alone. No-one seemed to understand me and I didn't blame them. I didn't even understand myself. I couldn't stand the thought of getting up in the morning and facing another empty, pointless day. I was sick of the pains in my stomach and the fear of another episode that would put me in hospital or worse. I couldn't ever imagine meeting someone. Who would want to be involved with me with my freakish body and constant health problems? I had no qualifications and no prospects.

I was in a total mess, crying and desperate. I grabbed a bottle of pills, opened the lid, poured half the bottle into my hand and threw the pills into my mouth. I was about to swallow when I realised what I was doing was wrong. What about my family? They'd feel terrible if they thought our fall-out had led to this. What about Alan? I'd committed to looking after him and now I was just going to leave him? I spat the pills out, laid my head down on the table and hated myself for not having the guts to go through with it. The misery was still ongoing.

A few weeks later, I bumped into an old friend of Mum's, Louise, who had two kids and a husband that worked away a lot. I started spending a bit of time at her house, helping out with the kids and babysitting and found that being away from my caravan, Nan's house and Mum's made me feel a bit less bogged down. I started to think getting a proper place of my own would be a good idea. Being at Nan's every day made me feel close to her, but with all her belongings still about and the house virtually unchanged, it was also a constant reminder of everything I'd lost.

A friend of Mum's was doing up some flats and said I could rent one. I knew, if I was going to do it, I'd need to save some money and that made me look at how much I was spending on booze. It started to occur to me that my drinking was becoming an issue. Although, I'd never got to a point where I was drinking in the day or even drinking every day, I was starting to rely on it. Grandad, Nan, Mum, Farmer, they were all big drinkers and I decided I was either going to drink big forever more or stop it altogether. I was spending loads of money and all I had to show for it was a headache. I wasn't even doing it to be sociable any more and just said to myself 'That's enough.' I decided that if I didn't drink at all, it couldn't cause me any pain.

I went on a night out with Mum soon after just to test myself and didn't have a drop of alcohol. I spent all night watching all these drunk people falling about and realised it's great when you are drunk but rubbish when you're sober.

I decided to leave them to it in future and didn't miss it at all.

I knew I was depressed and decided to go to see my GP and ask for some pills. I didn't really expect them to work, but, although there were still good days and bad, once I started taking them, they did seem to make everything seem less bleak.

The flat I was going to rent fell through, but I was so set on moving that I took myself up to the council and got put on the housing list. As 2007 came to an end, I felt as if the New Year would bring a new start and in early January, I got a call to say a flat in Spalding was coming up.

Viewing my flat, in a typical 1950s council estate, for the first time was very exciting. The estate was a mix of family semis and two-storey flats – ground floor flats like mine, with one flat above served by an external concrete staircase. It wasn't the best area, but all that mattered to me was that it was a place of my own.

An old man had lived in the flat previously and nothing had been done to the place in years. The front door was one of those the council put in in the 70s and was pretty rough. Inside, the council had ripped up all the carpets, in the kitchen there was nothing but a brick pantry and a free-standing stainless steel sink and the bathroom was 50 years old. The back door, off the kitchen, had a piece of wood nailed to it, covering a hole where there'd obviously once been a cat flap. None of it mattered to me and I immediately decided I'd take it.

For my birthday everybody bought me house things to help me get started and my dad gave me a cheque to buy two smart brown leather sofas. Things had been tight for Mum and Farmer and I'd leant them a bit of the money we'd been paid from the magazines, but I still had a few hundred pounds left to put towards the move.

I got the keys in early February and Mum, Farmer, Louise and I got straight in there and started decorating. The walls were full of cracks and holes and filling them took the best part of a week. I bought some laminate for the bedroom and living room, which Farmer laid for me and he found some offcuts of carpet for the dining room. The hallway was covered in broken and drilled out quarry tiles, too far gone to be made to look nice and the kitchen was just cement floors, but they had to wait.

We found some peach paint at Mum's which I used to cover the woodchip walls in the bathroom and I bought some tins of neutral paint for everywhere else. The council had fitted me one kitchen unit with a bit of work surface on it and I had the pantry in there too – depressing as it was. Someone gave me a decrepit old dining table and some chairs and I found a big ugly old desk that I threw a sheet over and put in my bedroom for somewhere to stand things. I took my television out of the caravan and spent the last of my money on an oak coffee table. I worked at the house from 8am to 8pm for a fortnight to get it looking okay.

I was so pleased to be moving into my own place, but leaving Nan's was difficult. Before I left I went up to her room and sat down at her dressing table, which still had – and still does have – all her stuff on it. I looked at the glass bowl with cotton buds in, the little bottles of lotion, drawers with bits and pieces of make-up in. Nan's still felt like home and I still say now that if I ever have enough money, I'll buy it and put it and the garden back to the way it was when I was little. I still go back regularly now to take John out and do bits of housework for him and occasionally I go and sit at Nan's dressing table just to feel close to her.

I'd packed all my stuff into boxes and was able to fit it all in the Zafira in one go. I put Alan in his carrier and set off, feeling full of hope. My plan was to get a job and start moving forward with my life.

Mum was looking for work at the same time and saw that a new windows company had set up in Spalding and wanted people for telemarketing. It was a five-minute walk from my new flat and they were looking for quite a lot of people so we both applied. We each got interviews, which pretty much consisted of 'Can you use a phone? You're hired.'

Mum took day shifts and I took nights, 4pm to 7pm five evenings a week, which fitted in with the restrictions attached to the benefits I was receiving. I was on incapacity benefit, but was allowed to do some restricted hours to see if my body was going to be up to it. I desperately wanted the sense of achievement and focus a job gives you and was keen to find a way to work.

I turned up for my first shift and was handed a pile of scripts and told to sit down in front of a phone and computer. The job was basically cold-calling to try to make appointments for sales people to go round to people's house. There was no training, it was just a case of you press this button to book an appointment and off you go. When I made the first call I didn't even know exactly what the company sold beyond it being windows, doors and conservatories. In my break I went and got some brochures and then read through them while I was on the phone, trying to give myself some clue of what I was talking about. That night I took the brochures home and studied them.

It was all very strict and we weren't supposed to deviate at all from the scripts we'd been given but one of the rules was that you had to make sure each call lasted at least ten seconds. It doesn't sound like a long time but often people would hang up before you even got to the end of the first script. You found yourself having ridiculous conversations just to keep the call time up. By the end of my second week, ten out of 12 people I'd started with had left and that's basically how it continued for the six months I was there. The staff turnover was just ridiculous. I got a call one day asking me to do the 10am to 3pm day shift as well as my night shift because no-one had turned up.

Often people only lasted one night, but I stuck with it and found myself quite enjoying it. I was getting a few appointments booked in and had a bit of a laugh with the colleagues who did last. To break up the monotony, we'd play games to try to get stupid words into the phone calls, like 'giraffe'.

Mum soon found something else and moved on, but I still saw her every day. She'd drop the kids at school then come round to the flat for a cup of tea. I think she liked to check that I was okay and I was quite happy to see her. She discovered that an old friend of hers, Nick, lived just around the corner from me and invited him over one day. Nick's mum and my nan had been great friends and Mum had known him forever. Nick and I got on really well and we found ourselves able to sit and chat for hours. He had been a secondary school biology teacher but had been forced to give it up due to ill health. We both had a lot of time on our hands and soon became best friends. Things were looking up.

CHAPTER TWENTY-TWO

It was only when my employers requested a copy of my full birth certificate, as part of the standard thing employers have to do now to make sure you are who you say you are and have the right to work in the UK, that I realised I'd never seen the full version of it. All I had was the short form version and the letter saying it had been resolved, so had to send away for it. What came back was my original certificate with a hand-written amendment to my name and gender.

Deep down it worried me that the amendment we'd fought so long for perhaps wasn't as 'official' as I'd thought it was, but I couldn't bear to drag it all back up again. Mum wanted me to go to see Dianne Miller and I knew I should but I never did. I just took the birth certificate into work as it was, took my boss to one side and gave him a brief explanation, which he was fine with and tried not to think any more about it.

That August, Pick Me Up got in touch and said they were interested in doing an update on me. They offered £500 for a quick over-the-phone interview and I couldn't help but be tempted. I loved the independence my flat gave me, but it was a struggle to keep up with the bills on my own and

I'd already had to give up my Zafira for a second-hand 1995 Golf to try to save a bit. There was still a lot I wanted to do to the flat and I'd started putting bits and pieces on credit cards which worried me.

I told the reporter I'd do the story for £1,000 and she agreed without hesitation.

'There's really not much to update you on though,' I warned her.

'It's fine, I'm sure there's something,' she said. 'We'll just have a chat about what you've been up to in the last few years. People will be interested to know how you have got on.'

'What I'd really like to talk about is my Nan,' I said. 'She helped me through everything that happened so much and I don't feel like any of the reports picked up on that.'

'Great, tell me about her.'

I told the reporter how important Nan had been to me and how precious I'd found the years I'd spent caring for her. It made me feel better to know the story would be a bit of tribute to Nan and all she'd meant to me.

I was concerned about featuring in the magazine because I felt like I'd got a bit of anonymity in Spalding that I'd never had in Pinchbeck and so I deliberately didn't mention the article to anyone other than Mum and Nick. On the day it came out, I went up to the newsagent's at the top of my road where I'd got to know the owners to chat to. I hadn't expected to feature on the front page and just thought 'oh dear'. I paid quickly and left, then didn't go back for a while! Luckily no-one at work mentioned the magazine and I got away with it without any fuss. It's not that I minded people knowing my past but it was easier if they didn't.

After Pick Me Up came out, I got a call from a BBC producer who said she was doing a half-hour documentary on people who had unusual health issues. To me, it was a big ask. I was private finally and didn't want to jeopardise that, but the producer said that if I took part she would make sure I got seen by a specialist who might be able to help with any ongoing issues I had.

My stomach had been pretty bad for months and I was going a week, sometimes two, without eating to get some relief from it. My system just did not seem to work and every time I ate, I'd end up in pain and bloated to the point where I couldn't really leave the house. It had become normal to have constant stabbing pains and feel sick all the time. I didn't class it as a bad day until I couldn't move with the pain and I'd had a number of bad days throughout that year. Sometimes it was a struggle to get to work, but I didn't ever call in sick. I just tried to plan things, knowing that if I wanted peace, I just didn't eat. If there was nothing going in, there were no problems and I was actually less drained than when I was eating because I didn't have the constant pain, but after a while the hunger would get to me.

I'd been worried about that and generally about not being under a particular hospital since the Christmas when I'd been taken in and no-one really knew what to do. My GP still hadn't ever got hold of my notes and it was a worry to me that if I had a car accident and was rushed to hospital, no-one would know what to do with me. It wasn't as if they could treat me in the same way as everybody else. I knew none of my organs were where they should have been and in an emergency they could end up causing me a lot of damage. The BBC seemed sure they'd be able to get my records and get me referred somewhere and it convinced me to get involved.

The producer of the BBC show, Agnes, came to meet me at my flat and my main rule was that I didn't want any filming to be done there. The last thing I wanted was camera crews turning up and making me the gossip of the neighbourhood. Agnes told me they'd got Natalie Cassidy, from EastEnders, to present the show and they were doing six other subjects as well as me. They would be particularly interested in trying to film some surgery, which quite appealed to me. I wondered if seeing inside my body might help me understand it a bit more.

I'd been thinking more and more about the Mitrofanoff and whether it would improve things for me and wondered if that was something I could explore again for the programme. Getting involved with the show was very much a means to an end for me and it didn't take long for the BBC to get me referred to a new hospital. They called and told me they'd found a specialist urology and gastroenterology team at University College London Hospital (UCLH).

I was able to speak to the hospital on the phone and we discussed some of the issues I faced. I mentioned the Mitrofanoff and they said they couldn't see any reason why something like that couldn't be offered. The prospect of finally leaving sores and nappies behind was exciting to me. I'd got my job and my flat and thought perhaps this would help me have a new start health-wise too.

I was given an appointment for October and the BBC said they'd pay for food and travel providing they could do some filming on the day, which I was fine with. Agnes and someone else came that morning and they were doing all the camera-work and sound themselves. We drove up to the train station and did an interview to camera out the front. It was all very embarrassing and Nick, knowing I was dreading it, deliberately drove by to have a look and laugh. Luckily, it was pretty early in the morning so there weren't too many people about.

We travelled down to King's Cross and did a bit of filming there just of me walking across the station. That was fine as no-one bats an eyelid there. You could be dressed as Mr Blobby and no-one would notice. At the hospital we did loads more filming out the front and in the lobby, which was huge and went up about four floors with all these glass walkways connecting everything up and big arty things on the walls. There was one embarrassing moment when Agnes and her assistant went up onto one of the walkways and directed me via an earpiece to walk across the lobby. I was all miked up and we were talking back and forth making sure they'd got what they needed.

A security guard came across looking quite concerned.

'Is everything okay?' he said.

It was only then that I realised I was walking through a hospital talking to myself and must have looked like a nutter!

I had an initial consultation with the specialist in private then mocked up something similar afterwards so the BBC could film it. The specialist and I discussed the problems I was having with my stomach as well as the Mitrofanoff and he said he wanted to take me into surgery for an exploratory so he could have a good look to see what was going on. He was very comfortable with the BBC being there and seemed quite pleased at the thought of being filmed for TV.

After the appointment I headed back to Lincolnshire and Agnes and her colleague stayed in London. Before we went our separate ways, we made a date for them to come up and do a bit of filming at Mum's, where we'd outline the background to my case and give them some footage to splice in with whatever else they got.

The BBC did the filming at Mum's and asked me to get in contact when I heard when my appointment would be. Initially I returned to London for some scans and then got the date for the exploratory. I called through to Agnes on the office number she had given me and left a message with someone there. When I didn't hear back, I called again and left another message, but again there was nothing. Bizarrely, I never heard from Agnes again and can only assume the programme was shelved.

The exploratory took place around November time. Mum came down to London with me and the hospital put us both up in a hotel. Under general anaesthetic they found I had stenosis, a narrowing of the colostomy from my stoma to a good five inches in. The area had almost completely closed up and because it wouldn't give like a muscle would they said they would need to cut it out. I discovered stomas generally need to be revised fairly regularly and mine had never been done. They booked me in for the operation in December and, as they couldn't be sure exactly what they'd find, told me my recovery could take anything from three days to a month.

Soon after the exploratory the problems with my stomach became worse than ever. I would have to take industrial loads of laxatives to get any relief and, because they had to be dissolved in water, even taking those would hurt like hell. I went to the GP and he prescribed some nutrient drinks to take four times a day instead of eating. The drinks made daily life more bearable but the weight started to drop off me.

Until that point I'd still been going to work but through a combination of how ill I was starting to feel and an increasingly unpleasant atmosphere in the office, I decided it was time to leave. It had never been a fantastic place to work, but I missed the sense of purpose having a job gave me and was determined that as soon I was well again I'd get something else.

Mum continued with her daily visits, I'd see Nick three to four times a week and Sam, my ex-colleague from the Spar, would often come over at weekends, which all kept me from becoming isolated. However, surviving on the nutrient drinks and a few mouthfuls of ice cream every now and again was making me very weak and I could feel myself starting to get down about it. I was just counting the days until the operation.

The day before the operation I knew I was very unwell. My stomach wasn't as bloated as it had been when things had got bad in the past, but the pain was crippling. In the morning, I pushed myself to gather up the things I needed for my hospital stay into a bag then spent the day on the sofa trying to deal with the pain.

Mum arrived mid-morning as always and knew immediately that things weren't good. She refused to leave me on my own and kept saying we ought to go to the hospital but I was determined to just get through to the next day. By late afternoon, I couldn't move and started being sick. Mum called Farmer and they took me to the doctor's, where they took one look at me and said I needed to go to hospital.

Peterborough was closest, but the journey was still one of the most agonising things I have ever experienced. I sat in the front of the car with my head hanging out of the window, continually being sick. Every vibration of the car, every bump, sent spasms through my entire body. Mum spent the entire 30-minute journey trying to get me to breathe and pant through the pain, like you would a woman in labour. Mum would manage to calm me down every minute or two and then the pain would start up again to the point where I couldn't breathe.

We got to the hospital and Farmer dropped us directly outside A&E. Mum was insistent she'd get me a wheelchair while, hunched over, I was determined I could try to walk. She went running off then came back with the wheelchair and scooped me into it. She rushed into the reception area calling for someone to help and I don't even really remember what happened next. One minute I was in the wheelchair and the next I was in a bed.

There were several nurses around me but they were all trainee military nurses and no-one seemed sure what needed to be done. I told them to get a cannula into me, which took them about ten attempts and left me covered in blood. The other pain was so bad that I couldn't even feel that. I told them my heart rate was always an issue during these episodes and they got me on a heart monitor then said they were going to put a tube down into my stomach. They tried to do that but it got stuck and I couldn't breathe, which was incredibly traumatic. They said they were going to try again but I put a stop to that.

I told them they needed to give me morphine, which they seemed to accept but as soon as a dose went into me, I was violently sick again and they started loading me up with anti-sickness drugs. I was so dehydrated from all the vomiting that my lips were cracking and bleeding. They gave me some of those little lollipops that are basically sponge sticks with flavours, which are awful really, but provided some relief at least.

I explained I was booked in for surgery at UCLH and told them I needed them to get me transferred down to there. Various faxes and phone calls were exchanged but UCLH didn't seem to have any record of me. In the end Peterborough said they were going to get an ambulance to take me down there. It took 13 hours for one to come free and UCLH were still saying I wasn't due in. My pain had eased to a degree but the thought of the two-hour journey was still frightening. The doctors gave me a big dose of morphine to get me through and thankfully I slept most of the way. Mum, who wasn't allowed to travel with me, got on the next train.

The confusion continued once I arrived at UCLH, where they maintained that they hadn't known I was coming. They put me into some kind of holding room until a doctor from gastroenterology came in and organised for me to be X-rayed. After about five hours they got me up to a ward, where a nurse said there was nowhere to put me. I ended up in a corner of the room with my saline drip taped to a wall.

I went to sleep and woke early the next day to find Mum sitting next to the bed. A surgeon came to see me and said they had still been unable to locate any record of the stenosis operation and as a result it wasn't possible to do it that day. Instead he proposed inserting a kind of balloon to stretch things as a temporary measure while the paperwork issue was resolved. I was so fed up that they'd messed up so badly but was willing to agree to anything for some relief. They took me down to theatre and during the process of anaesthetising me they had to push down on my neck to prevent any risk of regurgitation as a precaution because, even though I hadn't eaten for weeks, the operation was not planned and I had not been warned to have nil by mouth. It was a very unpleasant and frightening experience.

When I woke up, back on the ward, the area around my stoma was absolute agony. I had a feel around and could feel a huge pipe sticking out of it.

I managed to call out to a nurse.

'Help, please, you've got to get this thing out of me.'

It took about half an hour for a doctor to come and explain they'd left it in to see if it helped, by which time it was so painful I could barely talk. They yanked on this tube with no pain relief and I swear it was about two feet in. I'd never experienced anything like it. It was the final straw.

'That's it, I'm going home,' I announced.

They didn't seem to have a clue what they were doing and I was convinced if I stayed any longer they were going to end up killing me.

Mum begged me not to leave, but my mind was made up.

'Just get me the papers please. I'm discharging myself,' I told a nurse.

I was barely able to walk, was very pale, still in a lot of pain and was very angry. A nurse gave me some painkillers in an injection in my bum before I went, just to help me to get home. Just walking out of the hospital was so difficult because I was so bruised and sore where my bowel had been stretched, but I just wanted to be at home. I had lost all faith in the hospital and was terrified what they were going to do next.

Somehow Mum and I made it to King's Cross and got on a train. A group of teenagers were pointing and giggling at me, thinking I was blind drunk.

'Pack it in will you?' Mum yelled at them. 'She has literally just come out of surgery.'

I'd been in recovery at 5pm and was on the train by 7pm. I slept for most of the train ride and was so relieved when Mum and Farmer got me back to my flat. I laid down on the sofa and barely moved from there for two days. Mum did not want to leave me, but I insisted she go home at nights. I was so sick of being a burden to her.

I'd left UCLH on the Friday and on the Monday I got a call from them, saying I hadn't turned up for the operation I was scheduled to have. I could not believe it. It turned out that they have got several gastro teams and it seemed that when they kept saying they had no record of me, they hadn't checked if I was under another team. I was told there wasn't another slot for the operation until March.

I was convinced that I would not make it until then because I was just so weak. I'd lost well over 2st in the two months I'd been waiting and when I explained my concerns to the hospital, they found a slot on January 5. It was still almost three weeks away and the thought of all that time still not eating concerned me. I wondered whether I'd be strong enough for the operation or even if I'd make it that long. The nutrient drinks were literally all that was keeping me alive and, fearing the worst, I sat Mum down and talked to her about my wishes over funeral arrangements.

The night before the operation, I barely slept through nerves and excitement that things might be about to get better. I got to the hospital and was directed to a corridor full of people waiting with bags for one surgery or another. Everyone was quietly dealing with their own anxieties and after a few minutes of waiting I was called through to get gowned up. A lovely Nigerian nurse did a few pre-assessment checks and I admitted how scared I was, especially about having the anaesthetic after the previous time when they'd had to lean on my throat. She was such a warm character and said she would stay with me until I was out, which was such a comfort.

I was taken down at 8am and the last words I heard before drifting into unconsciousness were those of a nurse to a colleague.

'Make sure you take that off the bed. That's how things get left in people.' Very reassuring!

The surgery took three hours and the surgeon felt it had been successful though he'd had to take five or six inches of the large intestine away, which left me with very little. He explained that if there were further problems in the future, they might have to use the small intestine instead, which although it isn't uncommon worried me as nothing with my body works quite like it does in anybody else's.

The ward was full of women who'd had colostomy surgery and I got on with them all so well and the nurses were wonderful too. The lady in the next bed from me had just had hers put in because of cancer and was very concerned about how she would cope with it. We'd talk about it for a couple of hours every night and she seemed more confident afterwards. I ended up being in from the Tuesday to Friday and actually quite enjoyed it. Being able to eat again was amazing. As soon as I was strong enough, I went to the hospital shop and bought a chocolate bar and it tasted so good.

My 21st birthday was a few weeks after my surgery and Mum suggested we have a big party. It was a day that so many doctors, and in recent weeks I myself, had thought I wouldn't see. It really felt like a time to celebrate and for once I didn't even mind that I'd be centre of attention.

We decided to have the party at the social club and invited everyone who had been important in my life over the years. All my old friends, including Laura, Semrah and Daniel were there, Nick, my brothers and Farmer, my dad and Shirley, Mummy Mel and all that gang. I'm sure we asked Dianne Miller but I don't think she was able to make it, but we did have some of the Press photographers who had come to feel like friends over the years, including Woody from the Peterborough Evening Telegraph. I spent the evening walking around, smiling and chatting to everyone, all the time aware that on the wall, the framed photos of Nan were watching over us.

CHAPTER TWENTY-THREE

I'd been thinking for a while that I was almost ready to stop taking the anti-depressants, but hadn't quite taken the leap. My doctor had continued to supply them – swapping brands every now and again to keep them effective – since I went on them just before moving into my flat. Not long after my birthday, the brand was swapped once again. I didn't think much of it at the time and just kept taking them, still planning to call a halt to them soon.

It was great to be able to eat again and though I was still careful to avoid things that I knew had been a trigger for my problems in the past, I was enjoying food again. My stomach was working so well that I had a shock when I went to change my colostomy one time and found something solid and circular inside. On closer inspection I discovered it was a navy blue button exactly like the nurse's uniform button Mum had told had nearly killed me when I was tiny. I'm convinced this other one had been lying dormant somewhere in my system ever since and was finally flushed through thanks to my operation.

Nick and I were still spending a lot of time together and he had started teaching me guitar, which I really enjoyed. As big Dr Who fans we'd also begun a marathon of watching all the episodes from the beginning and it became a Saturday ritual for me to go over to his house, only a couple of streets away, to watch Dr Who and stuff ourselves with Reece's peanut butter cups.

I hoped I'd soon be strong enough to start looking for work again. Then I started getting backaches.

The aches started around February time and initially they were fairly mild and I did my best not to pay too much attention. It was in March, after a day turning soil in my garden, that the ache got more intense. It was a Saturday and I went round to Nick's as normal, assuming that I'd pulled a muscle.

As we watched TV, the pain started getting worse and I moved down to sit on the floor to try to ease the discomfort.

'You okay Jo?' Nick asked.

'It's my back, it's really getting to me today. I think I'm going to go home.'

It was only five minutes from Nick's house to my flat but he always walked me back and that night I couldn't get there quick enough. The pain was spreading up my back from the base and down into my legs. I just wanted to get back and be alone. I told myself that if I could get there and have a sleep it would be okay.

I said goodnight to Nick on the doorstep, grabbed my duvet and laid down on my sofa. I could barely move my legs and within two to three hours the pain had gone from sore to unbearable. I felt like my body was on fire, my back throbbing. I fell asleep on the sofa and woke up in the early hours, aware that I needed to get to the toilet to change my pad and bag.

I went to swing my legs off the sofa and the pain that shot through me was indescribable. The whole mid-section of my body, front to back was in agony. Even breathing hurt. I had to roll myself from the sofa onto the floor and crawl in the dark in blinding pain to the bathroom. I sorted myself out, grabbed a load of prescription and decided I'd take it back to the sofa with me so that I wouldn't have to move again. I crawled back along the hallway, biting my lip to stop myself screaming out in pain. I didn't want to wake the neighbour and cause a big scene. It took me an hour and a half in all to get to the bathroom and back to the sofa.

Mum arrived the next day as normal and found me crippled in pain on the sofa, Alan sitting quietly at my side as he always did when I was ill. He always knew and would sit and watch me constantly making sure I was okay.

'Jo, we need to get you an ambulance. You've got to have this checked out.'

'No, Mum. I've just overdone it in the garden, it'll sort out. I'm sick of hospitals. If I go, it'll just be hundreds of tests and they won't know what to do with me anyway.'

That day, I laid on the sofa slipping in and out of consciousness, unable to eat or move. I was in such pain that Mum was having to help with my toilet needs. I started to become confused, my heart was palpitating and I couldn't breathe, like I used to when I was having panic attacks. I felt like I was about to have a heart attack.

'We have got to get you to hospital!'

'No, Mum, I mean it. I'm not going.' I was terrified of being in hospital in that state and being that reliant on the nurses. Some of the experiences I'd had in the past hadn't given me great confidence in being well looked after.

'Right, well I'm calling the doctor at least.'

My GP came out and did a few checks – making sure I could feel my toes, which I could, though I couldn't move them because it hurt too much. He gave me some strong painkillers and told me to do my best to keep moving – standard advice for back pain. After he'd left, Mum was looking through the leaflets for the various drugs I was on and noticed that the latest anti-depressants listed a lot of my symptoms as potential side effects – palpitations, hot and cold flushes – it was all there. I was desperate to try anything to start feeling better and, convinced I didn't really need the anti-depressants any more anyway, I decided to come off them.

My heart stopped racing and all the breathlessness stopped from then, but the back pain did not go away. I laid on the sofa day in, day out unable to move or function. I'd watch CSI, Life on Mars and Dexter DVDs on repeat and started to lose track of whether it was night or day, just slipping in and out of sleep whenever the pain allowed. With a huge amount of effort and a lot of help from Mum, I was able to get to the bathroom for a wash round and that was about it. Mum kept trying to get me to go to hospital, but there was no way. It would just have been painful getting there, then while they prodded me about and they'd have no answers for me anyway. I preferred to be at home.

Mum came round each morning and looked after me all day before the same argument every night when I'd make her go home to be with Farmer and the boys. She would make me bottles of drink and leave all my prescription to hand then go out the door, saying she wished I'd just let her stay. She was already doing enough for me, running around after me all day, I couldn't allow her to stay at nights too.

Once Mum had gone, I'd often break down in tears. I had so much hope for the New Year and felt so defeated that things had gone so wrong. The nights seemed to go on so long and were not really any different to the days except that in the day, I'd lay looking out at my hallway, thinking this or that could do with being decorated again and knowing there was no way I could do it. Things got worse when I started to realise that my stomach was slowing up again too. Often after I'd eaten, I'd get the old bloating and feeling of sickness.

When it got to six weeks of me lying there, not getting much better, Mum arrived with Nan's old wheelchair.

'I'm not getting in that thing.'

'Are you going to lay there forever then? You won't go to hospital, you don't seem to be getting any better, at least if you insist on staying like this, in the wheelchair you can get out and have some air. It's doing you no good at all being in here every day.'

I wanted to argue but I didn't have the energy. Just getting into the wheelchair took a massive amount of effort, but when Mum wheeled me into the garden it did feel good to be outside. I could only manage ten minutes sitting before the pain got too much and Mum wheeled me back again.

I started to build up the amount of time I could spend in the chair each day and a few days after Mum first brought it, she took me into town in it. It was nice to be out but I didn't like being seen like that. I could see people looking and wondering what was wrong with me.

Gradually the pain in my back became slightly less overwhelming and Mum brought one of Nan's sticks for me to use. I was able to hobble about the house with it and could then use it to get around the supermarket if Mum drove me into town. It wasn't as bad as being out in the wheelchair but it still annoyed me that people would look at me. Some would even make comments or ask questions.

'You're a bit young to have that thing. What have you been up to?' an old guy asked me one day.

I couldn't believe people would actually say that sort of thing. 'Just a bit of a bad back,' I said, feeling furious.

A couple of months after my back problems had started I had a follow-up appointment in London for my stomach. Mum wanted me to go in the wheelchair but there was no way I was doing that. I went with the stick. It was very hard going because I got tired so easily with it, but I had set my mind to it. Just getting from King's Cross to the hospital was exhausting. I hobbled from the train to the taxi rank and got a cab and then once I got to the hospital there was a lot of walking to get to the building where my appointment was. Mum and I then had a two-hour wait before seeing the consultant. He listened to the problems I was still having with my stomach and suggested a few things my doctor could prescribe to try to ease things. The day felt like a marathon but it was quite a significant step that I'd managed to do it.

My back was still sore and uncomfortable right up to Christmas and New Year, though it had got a lot better. I was always aware of it and became very responsive to what my body was telling me. I knew the sensation that triggered the pain and had to be careful not to stay still for too long or do too much activity in one go because either could make it seize up. I could walk without the stick most days but the shop at end of street was about as far as I could get. I was very careful in everything I did because I just did not want to go back to those days stuck on the sofa. When my birthday came round again, I couldn't help but think back to how hopeful and positive I'd felt the year before.

I so wanted to get a job but I'd done the 'trial period' of work allowed while claiming incapacity benefit and if I did any more I'd have to be sure I was fit enough to work every day to earn a regular wage. I feared I'd commit to something, give up my benefits and then my back would go and I'd be left without an income and fighting to get the payments reinstated. My stomach was more of a problem again too and some days I'd wake up and the bloating would mean I could barely move. What job could I take that would allow me to turn up one day and then maybe have a week off sick? I felt trapped on benefits and I hated what that said about me. I felt sure people were judging me for sitting at home all day doing nothing and I didn't even blame them. I hated waking up each day and having no purpose, but I wasn't even allowed to get voluntary work because if I did it meant I was 'fit'. Part-time work wasn't an option either because if I wasn't on incapacity, my rent and Council Tax would go up to full whack. I knew there was no way. Some days I could do a 9-5 in an office, but others I was in pain all day and unable to function properly.

I was pleased to be off the anti-depressants and didn't want to go back on them and risk becoming reliant forever more, but the old feelings of hopelessness were starting to return. I could feel that old sense of anxious panic within me when I got up each morning. I tried to make sure I had things to do each day, some sort of aim, but nothing I did really mattered. Mum came each day and we'd chat and I'd see Nick, but there was no real reason to do it.

I'd look at the house and think 'I ought to vacuum,' but then I'd think 'what does it matter if I don't?' I'd keep telling myself to just do the cleaning, at least that was something practical to do, but the other side of me just could not see the point. I'd end up in a state of anxious panic, not knowing how to make myself feel better. My mind racing with 'what's the point?' thoughts. It made me feel angry with myself. How could I be anxious when I had absolutely nothing that I needed to do?

In the back of my mind was always the thought of the long-term, the future and what it had in it and I couldn't see anything. I knew I would never have a relationship, I couldn't get a job, I couldn't have a family. All the future was likely to bring was more illness and disappointment. I felt trapped in my own mind and would walk down the street seeing other people talking and laughing and feel so different to them that it was as if I wasn't entirely human. Being out, especially if there were too many people about, started to make me very anxious and panicky and I began to plan trips into town based on when I thought it would be quiet.

The constant whirr of thoughts and self-analysis left me feeling completely drained and stopped me from sleeping well, which made it worse. Very occasionally something would make me think about how unfeminine I was and for a second I'd feel a jolt of panic about that too. Make-up was a mystery to me and one I couldn't be bothered with. I couldn't be doing with messing about with my hair either and had got mine cut shorter and shorter because it was easier. I liked plain, simple clothes, long-sleeved T-shirts and jeans, never dresses, never anything floral or fancy. I'd quickly answer all the points in my head – a lot of women didn't wear make-up, a lot of women had short hair, a lot of women wore similar clothes to me. It wasn't like I wore male clothes, they were women's clothes, just simple ones. There were a lot more butch women than me. I wasn't actually butch at all, just not overly feminine. I told myself that none of it meant anything. My lack of interest in my appearance was more to do with the fact that I hated my body and my reflection. My body, covered in stitches and so alien to what it should look like, made me feel a bit sick.

A worry I couldn't switch off so easily was my financial situation. The credit cards I'd taken out when I moved into the flat had got a bit of a balance on them and that was a big concern. A lot of what I'd spent wasn't out of choice. Travelling to and from London for hospital appointments often cost me more than £50 a time.

My car wasn't reliable any more and I was constantly having to save for parts and ask Farmer to fix it for me. A lot of the time, it sat broken on the drive and when my back was bad I was even more isolated. I did have a bike and was sometimes able to use that to get about even when walking had become difficult, but it wasn't like I needed to be anywhere anyway. The fear of not being able to pay the bills on the house and the frustration over my car played on my mind a lot. I felt like I didn't want the responsibility of any of it. Everything just seemed so black.

Silly things would often make me boil with rage because I felt that everything I touched went wrong. One time I was trying to open a can of something for dinner and the can opener just would not work. I threw it at the disgusting back door in my disgusting kitchen and hated everything about myself and my life. If I didn't have some kind of head problem perhaps I could have got some qualifications and maybe I could have got a job and wouldn't be living in a place like this. If I had just dealt with things differently and hadn't got these stupid phobias. If I was just like everybody else.

I walked over to the kitchen drawer and ripped it open. Inside was a black-handled kitchen knife. I felt like I'd gone into a sort of daze where I wasn't completely in control anymore. I took the knife from the drawer and made my way into the bathroom where there were no windows for anyone to see in. I shut the door behind me and pushed my sleeve up above my elbow.

I started to slice at my arm. I didn't really know what I was doing or why, but I kept pushing the blade across my skin in a kind of autopilot until it broke through the skin. It hurt, but it also felt strangely good. My mind wasn't racing any more. I was focused on cutting. Blood started to trickle down my arm and to drip onto the navy blue and white diamond tile-effect lino that had been left behind by the old tenant. I sliced a little more, feeling a sort of achievement in seeing the wound open up a bit. As I bled, I felt all the anger and frustration kind of leaving me. It was as if it had been trapped and this was a way of letting it out.

I stopped before the cut became too deep – the last thing I wanted was to have to go to hospital and explain this to anyone. I dropped the knife into the big ceramic basin and grabbed some toilet roll to press onto the wound. I knew I needed to dress the wound and to clear up the mess and felt a strange calmness in having something to concentrate on. Once the bleeding was under control, I put some bleach on some paper and wiped the floor, then the sink and the knife. I took the knife back to the kitchen, put it back in the drawer and reached into the cupboard for a little first aid box I knew was at the back. I wiped my arm over with an antibacterial wipe, wincing a bit at how sore it was then pushed a compression pad onto the wound and strapped it on with some microfibre tape.

I didn't feel good about what I'd done and wasn't sure why I'd done it but, although it made no sense, it had made me feel better. It sort of broke the cycle of frustration and brought some relief. I felt a sense of calm that I hadn't had in days. I knew it was wrong and deep down it was just more proof of my 'head problems', but I'd discovered a coping mechanism.

CHAPTER TWENTY-FOUR

Cutting myself became something I'd turn to every few days. I knew I wasn't well and some days I felt as if I wanted to tell Mum and ask for help, but I was scared of being really honest about it. I often thought that I just couldn't cope with being in the world and felt like I needed to go into a mental health facility, but was convinced that if I did, I'd have crossed a line that I'd never fully step back over.

Evenings became the worst part of the day for me because they seemed so long and empty. I couldn't bear the thought of sitting in front of the TV watching another meaningless programme so I started going to bed at about 7pm. In the morning I never wanted to get up and have to face another day, but I knew Mum would be round and I didn't want her or anyone else to know how bad I was feeling or think I was mad. I'd get up and go and sit in my dining room in front of my computer watching the previous night's TV just for something to do.

Mum would burst in each day, always full of energy and tales of what was going on with the boys at home.

'Morning darling, how are you?'

'Not so good today.'

'What's wrong? Your stomach playing up?'

'Not really, I'm just feeling a bit down.'

'It's lovely out there today, you ought to get yourself outside.'

'I can't really see the point.'

I could see her getting angry. 'Come on Jo, you can't be like that. There's no point just feeling sorry for yourself.'

I knew I was hard work to be around and Mum's attempts to shrug my feelings off were her way of trying to pull me through it, but I felt like she just didn't understand me. Sometimes she'd get so angry with me, we'd row and she would storm out, but she'd always be back the next day. I learned to try to keep my thoughts to myself. It didn't help either of us to argue over it.

Eventually, sat in front of the computer oblivious to whatever programme was on in front of me one day, I came to the conclusion that there was no point in carrying on any more. Dropping in on me every day, checking I was all right and worrying about me was taking up Mum's time and she could have been doing something else. I was also a burden to Jarred, Chris and Farmer and Nick, who still kept popping round even though I barely had anything to say. I was no fun to be around and I was contributing nothing to the world. It didn't seem fair to keep dragging everyone else down. I'd been nothing but a problem to everyone from the moment I was conceived and felt the doctors had probably been right when they said I should have just faded away.

I walked across to the calendar that I got off the front of the Top Gear magazine which I subscribed to each year and flicked through to a few weeks ahead. I was thinking about the best way to make sure my family didn't have too much to sort out once I'd gone. I had various cupboards and drawers full of clutter and paperwork and decided I wanted to clear all those out and get rid of most of my clothes so they didn't have to do all that. I'd have to take a look at my finances and make sure everything was as in order as it could be. The family didn't need to be thinking about paying utility bills and things when they were trying to sort out a funeral. I looked at it in a very cold and logical way and it just seemed like the best thing to do.

I felt I'd have everything sorted by the beginning of April, but Mum's birthday was in April so decided to wait until May. I found a date, so insignificant in any other way that I don't remember which date it was and marked it with a cross. That was the day that I would kill myself.

I knew I'd have to be found by someone and I didn't want it to be too horrible for them so decided an overdose would be best. An overdose would also mean that I could be viewed okay, which I thought might be a comfort to my family. Seeing Nan after her death, so peaceful, had meant so much to me.

The next few times that I went into town I bought a packet of Paracetamol and put them away in the drawer under my coffee table. I wanted to make sure I had enough to do the job properly when the time came and was careful to make sure they weren't anywhere Mum might stumble across them.

The depression had got so bad that I felt almost completely unable to function at all. All I thought about was wanting to not be here anymore. My only hesitation was the impact my suicide would have on Mum, Farmer and the boys, which worried me a lot. I didn't want them to feel bad or guilty and, although I kept telling myself that once the shock of my death had settled, it would be a relief to them and they'd see it was for the best, it was a concern I couldn't easily shake.

I sat at the computer one morning with those thoughts going round in my mind and Mum arrived. Something just clicked in me and I couldn't hide my fear and misery any longer. As she walked into the room, I began to sob. I put my head down on the table in front of me and just cried and cried and cried.

'What is it love? What's wrong?'

'I can't do it any more Mum. It'd be better for everyone if I was gone.'

'Gone? What do you mean, gone?'

'Dead, Mum. I just want to be dead.'

Mum got her phone straight out and called my GP, which I didn't want her to, but Mum wouldn't discuss it. The doctor said she'd come out and I expected she would put me straight into an institution. Until she arrived, I sat in the same position, crying, while Mum busied herself around the house and kept coming back to check on me.

'I want to work through a questionnaire with you,' the doctor said. 'It helps give me a guide of just how low you are feeling.'

The questions were things like: 'Have you found yourself feeling hopeless?' 'Have you had trouble sleeping?' 'Have you thought about hurting yourself?'

I had to rate them all out of ten, with ten meaning very much so and 0 not really. I answered the questions honestly and was an eight or nine on most of them. There didn't seem any point in hiding anything. The doctor said I needed to see a psychiatrist, but it could take up to a year to get a referral through. She wanted to put me on anti-depressants in the meantime and to send me for some counselling. I wasn't really bothered what she suggested or how long she thought it would take because, after all this hassle and humiliation, I was more set than ever on following through with my plan.

The doctor handed Mum a prescription for some pills and they had a chat on the doorstep before she went. Mum went off to pick the pills up straight away and made sure I took the first one. Over the course of the next few days, she spent a lot of time at my flat and made sure I knew that she was willing me to get better. I wasn't expecting the pills to have any impact at all and was more amazed than anyone when, within a matter of days, I started to feel that things were not so bleak.

The pills were obviously very, very good because I suddenly just seemed to have my get up and go back and was able to focus my mind on doing stuff. The tablets lifted the darkness and stopped me from seeing bad in everything. Whereas before, the thought of doing the housework was crushing, I was able to get on with it and getting it done made me feel good. I just felt able to deal with each day.

Within a couple of weeks the appointment for an assessment with the counsellor came through and I actually felt like seeing someone and talking about things might be a good thing. I could talk to Mum up to a point, but always felt I had to dilute things to make sure I didn't upset or worry her.

The counsellor was based in an NHS mental health centre in a Victorian town house in a residential street in Spalding town centre. I went up there on my bike, looking forward to it. One or two others were sitting quietly in the waiting room, no-one wanting to talk or make eye contact. I flicked through a display of leaflets while I waited and picked up a couple about coping with depression that I thought might be useful.

The counsellor called me though and she was a youngish woman who introduced herself as Julie. The assessment turned out to just be a really honest talk and some more scoring, like when the doctor had come out to me.

'I feel as if the black cloud has really lifted since I've been back on medication,' I told Julie. 'The thoughts I was having about ending things aren't in my head so much now, but I do feel I need help.'

'Okay, that's good to hear. You're in a better place. What I'd like to do is to just get to know a little about you so that I can find out more about the types of things we can talk about in future. Would you, perhaps, be able to tell me a little about your childhood?'

I outlined the basics about my birth, my condition, the Press coverage, the problems I'd had at school and then how it had hit me when I lost Nan. It didn't take a rocket scientist to see that all those things had taken their toll on me and led me to this place. I was able to talk about it all with very little emotion. I've always been very good at being matter of fact about things. Even when I spoke about Nan, I didn't get upset, but it still felt like a huge weight was lifting. Even though that appointment was just an assessment, just being completely open and honest with someone made me feel like I was making headway.

Julie was almost open-mouthed as she listened. 'My goodness me, there's no wonder that you are depressed.'

I was quite taken aback when she said that. Here was a woman who listened to people talking about their problems all day long and she felt I was justified in being down. I had never considered that it was understandable for me to feel the way I did. After a lifetime of feeling like an oddity and freak, Julie's reaction made me think that maybe I was normal after all.

Julie told me to make an appointment to come back to see her in a couple of weeks for a proper session. It felt like a bit of a lifeline and I had that little lift of something to look forward to that could help to get me through. I hadn't yet got past the date I'd marked on the calendar, but I thought about it a lot less. It still felt like a bit of a safety net, a back-up plan, but it was fast becoming a date I just needed to get past.

I arrived for my next appointment still feeling pretty positive. Julie sort of categorised everything and said we'd take each category at a time and look at the problems relating to that. We covered health, family, money, everything really. I felt my biggest issues were my grief over Nan and not really having ever dealt with my very erratic and unusual childhood.

As a kid, when everything was going on, I remember everyone worrying about the impact all the media stuff was having on Jarred. There was a fear that he would feel left out or ignored. I was so good at hiding my feelings that it was as if everyone, myself included, didn't realise I had emotions. Counselling helped me to recognise that things did affect me and I was a proper person like everyone else. I'd always felt I was strange because things like my grandad dying didn't seem to cause any reaction in me, but the thought of being in a classroom made me a wreck. Things that should have bothered me didn't seem to and things that shouldn't bother me did. Julie helped me to see that I bottled things up and they came back at me in other ways, which was along the lines of what the psychiatrist had said when I was a kid.

I had three sessions with Julie and on the whole I found them so useful. A couple of times she tried things with me where I was supposed to do word associations with picture cards, that sort of thing and I never really got that. Devilment made me want to just pick anything that could be seen to be sexual! Talking about things, though, in a way I'd never really done before was a definite help. Ironically, the fact that I was feeling better seemed to work against me. Julie told me my scores on the assessments had improved so much that she felt able to decrease our sessions. I left our third meeting expecting to get another appointment through for a few months' time, but it never arrived. I think there was so much demand for counselling services that unless you were at the most extreme end of suicidal there weren't the resources to keep seeing you. I never expected to come back from the dark place I'd been to, but I had.

Keeping myself positive became a day-by-day battle and I always felt I was on a knife-edge, just hoping my mental state didn't get too bad. I consciously tried not to lock emotions away and to acknowledge feelings of sadness and anger and allow myself to experience them. I didn't always win the battle to stay upbeat and every so often I'd feel very low and trapped again.

I learned that if I was around anyone else when I felt that way, I tended to start offloading on them, then I'd feel guilty, which made me much worse. So, when I was down, I'd retreat a bit and allow myself some space to let it pass. When you are depressed you feel different to everyone else and not being around other people somehow stopped me from continuing to make the comparisons and I didn't seem to get so down. I actually withdrew quite a lot from everyone and only really maintained contact with my family and Nick.

One of the ways I made life bearable was to let go of a lot of the aspirations I used to have, which saved me from hurting over how unlikely those things were to happen. When I was a teenager, I constantly hoped to have a family of my own one day, but I decided not to allow my mind to go there any more. It was easier not to dream about those things than to deal with the devastating disappointment of not being able to have them.

CHAPTER TWENTY-FIVE

Something that really knocked me off balance happened when I was going through my post one day and glanced at the name on a letter and realised it was addressed to Joel David Holliday. The letter was something official from the local council in Spalding and I had two copies – one to Joel and one to Joella. I stood in the hallway and felt speechless for a second, then quite worried. I couldn't make out how that name was even in their system and it made me wonder again whether there was an ongoing problem with my identity.

I rang the council and explained that I needed to see someone, which was quite a battle in itself because I didn't want to go into it all on the phone. I was quite angry in a way because that identity should have been long gone. In a way, for me, it never really existed because I'd only been a year old when I'd stopped being Joel.

The person I saw at the council recognised my name and knew the background to my story and was very apologetic from the start. She explained that the letter had been automatically generated and there was obviously a gremlin in the system. She went off to see if she could work out which database the name still existed on and it turned out it was linked in some way to my National Insurance number. It made me think back to being sent the temporary number when I was 16.

I had to go to Boston to iron it all out and sat there in the middle of the Jobcentre, with everyone else milling about, trying to explain my background to a middle-aged guy who just didn't have a clue. He thought I'd been given a temporary number because I was from abroad, which he didn't seem to be able to grasp was not the case. In the end he scribbled an explanation on my forms and that seemed to put an end to it. The whole thing annoyed me because it was a big piece of my past that I preferred to be buried. The reminder wasn't welcome and dragged some of those old feelings of self-doubt to the surface again.

The following couple of years were dominated by health issues, which seemed to take up an amazing amount of time. The back and hip pain came back quite badly at the end of 2010 and I took myself off to A&E in Boston. They sent me for some X-rays, which showed that the bone density of my left hip was very diminished and my spine appeared to be leaning into it and trapping the nerves. They referred me back to UCLH, who sent me for physio at Peterborough and when that didn't work they referred me on to a spinal specialist in Nottingham. They felt the problem was all interwoven with the surgery I'd had on my pelvis when I was little and said there was nothing that could be done. They warned me it might deteriorate further over time and said there was a chance I could end up in a wheelchair.

My bowel was also a big problem again and pretty much didn't work at all unless I took about ten times the amount of laxatives I should have done. It was very hard to function with the degree of bloating and feeling sick, which happened every few days. I tried every tablet going and was referred for irrigation which eased it for a while then stopped having any effect. The only plus side was that there was a kind of freedom in the fact that it was so awful all the time. Whereas I'd previously been careful to try not to eat anything to aggravate it, at that stage it didn't seem to matter what I had so if I fancied a fry-up, I had it.

On the days when my hips were bad, I could barely get up to make a cup of tea without hobbling on my stick. Once it got like that, I knew it would be a few weeks of it being almost impossible to drive, difficulty in getting to the shops and functioning in any real way and there was no getting away from the fact that when I was ill and less able to do anything, I did dwell on things and feel down. I had a good bout of depression every few months that could last a few days or a few weeks. There was always a part of me that secretly felt maybe I would be better off dead even though I no longer had a serious plan to do anything about it.

On the good days, I tried to do things that would make me feel better about everything, like gradually decorating my flat. The council came in and redid my kitchen and bathroom which were really desperately in need. Finally, I had a proper shower unit fitted above the bath, which meant there was finally enough pressure for it not to be cold all the time and was a lot less depressing. I replaced the old offcuts of carpet I'd been given for the dining room when I moved in with laminate and ripped out the nasty old gas fire in the living room and had it replaced with a nice modern one.

Mum, who had finally started to do something with the psychic gift she had by doing readings as a medium, decided to open a spiritual café and helping to plan that and get it off the ground gave me another outlet for my thoughts. While I helped in the café, my mind wandered to the hormone tablets I'd been taking since I was little and I realised I'd not had them reviewed in years. I knew the hormones were important for the health of my bones and, with my hip problems being as they were, I decided to go along to the doctor's to ask them to check and make sure I didn't need a change in dose.

My doctor referred me to an endocrinologist at Boston hospital and I, a bit naïvely, went along for the appointment, thinking I'd just get a 'yay' or 'nay' on whether I was taking the right tablets. It hadn't occurred to me that we'd have to rake over the whole gender thing again. But, obviously, he looked at things from the point of view of being a specialist with a new patient and wanting to have all the information to hand before he began prescribing anything. I'd taken Mum along to the appointment with me and she was sitting next to me when the doctor told me he wanted me to run a string of blood tests, including a chromosome test.

There had always been so much doubt over whether I'd ever had a chromosome test when I was little and I half believed it wasn't actually possible to run a conclusive chromosome test after all the years of hormones I'd taken. I looked at Mum and realised that both of us had always wondered deep-down what the test would say. It was as if curiosity had finally got the better of us and neither of us commented as the endocrinologist filled in a form for the test to be done.

When we left the appointment, Mum and I walked straight down to the pathology lab for me to have bloods taken.

'Do you really want this chromosome one done?' Mum asked.

'I just want to make sure the tablets are right, so if he thinks it's necessary, I don't see the problem,' I told her.

'You know that whatever it says, it doesn't really mean anything? Even some people with fully formed female genitalia have XY chromosomes.'

'I'm fine with it, Mum. It'll be interesting to know what it says, but it doesn't really change anything.'

I felt the results had a lot less implications for me than they did for Mum because I knew for her they could throw up all sorts of feelings of regret and guilt. I told myself that, for me, they couldn't and wouldn't really change anything. Maybe if I hadn't had all the other health issues to deal with all my life, my gender would have seemed more important, but it was the one part of my condition that didn't cause me day-to-day problems. I'd never felt the need to look too deeply into a chromosome test because whatever the result, I couldn't see that it would make my life any different or make me any happier. While I awaited the results, I considered that maybe I had started off life as a boy, but told myself that even if that were true, a clinical decision had been made to make me a girl and I was therefore female.

It took quite a few weeks for the results to come back and, although I was keen to see what they would be, I was concerned how Mum would react to them. I told her that in the same situation as she'd been when I was little, I'd have made the same decision she had and so would anyone else. It was what the doctors told her she should do, so how could she have done any other? I think Mum was expecting, maybe hoping, it would be an inbetween result, an XXY, intersex result, but I was trying to prepare myself for it to be male, XY.

It did cross my mind that if the result was XY, I could perhaps just not tell Mum and save her the guilt, but it wasn't really practical. She'd always liked to come to hospital appointments with me, both to support me and because she had more knowledge of my condition than anyone. I worried that if I didn't take her to the results appointment she might feel hurt and in reality I wouldn't have wanted to lie to her anyway.

I'd had a reasonable week emotionally when we went for the results and we were both quite relaxed. Being at hospital is so normal to us that it was just like a regular day.

'So, I've had a look through everything and we weren't far out on your hormone tablets before, but I think a slight adjustment is going to be in order,' the doctor began. 'I'm going to change your prescription slightly and see how you get on and I'm going to want to see you back here regularly to keep a monitor on it. Getting this hormone balance right will almost certainly help to address some of the depression issues you have spoken of.'

While he talked the doctor was flicking through my notes on his desk, glancing down at results of the tests I'd had, but it didn't seem he was going to actually address them. I was aware of what he was saying, but really wanted to know what the chromosome result had been. I scanned the paperwork in front of him and then my eyes fell upon the letters 'XY'.

'Could you tell me the outcome of the chromosome test please?' I'd seen it but needed to have confirmation. 'It was XY, wasn't it?'

'The chromosome test, like everything else we look at, should not be treated in isolation. The notion of there being two distinct and separate genders is becoming very outdated thanks to today's science so we really must treat these results as a small part of the entire picture.'

'But they were XY?'

'Well, yes they were XY, but, due to the cloacal exstrophy, your reproductive organs never developed and the female classification was made, quite properly.'

'But if I hadn't have had cloacal exstrophy, I would have been male?'

'That is one way of viewing things, but it can be unhelpful to deal in hypotheticals. I think what we need to focus on is today's position and how best to ensure you are getting the right treatment to keep you well.'

I didn't disagree with him, but just needed to have my status confirmed. When I think back to the appointment, I can still see the XY written on the sheet in front of him.

'Is there some counselling Jo can access to help her deal with these results?' Mum asked.

'It's not something that is within my remit, but I should think we can give you some numbers for the mental health teams,' the doctor said. He was compassionate and very nice, but seemed keen to focus on the medication rather than sifting over the decisions that had been made in my past and, in a way, I agreed with him. We talked a bit more about adjusting my hormone tablets and then the appointment was over. I didn't bother asking for any numbers for the mental health team because I didn't see the point. A decision had been made for me when I was tiny and that was it. Nothing had changed.

On the way back to the car, Mum asked if I was okay.

'I'm fine, are you?' I said.

'I am, yeah, course. You could still be intersex you know, chromosomes don't mean everything.'

'Mum, XY means male. That's what I was, but it's fine, okay? You shouldn't feel bad about it.' The truth didn't bother me but I didn't want to keep pretending. We didn't discuss it any more.

A few days later, I went round to Mum's and had a game of pool with Jarred. I knew Mum had spoken to him and Farmer about the results and, still concerned for her, I asked Jarred if she was okay and he said she was.

When I won the game, Jarred joked about it without thinking. 'Beaten by a girl,' he said.

'Well not technically, I suppose,' I said and we laughed. I just did not want to see it as a big deal.

Regardless of my determination that the result was insignificant to my life, I did find that my mind wandered at times to what might have been if I'd never had cloacal exstrophy. It would have meant that I would have grown up to be a man, I wouldn't have had a childhood that was so strange, I could have survived school, maybe gone to university, I might be married with kids. It made me feel a bit envious of the life I could have had. I wondered whether I'd be working and what I'd be doing.

I began to wonder about the whole issue of gender and started to think that perhaps I didn't necessarily need to have a gender. Some other countries have legislation now to recognise that some people are inbetween sexes and I started to consider whether I could view myself, as Mum had suggested, as intersex. With my short hair and neutral clothes, on more than one occasion, I'd had people accidentally call me 'sir' at first glance before quickly correcting themselves. It had always stung a little when that had happened but I'd felt more embarrassed and awkward for them than anything.

From the internet I could see that there are all sorts of 'differences of sex development' conditions – as they are now beginning to be called instead of 'intersex'. Doctors and people with the conditions are just beginning to get others to understand that gender is like a sliding scale. All babies start off with a womb but in a 'typical' male there is an X chromosome and a Y chromosome. The Y chromosome tells the body to create testes and they release testosterone and cause the penis and scrotum to grow. The Y chromosome also tells the body to get rid of the womb. A 'typical' female has XX chromosomes and, instead of testes, ovaries form, as do a clitoris and labia and the womb remains. Gender is a spectrum with males that have a penis, testes and XY chromosomes at one end and females that have a clitoris, labia, womb and XX chromosomes at the other and all kinds of variations in between.

When I thought about my childhood, I was in no doubt that all the birth certificate stuff had caused me a lot of problems. I felt angry that my family had been forced to fight for my birth certificate in the way they had. I even wondered if I'd have got better medical care if the birth certificate battle hadn't been necessary because perhaps the doctors were scared to treat me with the constant fear we might be about to run off to the lawyers or Press.

If it hadn't been for the birth certificate fight, maybe I'd have been given surgery to at least give me the appearance of a female rather than just being left stitched up and neither one way nor the other. Maybe there would have been earlier intervention around my hips and something could have been done to lessen the chances of them giving up on me completely one day. I didn't blame my family for fighting for the birth certificate – it was another thing that I don't feel as if Mum had any choice but to do – but I did blame the system for forcing me to be dragged through all of that.

The issue of gender and the facts relating to my gender started to go round in my head whilst I helped out at the café. I began to allow thoughts that I'd never dared to allow to surface before come into my head and stay there for a moment. With the benefit of hindsight, I even decided that it would have been less psychologically damaging to have been a boy without a penis than a girl who had to fight for recognition as female.

In childhood, I'd had moments of wondering if my love of cars and football was significant but had always told myself that loads of girls like those things and I didn't subscribe to basic gender stereotypes. I'd hated all girly clothes, but I'd always told myself it was because they were impractical for me. It was true that skirts did not support my colostomy in the way leggings and trousers did. I always wanted to play outside, to run and climb. So did lots of girls. I'd never felt comfortable with long hair and make-up. Loads of women had short hair and didn't wear make-up. I'd always adopted male roles in play, wanting to be the fireman, policeman and hero, never the princess. So? I was attracted to women not men, but thousands of people are gay. I always felt like I didn't fit, like I was different, like something was wrong.

It occurred to me that I'd spent my life being told by others and telling myself that I was a girl, but had never been able to suppress who I really was. Over time, the one thought I'd never allowed myself to have bubbled up. I was a man and I was living a lie.

EPILOGUE

When I was looking after Nan, I lived in fear every day of finding out that she had passed in the night, but when she actually died, the moment wasn't as frightening as the thought of it had been. Accepting that I was male was much the same. It was one of those things I had been so terrified of that I'd buried it so far down to avoid ever having to face it, but once it happened, even though it was a big thing, it wasn't as horrible as I'd always thought.

Through the internet, I discovered a man who lived in Tasmania, who had been born with cloacal exstrophy and was raised as a girl until he finally discovered the full truth of his past in his early twenties. Although he'd never had to endure the birth certificate battle or anything like that, a lot of what he'd been through in his life – the confusion over his self image, the operations and the depression – mirrored mine. We got in contact with each other and the emails and texts we exchanged really helped me. My biggest remaining concern was how my decision would impact on Mum and I was able to email my friend in Tasmania and ask how he'd broached the subject with his family and how they'd reacted. His responses reassured me a lot.

Much like when I'd been trying to tell her I was gay, Mum seemed to guess what I'd decided about my gender.

'Do you ever consider going back?' Mum asked during a discussion about my health and the test results I'd had.

'I have been thinking about it a bit lately,' I admitted.

'I thought so,' Mum said. 'You know we'll support you whatever you want.'

I think dealing with the emotions of whether she'd done the right thing by me as a baby did bother her quite a bit and I know she felt a lot of anger at herself and the doctors, but she played it down to me. She wanted me to be able to get on with what I needed to do.

For so long I'd struggled to form relationships and friendships with other people and I think it was partly because I didn't really know who I was. I always felt a bit as if I was trying to pretend to be someone I wasn't, but I hadn't realised it was gender-related. I'd always put it down to the 'head problems' and depression, but once I started to commit to the idea of returning to being male, I felt easier in myself. All the anxiety I used to carry around all the time, even when I was just walking along the road, started to seep away. So many things that had bothered me about not seeming to fit in were easily explained once I accepted it was because I was male.

When I bumped into the dad of my old friend from the Spar, Sam, I stopped and chatted and when he gave me her new phone number, I found that I wanted to text to see how she was. For so long, I'd avoided maintaining friendships but I didn't feel like I had to keep away from everyone any more. I wasn't getting the regular bouts of all-consuming depression I'd come to accept as part of everyday life. Although I still had the odd down day, it wasn't 'depression'.

I started to think about how I could improve my life and the Mitrofanoff came back to mind yet again. All my other health problems had meant it had been pushed to the back-burner for a very long time but I got an appointment about it at UCLH and while I was there I told my urologist I was considering returning to male.

I was at first surprised and then shocked and angry to discover that my urologist had dealt with cloacal exstrophy cases before where people had been assigned to female and had to return to male. It meant he was very comfortable with the subject, which was good in terms of helping me get to where I need to be, but I can't believe how many people this must have happened to. Until very recently medical wisdom was that boys born without a penis should just be raised female. From what I understand, there are old-school clinicians out there who still believe it and are still doing it. We never hear about the children or what happens to them because, unlike me, they are given female birth certificates from the start.

I understand that there was once research that suggested it was the right thing to do but surely now there's enough evidence that it just doesn't work? I think the decisions are generally taken much more carefully now but how can any doctor actually believe that babies become the gender they are told they are? I think my case proves that gender is far more than a matter of clothes or conditioning. I was raised a girl in every way but I was absolutely a boy.

My urologist suggested getting all of my care moved to UCLH where they had teams of psychologists to discuss my gender decision with me as well as surgeons who could help make it happen. At my first psychologist's appointment we talked through all of my past. The psychologist got quite philosophical about gender and the variations of male and female there are, which was interesting, but the more I discovered about my own situation the more straightforward I thought my case was.

As far as I am concerned, cloacal exstrophy isn't even an 'intersex' condition. All I ever was was a boy without a penis and my biggest problem was caused in spending so many years trying to convince myself and everyone else that I was female. Getting the chromosome results undid so much of the confusion and damage.

I finally got to see my medical records during one of my trips to London and it really confirmed that returning to male was the right decision. My new UCLH endocrinologist had given me my notes to take with me to my urology appointment, which was a few hours later and it was too enticing an opportunity to miss. I went straight to the café, got myself a drink and sat down to have a good read. There were dozens of references to the testicles that had been removed when I was a baby and some of the notes stated that they'd been attached to a healthy male reproductive system. One specialist had even written to the Registrar General to say it would be wrong to change my birth certificate to female because I had definitely been born male. Some of the letters described what they'd taken away in surgery and stated that it had been done because it would be easier to construct female genitalia than trying to form something male.

A part of me felt extremely angry that they'd made that decision based on what would be 'easiest' from a surgical point of view. The irony is that they never even completed the job of constructing female genitalia. I was never even made to be a woman. I was just left somewhere in between.

It is still not clear whether my body is going to be up to having the Mitrofanoff, which would involve some of my intestine being used to create an inlet into my bladder and to enlarge it. I'd then have a little opening on the opposite side to my stoma where I'd be able to insert a catheter at intervals to drain the contents. It's something I'm still exploring.

Hormone-wise, I have made the switch from taking oestrogen to testosterone and I am on the list for surgery to construct a penis. It has been strange seeing my body shape change, the arrival of facial and body hair and my voice deepen, but it feels right.

Some of my lifelong fear over contemplating being male was based, I think, on all the trouble everyone went to to get me my birth certificate and feeling like a bit of a fraud over it. I've had to keep telling myself that an important legal point was being made and it wasn't a waste. Having said that, I feel strongly that I want my birth certificate to be returned to Joel. I feel as if my identity was stolen away from me when I was a year old and I want it back. There's a lot of others out there who were registered as girls from the start even though they were clearly male and I think those that have gone back to being male deserve to have their identities recognised too. Perhaps the battle already fought over my birth certificate will make it easier for that to happen for them and me.

One of the biggest challenges I faced in transitioning back to male was in deciding when and how to stop living as 'she' and start being 'he.' It was like a lot of little hurdles. Initially I became very careful over the types of clothes I bought and buying a pair of men's shoes was one of my first milestones. I gave my family time to get their heads around it and to start seeing me as a son and brother instead of a daughter and sister.

I never had a big heart-to-heart with Farmer or the boys about my decision, I don't think that's us really, but they have been very accepting. We joke about it more than anything, as I have with Nick, though Farmer told me the other day that I'm suiting the stuff I'm buying now, which was good to hear.

I'm 27 now and know it's a long road ahead, emotionally and physically. I'm thinking, hopefully by the time I get to 30, I will have accomplished what I am trying to physically. I am not set into a vision of the future being a certain thing, I am just hoping to be more comfortable in myself. I do feel as if my life will start more once this is all complete because I feel I'll have more confidence to go out and do things. I have been thinking about doing some online studies or perhaps getting involved in some kind of support work relating to my experiences.

A while back, a thought flashed through my mind: 'What if something happens to me before I get all this done?' The thought frightened me and suddenly I realised I was looking forward to the future. It was then that I knew I was definitely doing the right thing. That was the moment I knew I was all right.

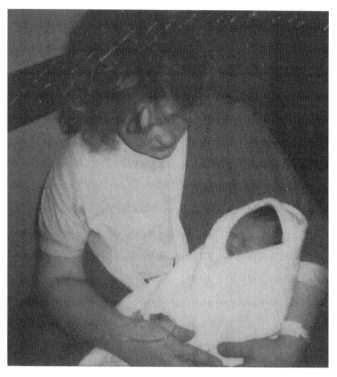

First ever photo, taken before I went into
surgery. Mum didn't know if I would survive.

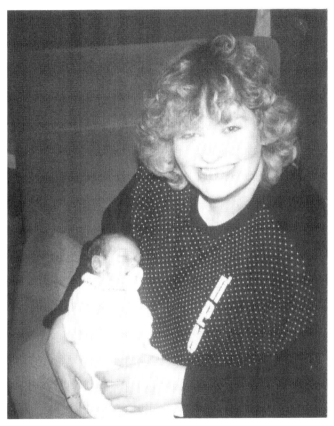

Mum looking much happier, with a tiny me.

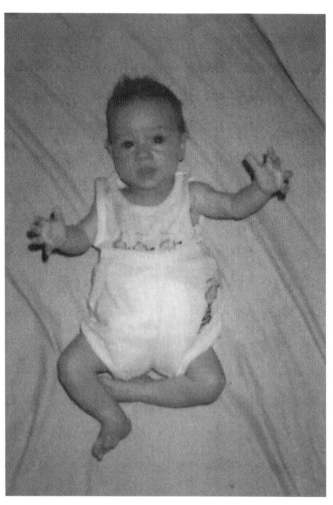

Underneath the giant nappy and layers of dressings I still had a huge
hole in my abdomen. It wasn't sealed until I was 18 months old.

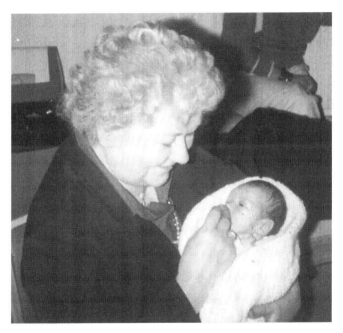

My wonderful nan with baby me.

Me as Joel, before doctors told Mum I should be raised a girl.

Mum and I trying on our outfits before she married Farmer. I was four.

A rare 'girly' moment in my bridesmaid dress on Mum's wedding day.

With Jarred. I'd chosen to play with a car, no
surprises there! I would have been five or six.

Jarred and I.

In a beer garden with Farmer, the man I call Dad.

Nan was my favourite person in the world.

You could never get a sensible photo of Grandad!

Me with Mum in 2013. I still very much believed I was a
woman at this stage but had long since given up with long
hair and make-up – I was never comfortable with it.

Me now, aged 27, finally aware that I am a man and
living the life I always should have been. Photo: By Tony Jones

19634538R00183

Printed in Great Britain
by Amazon